THE COMPLETE IDIOT'S GUIDE TO

World Conflicts

by Steven D. Strauss

ALPHA

A Pearson Education Company

To my dear friend, Raphael Goodblatt

Copyright © 2002 by Steven D. Strauss

International Standard Book Number: 0-02-864366-6
Library of Congress Catalog Card Number: 2002106339

04   03   02   8   7   6   5   4   3   2   1

Interpretation of the printing code: The rightmost number of the first series of numbers is the year of the book's printing; the rightmost number of the second series of numbers is the number of the book's printing. For example, a printing code of 02-1 shows that the first printing occurred in 2002.

Printed in the United States of America

For marketing and publicity, please call: 317-581-3722

The publisher offers discounts on this book when ordered in quantity for bulk purchases and special sales.

For sales within the United States, please contact: Corporate and Government Sales, 1-800-382-3419 or corpsales@pearsontechgroup.com

Outside the United States, please contact: International Sales, 317-581-3793 or international@pearsontechgroup.com

Publisher: *Marie Butler-Knight*
Product Manager: *Phil Kitchel*
Managing Editor: *Jennifer Chisholm*
Acquisitions Editor: *Mike Sanders*
Development Editor: *Michael Koch*
Production Editor: *Katherin Bidwell*
Copy Editor: *Rhonda Tinch-Mize*
Illustrator: *Jody Schaeffer*
Cover/Book Designer: *Trina Wurst*
Indexer: *Tonya Heard*
Layout/Proofreading: *Megan Douglass, Mary Hunt*

Contents at a Glance

Contents

Foreword

The great Buckminster Fuller was one of the first visionaries to look at the whole Earth and ask what are the greatest problems facing humanity, particularly the poor, and where are we all collectively heading.

Steven Strauss, the author of this book, takes up Bucky's legacy, and would make Bucky proud. Strauss, who wrote about Fuller in his book on modern business innovations, The Big Idea: How Business Innovators Get Great Ideas to Market, does an exemplary job of examining the idiosyncratic contexts of today's greatest crises, effectively covering the entire world, and, again in justice to Fuller, asking where future crises might occur.

More than at any time in the past, what goes on in one part of our world now affects every other part. Yet, while journalists report on each foreign war as isolated news, it's important to see the whole tapestry, to understand the patterns and trends, the causes and results.

An understanding of world conflict is vital in order to prevent future wars and thereby forestall their consequences: famine, massacres, mass displacement, persecution, collapsed governments, genocide, wartime deaths, and retribution killings.

Violent conflict still is the dominant condition for tens of millions of people and, alongside progress in governance, defines the momentum of history for most of the world's peoples. Most of today's wars are in the poorer countries of the world. As well, where one finds violent conflict one also finds authoritarian governments.

Until recently, wars in distant countries were unknown to Americans because, in large part, the distant lands themselves were mysteries. Only after international aid agencies succeeded in gaining attention to places like Somalia, Mozambique, Burma, Tibet, and Bosnia did these countries begin to appear more regularly on the radar screens of news agencies, pundits, Hollywood filmmakers, and government policymakers.

In recent years, violent conflict has become the leading cause of excess deaths of people. For thousands of years, famine, caused by drought or chill, was one of the great and terrible threats. Since the early 1970s, however, famine has only struck countries at war, where economies are disrupted and access to world supplies are denied to populations. The arguable exception is North Korea, were 200,000 starved to death in the 1990s, but this in a country on perpetual war-footing, which still devotes an enormous share of its national economy to propping up an artificial dictatorship under the pretext of defending itself against its southern neighbor. In Africa and very poor countries such as Afghanistan, war and famine continue to fuel each other in vicious cycles. The combination killed three million in the Greater Horn of Africa, over 200,000 in Central America, and some two million in South East Asia since the 1970s.

It is a current myth that only modern wars kill predominantly civilians, while wars of the past only harmed uniformed combatants. Most of the 50 million deaths attributed to World War II were of civilians or ex-combatants. In centuries past, civilians were starved or massacred as they are today. The difference is that we finally have credible information about the inhumanities that result from war, from torture to landmines, from forced migration to epidemics.

Inevitably, there will be more horrible wars and innovations in mass destruction. War continues to be part of the birthing pain of emerging democracies, just like it was in the United States' most lethal war, the Civil War, in which 600,000 died. Particularly in sub-Saharan Africa, violent conflicts both cause poverty and are the result of stalled economic growth, and inhibit global campaigns to stamp out diseases like polio, meningitis, and measles.

The Complete Idiot's Guide to World Conflicts has done an admirable job of pulling together the most salient information about recent historical experience with complex emergencies. Further data on individual crises, trends in military spending, and the like can be re-searched on the Stockholm International Peace Research Institute website (www.sipri.org).

This book reviews three important aspects of war—the patterns of war worldwide, the history of recent wars, and the prospects for future wars, in places of high tension such as Taiwan, the Spratley Islands, Kashmir, the Balkans, and Central Asia.

Steven Strauss also does a terrific job of casting light on the front lines of tension between Muslim states and their neighbors, which appear to be dominating the global statistics of war—whether between Islamic factions, such as between Iran and Iraq, or between countries with huge Muslim populations mixed in with others, as in India, China, and Indonesia.

Peace in our time will depend, in part, on a broader international understanding of these problems, which can be promoted by more people reading books like this.

Steve Hansch
Editor, *The Humanitarian Times*
www.humanitariantimes.org

Introduction

Although September 11 changed America forever, the rest of the world has, for many years, been engaged in conflicts that dwarf the destruction of the Twin Towers. In Africa alone, civil wars have killed literally millions of civilians, and made refugees of millions more. In the Middle East, terrorism is a way of life. So you may excuse the rest of the world if they think that the death of 3,000 Americans is not the worst tragedy they have ever witnessed, because it's not.

But even beyond the sheer numbers of these conflicts, it is the tales of war and peace that are so fascinating. From the old—the Cuban Missile Crisis, for example—to the new—the War on Terrorism—learning what happened and why they happened makes for some great reading.

The good news is that although conflict and war abound, peace still finds a way. Israel and Egypt, the most bitter of enemies, have forged a delicate peace. Protestants and Catholics in Northern Ireland are seeking a peaceful solution to their age-old conflict. The former Warsaw Pact countries of Hungary, Poland, and Czechoslovakia threw off their Soviet master and have, amazingly, since joined NATO. There is reason to hope.

What's in It for Me

The Complete Idiot's Guide to World Conflicts is your chance to learn the facts. Why is it that the rest of the world seems to hate the United States? After reading this book, you will see why America is often perceived by others as a big bully. By the same token, you will also see how the United States has often made the world a safer, better place. This book allows you to understand the whole world, not just your own.

The Complete Idiot's Guide to World Conflicts is intended to make these sometimes complicated matters (just who are the bad guys in the Balkans, anyway?) easy to understand and interesting to read. As such, the book is divided into geographic regions so that you can grasp an entire continent's issues easily and quickly.

Is war inevitable? Is peace possible? Read on, and decide for yourself.

How This Book Is Organized

This book is divided into six parts or geographical regions:

Part 1, "The Middle East and North Africa," begins with a broad overview of the state of conflict in the world today, and then goes on to analyze that most problematic of places, the Middle East. Here you will see that, although peace is possible, the likelihood of further conflict is even more probable.

Part 2, "Central and Southern Africa," might be the most gruesome part of this book. It is simply unbelievable how widespread, how redundant, and just how wanton the violence in this part of the world can be. With civil wars that seemingly never end and mayhem as a tool of destruction, Africa has been devastated by conflict.

Part 3, "Asia and the Pacific," not only recounts some of the largest conflicts of our time (Korea, for example), but it also examines the likelihood of further conflict in the region, and what might set those conflicts off. With China growing as it is, and as repressive as it remains, the chance for even more conflict in Asia grows daily.

Part 4, "Europe," examines the continent that was the cause of the most war, grief, and destruction during the twentieth century. Besides looking at historical conflicts, this section explains in an understandable way more modern conflicts: the breakup of the Soviet Union, what happened in the Balkans, and the chances for a successful peace in Northern Ireland.

Part 5, "South America and Latin America," looks at the long-running war in Columbia and analyzes the prospects for peace there. It also looks at the terrible tragedy that Papa Doc and Baby Doc Duvalier brought to Haiti, as well as smoldering conflicts in Peru, Ecuador, and Paraguay.

Part 6, "North America," looks at the many conflicts that the world's last superpower—America—has been and is currently involved in. It also looks at problems in Mexico and Canada, and then concludes with the prospects for an overall more peaceful world.

The appendixes at the end of the book will lead you to further pertinent information, and the glossary will help you understand the jargon of conflict a bit better.

Extras

Throughout the book, you will also encounter many more tidbits of information that have been highlighted by friendly icons. Here's what to expect:

Diplomatic Dialogue
The jargon of war and peace can often be confusing. This section translates it into plain English.

Landmine!
Especially gruesome facts, or problems to be on the lookout for, are discussed in this sidebar.

Reliable Resources
Insider information, facts, knowledge, and quotes of interest can be found here.

Peacekeepers
Tips and hints can be found here.

Acknowledgments

I would like to thank Maria for everything, but especially for marrying me. Lili was her usual funny, bratty self, Hoop Girl was typically sweet and great, and Mai Mai was, as always, wonderful, and very patient as she waited for me to finish this book.

I would also like to thank Steve Hansch, Michael Koch, Rhonda Tinch-Mize, and Katherin Bidwell for making this book much better than it otherwise would have been.

Special Thanks to the Technical Reviewer

The Complete Idiot's Guide to World Conflicts was reviewed by an expert who double-checked the accuracy of what you'll learn here, to help us ensure that this book gives you everything you need to know about world conflicts. Special thanks are extended to Steve Hansch, editor of the *Humanitarian Times*, www.humanitariantimes.com.

Trademarks

Part 1

The Middle East and North Africa

Of all the conflicts in the world today, the ones raging in the Middle East are both the most publicized and the most dangerous, if not the bloodiest. The possibility of major escalation rightly keeps the problems in the Middle East on the front pages.

Israel's long conflict with her neighbors is just the tip of the iceberg. Iraq has been a major source of conflict, and the problems of the Kurds are not going away any time soon. Throw in the growing threat of radical Islamic fundamentalism, and all the necessary ingredients for setting off a world war are present.

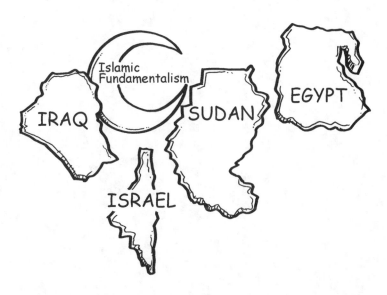

Chapter 1

The World at War

In This Chapter

- ◆ The world is getting smaller
- ◆ The state of things today
- ◆ Why people go to war
- ◆ The potential for peace

The world is a crazy place, and it seems to get crazier by the moment. If Islamic extremists aren't attacking the United States, then the Serbs are attacking Kosovo, the Palestinians and Israelis are killing each other, or Protestants are blowing up Catholics. North Korea is digging what former President Clinton has called "a big hole in the ground," supposedly to hold nuclear weapons intended for use against their estranged brethren in the south.

Many of these conflicts are well known: India hates Pakistan, China has it in for Taiwan. Many more are not: The Tutsi and the Hutu in Rwanda have been at it for years (almost one million Tutsi were murdered in 1994 alone). Did you know that Iraq made its first claim to annex Kuwait in 1961 but was rebuffed by the presence of British troops? Who hates whom?

In this chapter, I explain the state of conflict in the world today, examine who goes to war the most and why, and conclude by analyzing the potential for peace.

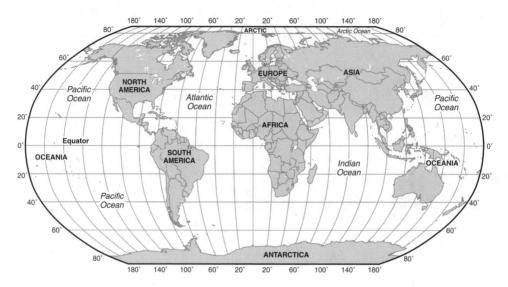

The world is getting smaller.

It's a Small World After All

The attacks on New York City by Osama bin Laden exemplify how these festering animosities around the globe can suddenly erupt, seemingly without notice. Take for example the simmering crisis in Spain.

What crisis in Spain, you ask? That's the point. Basques in Spain are racially and culturally different from the rest of the Spanish population. These so-called Basque separatists have been striving for independence for much of this century, and their struggle has created some of the most violent incidents in post-war Europe. Should their struggle erupt again violently, all Europe could be affected.

Reliable Resources

As stated on the Unrecognized Nations and Peoples Organization (UNPO) website (www.unpo.org), "UNPO is an international organization created by nations and peoples around the world who are not represented in the world's principal international organizations, such as the United Nations. Founded in 1991, UNPO today consists of more than 50 members who represent more than 100 million persons, including Basque separatists. UNPO offers an international forum for occupied nations, indigenous peoples, minorities, and even oppressed majorities, who currently struggle to regain their lost countries, preserve their cultural identities, protect their basic human and economic rights and safeguard the natural environment."

Not only is the world getting crazier, but it is also getting smaller; thus the need to understand it is ever increasing. The Internet and the advent of instantaneous global communications, when combined with more and more economic interdependence, have made the Earth a very small place indeed.

A few years ago, Thailand made some economic mistakes that affected the entire Southeast Asian economy. The entire Pacific Rim was then jarred, and for a while, the whole world was on the verge of recession. The downturn in the Asian economy then caused an already hurting North Korea to become even more aggressive toward its rival South Korea.

Similarly, a recent article in *The New York Times* explained that the aftermath of the World Trade Center (WTC) attack would eventually cripple the sub-Saharan economy. So conflict in the twenty-first century is sure to hit closer to home as the world becomes an ever-increasingly smaller place.

By the way, it is important to understand that conflict and war are not necessarily the same thing, although they sure are close. For example, when the United States attacked the Taliban in Afghanistan after the attacks on September 11, 2001, no formal declaration of war was ever passed by the United States Congress; but that the conflict was a war is no surprise. A formal declaration of war is not necessary for a war to be a war.

Even so, there are conflicts that are not wars. For example, although the Armenians and Azerbaijanis are still in conflict to this day, they are not now at war; however, they could be at any time. Therefore, throughout this book, I will use the terms "conflict" and "war" interchangeably.

The challenge is to understand why conflict and war seem so inevitable, so commonplace, as well as how they might be reduced.

War Today

There are 192 countries on Earth, and in the past half century, almost every one of them has been involved in more than one conflict. Some have had many.

Which country do you think has had the most wars and conflicts in the past 50 years? The answer is, the United States. Not only has it engaged in five wars (Korea, Vietnam, the Cold War, Iraq, Afghanistan), but it has also been involved in three incursions and invasions (Laos, Cambodia, and Libya), two liberations (Grenada and Bosnia), six peace-keeping operations (Dominican Republic, Lebanon twice, the Gulf, Somalia, Kosovo), two rescue missions (Mayaguez and Iran), and one ouster (Panama).

Who's next? If you guessed Israel, you would be right. Since the end of World War II, the tiny Jewish state has been involved in no fewer than seven wars:

- ◆ The War of Independence (1948)
- ◆ The Suez War (1956)

- The Six-Day War (1967)
- The War of Attrition (1967–70)
- The Yom Kippur War (1973)
- The War in Lebanon (1982)
- The Palestinian Intifada (1987–?)

> **Peacekeepers** _____
>
> Israel is the only democracy in the Middle East. It proclaimed Jerusalem to be its capital in 1950, but the United States, like nearly all other countries, maintains its embassy in Tel Aviv. The Israeli president is elected by the 120-member Knesset for a five-year term, but the real power lay with the prime minister, who traditionally was elected by popular vote for a four-year term. In 2001, however, the Knesset voted to restore the previous method under which the legislators will choose the prime minister.

But the United States and Israel are not the only countries that have been heavily involved in armed conflict during the past half century. Not surprisingly, the next most warring country has been Israel's one-time enemy, Egypt. In the past 50 years, the number and types of conflicts that Egypt has been involved in are numerous as well:

- Six wars (five with Israel and one with Yemen)
- Three international missions (Cyprus, Malta, and Western Sahara)
- One border incident (Libya)

The parade of warring Middle East countries continues, with Iraq coming in as the fourth country involved in the most number of conflicts, with five major wars (three with Israel, one with Iran, and one with Kuwait/the United States), several border incidents (with Iran, Syria, and Turkey for example), and an internal battle against the Kurds and Shiites.

Pakistan is the next most warring nation, with four major wars (three with India and one with Bangladesh), several incidents with bordering neighbors (Afghanistan being but one example), and numerous internal security problems (Islamic fundamentalists and Baluchis, to name just two).

> **Landmine!** _____
>
> In 2000, India's population topped the one billion mark.

India is tied with Pakistan, having had four wars (three with Pakistan, one with China), numerous problems with its island neighbor Sri Lanka, numerous annexations (Kashmir) and a multitude of internal security problems.

Russia (and the old Soviet Union) has had three wars (Hungary, the Cold War, and Afghanistan), numerous incidents and problems with her old Warsaw Pact allies (Czechoslovakia, Poland, and Berlin), several internal "wars" (Chechnya, for example), numerous border incidents with China, and a few problems with foreign airliners (KAL 007).

A Global Perspective

In short, war and conflict are part of modern life. This is made all the more obvious in the following table, provided by the United Nations. It examines conflicts in the world at the dawn of the twenty-first century.

Conflicts in the Twenty-First Century

Region	Number of Countries in Region	Conflicts (in %)	Countries with Conflicts (in %)	Percent of World Conflict
Africa	50	13	26	36
Asia	42	13	26	36
Europe	42	1	2	3
Americas	44	2	5	6
Middle East	14	7	43	19
Totals	192	36	16	100

What does this tell us?

- ◆ Not surprisingly, the region hosting the most conflicts was the Middle East, with fully 43 percent of its countries at war.
- ◆ The most stable region was Europe, accounting for only 3 percent of all conflicts, followed by North and South America, with only 6 percent of all conflicts.
- ◆ A quarter of both Africa and Asia was at war.

The real question though is not how many conflicts there are at any given time around the globe, but rather, why are there so many conflicts?

Johnny Got His Gun

Although reading this list of recent wars might be depressing, it surely is not surprising, given just how much money is spent on arms shipments every year.

Annual Arms Shipments

Biggest Exporters of Arms (in billion dollar/year)		Biggest Importers of Arms (in billion dollar/year)	
United States:	$18	Iraq and Iran:	$6
Russia:	$4.5	Saudi Arabia:	$3
France:	$4	India:	$3
Cuba:	$2	Vietnam:	$2
China:	$2	Angola:	$2
Czechoslovakia:	$1	Libya:	$2
Poland:	$1	Egypt and Syria:	$2
Germany:	$1	Australia and Japan:	$1

Landmine!

According to the Council for a Livable World: "The United States spent approximately $2.50 per person (non-U.S. residents) on foreign aid in Fiscal Year 1997. Of this, military and security assistance totaled $1.25 per person (non-U.S. residents), while peacekeeping and humanitarian intervention accounted for another $0.40 per person. The remainder, approximately $0.85 per person, was spent on development aid. Meanwhile, in the same time period, the United States exported weapons worth more than $2 for every person on earth. This is based on conservative estimates of total weapons transferred in that year."

So war is big business. With countries around the world importing more than $30 billion worth of arms every year, it is no wonder that so much armed conflict exists around the globe.

Moreover, with technology increasing as rapidly as it does these days, industrialized countries such as the United States are inventing ever more sophisticated ways to kill human beings. And the military in those countries importing these weapons are anxious to try them out on their alleged enemies. Thus there are both financial and military reasons behind war.

Yet, although the manufacture and selling of arms is undoubtedly a large reason why there seems to be so much conflict in the world today, it is by no means the only reason.

War—What Is It Good For?

War has been around as long as man has been alive. If you have ever seen the movie *2001: A Space Odyssey*, you will recall that the prehumanoids in that film fought a war, with the ones who used bones as tools being the winner. It isn't hard to imagine that something similar occurred time and again in real life. Man has always fought and has always looked for better ways to kill his fellow man.

Mankind fights for many reasons: survival, hate, anger, greed, need, miscalculation, power, insecurity—the list is probably as lengthy as the list of human emotions.

However, just as long as man has been at war, so too has he been trying to understand and end it. Woodrow Wilson said that World War I would be the "war to end all wars." George W. Bush said that the purpose of the War on Terrorism was to "wipe out evil."

Indeed, mankind has been discussing the causes of war from a very early date. The first great work of history, Thucydides's *History of the Peloponnesian War*, written in the fifth century B.C.E., is an analysis dedicated to discussing why men fight. Thucydides did not ask whether war was right or wrong. To him, war was a fact of life—men fight for survival. The author's message was that if one fights, one risks death; but the country that refuses to fight will undergo death as the penalty.

Landmine!

War has been waged against us by stealth and deceit and murder. This nation is peaceful, but fierce when stirred to anger. This conflict was begun on the timing and terms of others. It will end in a way, and at an hour, of our choosing.

—President George W. Bush, Speech at National Cathedral, September 14, 2001

Certainly, as researcher Walter Fritz points out in his online article "Peace between Nations," beyond emotion and survival, there are other subjective reasons for war, including

- The belief that the war will be beneficial to society in the long run.
- Errors of appreciation of the political, economic, and social situation of its own society and of the adversary.
- Accidents in which a critical situation gets out of hand.
- A fight over resources.

Maybe more than anything else, war is seen as a means to achieve an end, the end being the perceived betterment of the nation. Maybe that is why capitalistic democracies do not go to war against one another.

Democracy and capitalism are shared values, and, when combined with an ever-increasing interdependent economic system, it is rarely in the interest of one such country to harm another because the net result will be a diminution of both. As such, one of the best things that can be done to promote world peace is to promote capitalistic democracies. Far from being jingoistic, this is simply a conclusion drawn from the facts: Democracies don't go to war.

As R. J. Rummel, professor of political science at the University of Hawaii, observes, for the years 1946–1986, "when there were the most democracies and thus the hardest test of the proposition that democracies do not make war on each other, there were 45 states that had a democratic regime; 109 that did not. There were thus 6,876 state dyads (for example, Bolivia-Chile), of which 990 were democratic-democratic dyads. None of the 990 fought each other. Thirty-two nondemocratic dyads engaged in war. Thus the probability of any dyad engaging in war from 1946 to 1986 was 32/6876 or .0047; of not engaging in war was .9953. Now, what is the probability of the 990 dyads not engaging in war during this period? Using the binomial theorem, it is .9953 to the 990th power or .0099, which rounded off, equals .01. This is highly significant. The probability of this lack of war between democracies being by chance is virtually 100 to 1."

Reliable Resources

It will not be quick and it will not be easy. Our adversaries are not one or two terrorist leaders, or even a single terrorist organization or network. It's a broad network of individuals and organizations that are determined to terrorize and, in so doing, to deny us the very essence of what we are: free people.

—Secretary of Defense Donald Rumsfeld, Press Briefing, September 18, 2001

War and Poverty

According to a report by Radio Free Europe journalist Anthony Georgieff, the Center for War and Peace Research in Uppsala, Sweden issued a report which stated that most armed conflict today occurs within a country's own borders, whereas in years past, most wars were fought *between* different countries.

What is even more interesting, according to the report, is that poverty was the major cause of about 80 percent of today's wars. Poorer countries were found to be three times at greater risk of war than richer countries. Indeed, throughout the decade of the '90s, most wars were fought by countries with severe economic problems.

Yes, ethnicity was a factor, but not as big a factor as you may believe. It is when ethnicity is tied to poverty that war often results. In richer countries, those ethnic divides are more easily breached without violence and war.

War According to the United Nations

United Nations Secretary-General Kofi Annan has another idea when it comes to the causes of war. In an article summarizing Annan's annual report to the 54th session of the UN General Assembly (September 1999), InterPress journalist Thalif Deen characterizes

Annan's stance as follows. Although Annan acknowledges that poverty does play a role in many contemporary standoffs, he would like us to shift our focus of attention to the lack of equality and power many domestic social groups face in the world today: "It is this [inequality], rather than poverty, that seems to be the critical factor."

Regardless whether the inequality is based on ethnicity, religion, national identity, or economic class, according to Annan, "it tends to be reflected in unequal access to political power that too often forecloses paths to peaceful change." Another factor that fuels the fires of violent conflict today, according to the United Nations, is the disturbing rise in ethnic, or so-called "identity politics." According to the United Nations, "fewer than 20 percent of its 185 member states are ethnically homogeneous." This diversity can easily cause friction within a country, and political demagogues thus have little difficulty finding targets of opportunity and mobilizing support for bigoted causes. Says Annan, "The upsurge of ethnic cleansing in the 1990s provides stark evidence of the appalling human costs that this vicious exploitation of identity politics can generate."

The good news from the United Nations is its conclusion that peace agreements are on the rise. In the 1990s, three times as many nations signed peace agreements than in the previous three decades, reflecting, as Deen reports, " a more than 30 percent decline in the overall number and intensity of armed conflicts worldwide from 1992 to 1997." Not surprisingly, Annan believes that it is better and cheaper to prevent crises before they break out, but knows that it is difficult to do so. Quoting an ancient proverb, he says "it is difficult to find money for medicine, but easy to find it for a coffin."

> **Landmine!**
>
> According to *The New York Times*'s journalist Barbara Crosset's summary of the UN Human Development Report 1998 (September 27, 1998): "The richest fifth of the world's people consumes 86 percent of all goods and services, while the poorest fifth consumes just 1.3 percent. Indeed, the richest fifth consumes 45 percent of all meat and fish, 58 percent of all energy used and 84 percent of all paper, has 74 percent of all telephone lines and owns 87 percent of all vehicles."

War and Resources

It is common knowledge that the Gulf war was a war over oil, and who would control it. The United States was loathe to cede that power to Saddam Hussein. So clearly, resources are another reason that countries go to war.

Similarly, wars on a much smaller scale are often fought over specific areas; areas that are usually rich in resources. Once this land is conquered, resources such as oil, diamonds, and timber can be looted and sold for hard currency. Be that as it may, most states at most times get the natural resources they need by means other than war.

As such, fighting over resources is a relatively rare reason for countries to go to war. As in the case of the Gulf War, it is the *power* to control the resource, and not the resource itself, that is usually the reason for war.

Freedom

Needless to say, one of the oldest reasons for war is that it allows a people to free themselves from what they consider to be tyranny. Consider these words:

> When in the Course of human events, it becomes necessary for one people to dissolve the political bands which have connected them with another, and to assume among the powers of the earth, the separate and equal station to which the Laws of Nature and of Nature's God entitle them, a decent respect to the opinions of mankind requires that they should declare the causes which impel them to the separation.
>
> We hold these truths to be self-evident, that all men are created equal, that they are endowed by their Creator with certain unalienable Rights, that among these are Life, Liberty and the pursuit of Happiness. That to secure these rights, Governments are instituted among Men, deriving their just powers from the consent of the governed, That whenever any Form of Government becomes destructive of these ends, it is the Right of the People to alter or to abolish it ....

Those words, from the Declaration of Independence, might be the most elegant ever put to paper explaining why men sometimes feel the need to take arms against other men.

> **Reliable Resources**
>
> The actual day of American independence is July 2, 1776, when the Continental Congress passed the resolution for independence. Congress approved the declaration two days later.

In the world today, there are many such people who feel similarly: Palestinians, young Chinese, Cubans. One side's freedom fighter is another side's terrorist. Who is to say which is which?

In the end, history determines who was right and who was wrong. As they say, the winner writes the history books. But if one thing is clear, it is this—freedom usually finds a way. The forces of oppression are mighty indeed, but the yearnings of a people to be free is a force difficult to stop. Freedom usually finds a way.

All We Are Saying

Whatever the cause, one thing is certain: The twentieth century was the bloodiest, most violent century in recorded history. It is estimated that World War I caused more than 30 million deaths. World War II caused about 60 million deaths, almost half of those were civilians.

Something must change. The means of killing other people are becoming so sophisticated that whereas a conflict a hundred years ago might have resulted in 10,000 deaths, the weapons of mass destruction that are so readily available today could now result in ten times the deaths for the same conflict. As technology advances, the potential for devastating destruction accelerates.

But peace is possible, albeit never simple. To paraphrase the late Israeli Prime Minister Yitzhak Rabin, "You don't make peace with your friends. You make peace with your enemies." It's not easy, but it is possible. Catholics and Protestants in Northern Ireland proved it is possible. Israelis and Egyptians proved it is possible. Eastern Europe proved it is possible.

If the twenty-first century is to not be like the one preceding it, bravery will be required. It used to be that going to war was considered courageous. Yet today, with the stakes ever increasing, with lethality ever growing, the courage to *not fight* might be what will be required; the new badge of honor.

The Least You Need to Know

- ◆ The world is getting smaller and weapons are getting deadlier.
- ◆ More than 33 percent of the world is usually engaged in conflict at any one time.
- ◆ War serves many purposes, some noble, some not.
- ◆ You don't make peace with your friends. You make peace with your enemies.

Chapter 2

East Is East and West Is West

In This Chapter

- ◆ Understanding Islam
- ◆ The Afghan connection
- ◆ The roots of Jihad
- ◆ Terrorism against the United States
- ◆ The culture clash between East and West

Like December 7, 1941, September 11, 2001, is a day that will live in infamy. On that day, 19 fanatical terrorist followers of Osama bin Laden hijacked four American jumbo jetliners, flying two into the towers of the World Trade Center in New York City and one into the Pentagon, while another crashed into a deserted field in Pennsylvania.

The shock from those events changed how America sees itself and its place in the world. A seemingly once-lightweight President George W. Bush found his *raison d'être*. Transformed into a man of purpose, he was determined to root out terrorism wherever it could be found. The United States discovered patriotism again for the first time in two generations, and the world will never be quite the same.

How this conflict will end is difficult to say. Without a doubt, there will be more bloodshed and many more lives lost before this suicidal, militant form of Islamic terrorism is thwarted, if ever. Yet although the outcome is not certain, how we got to this point most certainly is, as you'll learn in this chapter.

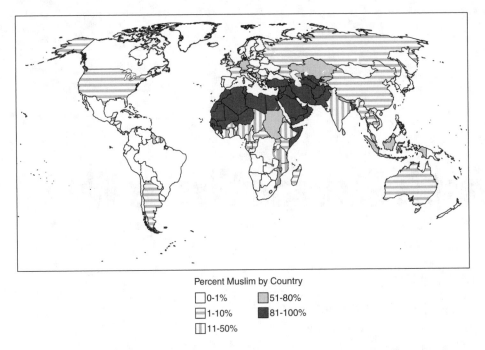

Percent Muslim by Country

☐ 0-1%   ▨ 51-80%
▤ 1-10%   ■ 81-100%
▥ 11-50%

Islam is the world's fastest growing religion.

Islam

The word Islam is an Arabic word: The root of which is Silm and Salam. Among other things, it means peace, greeting, salutation, obedience, loyalty, allegiance, and submission to the will of the Creator of the Universe. The religion was begun by the prophet Muhammad in the sixth century Arabia. A Muslim (that is, a self-surrendered one) is a follower of this faith, and nearly one in every seven persons alive on Earth today is a Muslim. It is among the fastest-growing religions in the United States.

> ### Reliable Resources
>
> Six to seven million Americans consider themselves Muslim, and they worship in 1,209 mosques from coast to coast. African Americans are the dominant Muslim population in the United States, accounting for 27 percent of the religion. Arab Americans account for only 15 percent.

Islam has two basic foundations: The holy book, or *Qu'ran*, (or Koran; from the Arabic word for "recitation"), and reports about Muhammad's life and work called the *Hadith* (from the Arabic word for "report"). The Koran as a book is comparable in length to the Gospels of the Christian Holy Bible.

According to religious scholar Karen Armstrong, when the prophet Muhammad brought the Koran to the Arabs, a major part of his mission was devoted to bringing an end to mass slaughter. Pre-Islamic Arabia was caught up in a vicious cycle of warfare in which tribe fought tribe in a pattern of vendetta and counter vendetta. Muhammad had to fight a deadly war in order to survive, but after achieving victory, he then devoted himself to building a peaceful coalition of tribes. By the time of his death in 632, he had almost single-handedly brought peace to war-torn Arabia.

By and large then, Islam teaches peace. Yet part of the problem in the modern world is that Islamic fundamentalists have been using a term found in the Koran—*jihad*—to justify murder. A jihad is supposed to be a holy war; a misnomer if ever there was one, raising the question: Just what does the Koran say about jihad?

The Koran and Jihad

As Armstrong points out in her essay "The True, Peaceful Face of Islam," the only permissible war in the Koran is one of self-defense. Muslims may not begin hostilities (2:190), but may fight in self-defense (2:191; 2:217) or to preserve decent values (4:75; 22:40). (For those of you who are unfamiliar with the preceding notation, the first number notates the chapter, and the second number notates the verse in the Koran where the teaching can be found.)

Accordingly, the Arabic word jihad does not mean "holy war," but rather, "struggle." Even so, Islamic scholars have even been divided on how the word "struggle" should be interpreted. According to Middle East analyst Fiona Symon "For some, it means the struggle to defend one's faith and ideals against harmful outside influences. For others, it has come to represent the duty of Muslims to fight to rid the Islamic world of Western influence in the form of corrupt and despotic leaders and occupying armies."

Under modern Islamic thought, there are in fact three levels of jihad:

- **Personal jihad:** This jihad is the struggle to purify the soul of negative influences; to cleanse one's spirit of sin. This is typically the most important level of jihad.

- **Verbal jihad:** Mohammed encouraged raising one's voice in the name of Allah on behalf of justice, stating, "The most excellent jihad is the speaking of truth in the face of a tyrant."

- **Physical jihad:** This is the type of jihad that is at issue today. This jihad refers to combat waged in defense of Muslims by the enemies of Allah. This "jihad with the hand" is the aspect of jihad that has come to be widely accepted among the more militant Muslim groups, although most would not agree with the methods adopted by Osama bin Laden and his al-Qaeda movement.

Modern Jihad

For much of its history, Islam was not interpreted to allow this last form of jihad as an excuse to wage war and kill innocent people. Jihad as a tool for terror is not part of historic Islam. As such, the origins of bin Laden's radical concept of jihad is a recent phenomenon that must be traced back to two early twentieth century figures who started powerful Islamic revivalist movements in response to colonialism and its aftermath: Hassan al-Banna's Muslim Brotherhood in Egypt and Syed Abul Ala Maududi's Jamaat Islami in Pakistan.

In Symon's analysis, these men blamed the Western idea of the separation of church and state for the decline of Muslim societies, believing that in Muslim societies, church and state should not be separate entities. Thus, they thought, the negative effects of colonialism could be corrected through a return to Islam in its traditional form—in which society was governed by a strict code of Islamic law. This belief would later form the basis of Afghanistan's Taliban.

> ### Peacekeepers
>
> During the ninth month of the lunar Islamic calendar, Ramadan, Muslims who are old enough and healthy enough fast for 29 or 30 days from sunup to sundown.

> ### Diplomatic Dialogue
>
> In the Islamic culture, an infidel is an unbeliever.

In addition to promoting the creation of pure Islamic states, these two men also instigated a new concept of jihad, proffering the theory that "holy war" was a viable Muslim method for ending foreign occupation of Muslim lands.

This idea was taken a step further in the 1950s, In Symon's analysis, when a man by the name of Sayed Qutb, a prominent member of Egypt's Muslim Brotherhood, theorized that all non-Muslims were *infidels*. Qutb predicted an eventual clash of civilizations between Islam and the West.

Qutb's words struck a chord with an Islamic populace that was increasingly ready to rid themselves of Western influence. Indeed, his radical notion of Islam inspired a whole generation of Muslims, including Ayatollah Khomeini, who developed an Iranian version of fundamental Islam in the 1970s. In 1966, Qutb was executed by Egyptian President Gamal Abdel Nasser.

Jihad and bin Laden

Osama bin Laden would be introduced to the radical ideas of Qutb and the growing Islamic fundamentalist movement by Abdullah Azzam. Azzam was a Palestinian scholar who had fought with the Palestinian Liberation Army (P.L.O.) in the 1970s, but became disillusioned with the PLO leadership because of its secular outlook.

Azzam had studied Islamic law in Cairo, where he met the family of Sayed Qutb. He then went on to teach in Saudi Arabia. It was there that he met and taught a sharp university student named Osama bin Laden, who quickly became enamored of this emerging fundamentalist philosophy.

Afghanistan Ho!

In 1979, the Soviet Union invaded its neighbor Afghanistan. The Afghans, long accustomed to invasions and intruders, began to actively resist the mighty Soviet Army. This battle to liberate the predominantly Muslim Afghanistan from Soviet occupation gave Abdullah Azzam an opportunity to put his revolutionary Islamic ideals into practice. Dubbed the "Emir of Jihad," he was one of the first Arabs to join the Afghan *mujahedeen*, along with Osama bin Laden.

Diplomatic Dialogue

A **mujahedeen** is someone who actively fights for Islam.

Together they set up a base in the country, where they recruited and housed Arabs who had come to join the jihad. Azzam taught that it was the moral duty of every Muslim to undertake jihad, and he traveled the world calling on Muslims to join the fight.

The ruling family of Saudi Arabia, which had long been criticized for its pro-Western views, seized the occasion of the Soviet invasion of Afghanistan to deflect internal criticism. The kingdom threw its political and financial weight behind the Afghan jihad—which was also backed by Pakistan and the United States under the apparent premise that the enemy of my enemy is my friend—against the Soviet Union.

The upshot of the decade-long war in Afghanistan was that a mentality of jihad emerged that many mujahedeen found difficult to abandon. Followers of the Egyptian Islamic Jihad movement, an extremist offshoot of the Muslim Brotherhood, believed that Afghanistan should be a template for the liberation of the entire Muslim world.

After the victory in Afghanistan, Osama bin Laden returned to his native Saudi Arabia to continue the fight against the government there. The Saudis were not disposed to tolerate his calls to insurrection, and in April 1994, his Saudi citizenship was revoked for "irresponsible behavior," and he was expelled from the country.

Together with his immediate family and a large band of followers, bin Laden moved to the Sudan where he set up several businesses to help continue to fund his war against the

West. Among bin Laden's numerous Sudanese commercial interests were a factory to process goatskins, a construction company, a bank, a sunflower plantation, and an import-export operation.

However, Sudan was on the U.S. State Department's list of state sponsors of terrorism, making it an outlaw nation. Because the country was in much need of help, it decided that the United States would be a better friend than Osama bin Laden could ever be. So, as a gesture toward the United States, the Sudanese government requested that bin Laden depart. In May 1996, running out of places to go, the terrorist moved back to Afghanistan.

> **Reliable Resources**
>
> Centuries before the women's movement in the West, Islam granted women the right to own property, to be educated, and the right to inherit. In the West, in many instances, women did not receive these rights until centuries later.

The Gulf War and Its Aftermath

In the meantime, the 1991 Gulf War had brought U.S. troops to Saudi Arabia. After devoting their lives to the liberation of Muslim territory, this was a bitter blow for bin Laden and his Arab brethren, seeing the land they regarded as sacred being occupied by American infidels.

For bin Laden, the continuing presence of American troops so close to the Islamic holy sites of Mecca and Medina were the last straw. So, in February 1998, he announced the formation of an umbrella organization called "The Islamic World Front for the struggle against the Jews and the Crusaders."

> **Diplomatic Dialogue**
>
> A *fatwa* is a legal opinion or decree on a specific issue.

He then issued a *fatwa*, and declared war on the United States, though few knew of the declaration. It was this so-called fatwa that paved the way for the terrorist attacks on American targets that followed.

Fatwa This!

On February, 23, 1998, Osama bin Laden, his top aide, Egyptian Ayman al-Zawahiri, and his group, al-Qaeda, issued the following proclamation:

> Praise be to Allah .... The Arabian Peninsula has never ... been stormed by any forces like the crusader armies spreading in it like locusts, eating its riches, and wiping out its plantations. All this is happening at a time in which nations are attacking Muslims like people fighting over a plate of food. In the light of the grave situation and the lack of support, we and you are obliged to discuss current events, and we should all agree on how to settle the matter.

No one argues today about three facts that are known to everyone; we will list them, in order to remind everyone:

First, for over seven years the United States has been occupying the lands of Islam in the holiest of places, plundering its riches, dictating to its rulers, humiliating its people, terrorizing its neighbors, and turning its bases in the Peninsula into a spearhead through which to fight the neighboring Muslim peoples. The best proof of this is the Americans' continuing aggression against the Iraqi people.

Second, despite the great devastation inflicted on the Iraqi people by the crusader-Zionist alliance, and despite the huge number of those killed, which has exceeded 1 million … despite all this, the Americans are once again trying to repeat the horrific massacres, as though they are not content with the protracted blockade imposed after the ferocious war or the fragmentation and devastation.

Third, if the Americans' aims behind these wars are religious and economic, the aim is also to serve the Jews' petty state and divert attention from its occupation of Jerusalem and murder of Muslims there.

All these crimes and sins committed by the Americans are a clear declaration of war on Allah, his messenger, and Muslims. And ulema have throughout Islamic history unanimously agreed that the jihad is an individual duty if the enemy destroys the Muslim countries.

On that basis, and in compliance with Allah's order, we issue the following fatwa to all Muslims:

The ruling to kill the Americans and their allies—civilians and military—is an individual duty for every Muslim who can do it in any country in which it is possible to do it.

> **Reliable Resources**
>
> In 1989, Ayatollah Khomeini issued a fatwa against British author Salman Rushdie for his book *The Satanic Verses*. A multi-million dollar bounty was offered for the author's death (talk about your bad review!), and Rushdie went into hiding. Britain spent years trying to get the fatwa revoked, and finally succeeded in 1998.

Understanding bin Laden and Al-Qaeda

Al-Qaeda is a network of many different organizations in diverse countries that are willing to use terrorism for the attainment of their political goals. Those goals include the overthrow of governments in their respective countries, and the establishment of Islamic governments in their place.

According to the International Policy Institute for Counter-Terrorism, much of the philosophy behind al-Qaeda was formed during the Afghan war when bin Laden came to see the world in black or white: You were either a believer or a heretic. Here, "heretics" includes pragmatic Arab regimes (including his homeland, Saudi Arabia), as well as the United States.

So bin Laden's fatwa was no idle threat. By the time he issued it, he and al-Qaeda had already proved to be deadly serious. Indeed, according to the U. S. Department of State, prior to 1998, bin Laden and his groups were responsible for, among other things …

◆ Conspiring to kill U.S. servicemen in Yemen who were on their way to participate in the humanitarian mission "Operation Restore Hope" in Somalia in 1992.

◆ Plotting the deaths of American and other peacekeepers in Somalia who were there to deliver food to starving Muslims.

◆ Assisting Egyptian terrorists who tried to assassinate Egyptian President Mubarak in 1995 and who have killed dozens of tourists in Egypt in recent years.

◆ Bombing the Egyptian embassy in Pakistan in 1995; a blast that killed more than 20 Egyptians and Pakistanis.

◆ Conspiring to kill the pope.

◆ Bombing a joint U.S. and Saudi military training mission in Riyadh, Saudi Arabia in 1995.

Then, in May 1998, soon after his fatwa was issued, bin Laden stated at a press conference in Afghanistan that the world would see the results of his latest threats "in a few weeks."

The Embassy and *Cole* Bombings

On August 7, 1998, American embassies in Nairobi, Kenya and Dar es Salaam, Tanzania were bombed, killing many civilians in the process. Although bin Laden was the prime suspect, conclusive proof was hard to come by until a cohort, Mohammed Sadiq Odeh, was arrested at Karachi International Airport in Pakistan. Odeh spilled the beans, describing in detail bin Laden's international network and his role in the bombing of the American embassies.

CAUTION

Landmine! _____

Proof of just how much the United States underestimated its foe can be seen in a 1998 statement by Clinton National Security Advisor, Sandy Berger: "Osama bin Laden *may be* the most dangerous nonstate terrorist in the world."

With conclusive proof that bin Laden was the culprit, the United States struck back against him and al-Qaeda on August 20, 1998. The targets included six training camps belonging to al-Qaeda and a pharmaceuticals factory in Sudan that intelligence sources suspected of producing components of chemical weapons.

These counter-attacks by the Clinton Administration were mostly seen as a little more than a gesture. Critics complained that they would do little to deter bin Laden, and they were right. In fact, this limited retaliation likely encouraged the terrorists, giving them reason to conclude that the United States did not have the stomach for a "real fight."

On October 12, 2000, a small boat pulled up alongside the USS *Cole* while it was refueling in Yemen. Witnesses said they saw two men in the boat stand at attention, and then an explosion ripped a hole in one of the most advanced destroyers in the U.S. Navy, killing 17 sailors and injuring 39. What few realized at the time was that even if no one else was taking bin Laden's fatwa seriously, he certainly was.

The next year, 2001, a videotape began to circulate around the Middle East. The tape represented the clearest public link between bin Laden and the *Cole* bombing. In the tape, bin Laden's masked men are seen training in an Afghan terrorist training camp (since destroyed by the U.S. military) and singing a song that says in part: "We thank God for granting us victory the day we destroyed *Cole* in the sea." In the tape bin Laden appears repeatedly preaching at a mosque and talking to his men in the field. In an address to Palestinians at the end of the tape, bin Laden calls for "blood, blood and destruction, destruction."

September 11, 2001, was the day when that desire came to fruition.

So if the United States was unprepared for the September 11 attacks, it certainly wasn't because it hadn't been put on notice; bin Laden had loudly declared jihad against the United States and was steadily escalating his side of the war.

Reliable Resources

The World Trade Center towers were constructed by the Port Authority of New York and New Jersey in the early 1970s. At the time, they were considered the best-known examples of "tube" buildings, which are strengthened by closely spaced columns and beams in the outer walls. Although the towers were in fact designed to withstand being struck by an airplane, the resultant fires of the September 11 attack weakened the infrastructure of the buildings, causing the upper floors to collapse. The weight was too much to bear for the lower floors, which pancaked upon themselves.

Never the Twain Shall Meet?

The United States remained oblivious to the actual nature of the threat it faced until September 11, 2001, when it learned the hard way that many of the world's more than one billion Muslims intensely disliked America and its Western way of life.

Certainly these animosities are not one-sided. Westerners, too, have long not understood Muslims: women in burquas, fanatical followers, suicide bombers, and undemocratic regimes (even though the West has had more than its share of extremists as well). As such, the question becomes: Can East and West live in peace?

Samuel Huntington is a Harvard professor and was part of the National Security Council during the Carter Administration. Huntington says that "the clash of civilizations will be the battle lines of the future" and will result in decades of conflict and violence. "Ultimately the West can prevail," he predicts, "but the outcome is not a forgone conclusion."

A significant reason for this conflict is that the Eastern and Western cultures are so very different. The West upholds values such as a free press, freedom of religion and assembly, and open thought. These are far less important in Muslim countries, where values such as tradition, respect, and religion are far more important.

Undoubtedly, much of this Arab anger stems from American foreign policy. Middle Easterners greatly resent the United States' unswerving support of Israel and the resulting repression of the Palestinians, the stationing of U.S. troops in Saudi Arabia, the sanctions against Iraq, and America's previous support of the Shah of Iran. They also resent and find hypocritical the American tendency to trumpet democracy, all the while supporting corrupt or oppressive governments in Egypt, Bahrain, Pakistan, the United Arab Emerites, and Saudi Arabia.

Arab Muslims also resent having, from their perspective, unwanted American values and materialism shoved down their throat. Billboards, television, and magazines in their own countries often are full of Western culture and the American way of life; lifestyles that are usually at odds with Muslims' more traditional way of life. Many Muslims are unhappily forced to constantly deal with the unwanted intrusion of western commercialism and its values in their traditional, everyday lives.

With all this mutual animosity, it might be hard to see how East and West can ever meet in peace. But maybe they can; hate is not a foregone conclusion for several reasons.

First, not all Muslims are created equal. Even though a few support bin Laden, the vast majority do not. Like Americans, most Muslims have a deep respect for life.

Indeed, Islam is not so different from Christianity and Judaism. All three religions began in the Middle East, all three are monotheistic, and Islam sees itself as linked to Christianity and Judaism: It recognizes all the Old and New Testament texts and prophets, and both Jews and Muslims recognize Jesus as an important prophet. Moreover, Christians, Jews, and Muslims all consider themselves to be children of Abraham. All three religions place great emphasis on piety, kindness, and peace. In essence, they are three spokes on the same wheel, all leading to the center (God) in their own way, but all headed in the same direction.

> **Diplomatic Dialogue**
>
> The **Crusades** were a series of wars begun in 1095 fought by Christians to take back the Holy Land from the Muslims who had come to control it.

Is there an answer? Certainly in the post September 11-world, it would behoove the United States to examine how there came to be such hatred for it, however misguided, and why much of the world thinks that America acts like a big bully. The question that Americans must answer is whether its perceived heavy-handed foreign policy serves America's interests in the long run.

By the same token, if there is to be peace, Muslim clerics and leaders must also do their part. They must loudly, and often, decry the violence wrought by those who murder innocents in the name of Allah. They must remind their flock that Islam does not condone such actions.

But even if that happens, part of the problem may simply be systemic. Little can change the fact that as long as the United States is the sole superpower, ready and willing to flex its might around the globe, there will be people who will resent that. That is the nature of people and politics.

In the end, the best hope seems to be twofold. First, the United States needs to show the people of the Middle East that it understands their needs and anger, and that it is willing to try and use its might to alleviate some of their suffering. By the same token, Muslim nations must begin to take more risks on peace, publicly decry their most extremist elements, and teach respect and tolerance for those with whom they disagree. Maybe then, the root causes of terrorism can be reduced.

The Least You Need to Know

- Islam is a religion of peace.
- The Soviet invasion of Afghanistan gave rise to Osama bin Laden.
- Jihad is not traditionally thought of as a "holy war."
- Osama bin Laden declared war on the United States in 1998.
- The culture clash between East and West is not insurmountable.

The Middle East Mess

In This Chapter

- ◆ Sharing a small plot of land
- ◆ The birth of Zionism
- ◆ War and more war
- ◆ The Oslo Peace Accords

Of all the conflicts affecting the world today, none is more problematic, more irreconcilable, and likely more difficult to solve than the one in the Middle East. It combines high emotion with limited territory and years of bloodshed with sworn enemies.

Yet, there is also reason to hope. Israel and Egypt, countries that have gone to war too many times, found a way to put their animosities aside and make peace. Israel has been able to do the same thing with Jordan. The Israelis and the Palestinians were almost able to create peace in 2000, and still might do so.

But to truly comprehend the complexity of this regional conflict, one must go way, way back. Understanding why every party thinks it is right requires a bit of a history lesson, for if anything is true in the Middle East, it is that the past is prologue.

The Middle East: Fighting over a small plot of land.

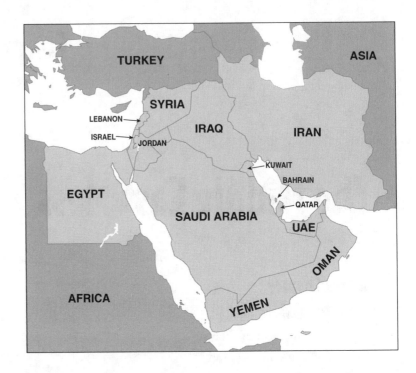

A Long Time Ago, in a Land Far, Far Away

The area fought over by Israel and the Palestinians is only 10,000 square miles. Today, the State of Israel formally occupies all the land from the Jordan River to the Dead Sea, bound by Egypt in the south, Lebanon in the north, and Jordan in the east.

Landmine!

To get an idea of just how small Israel is, consider that it is about half the size of Maine, a quarter of the size of New Zealand, and about the same size as Vancouver Island.

However, these officially recognized borders of Israel only constitute about 78 percent of the land that today makes up all of Israel proper, as noted by Ami Isseroff in an article on mideastweb.org. The other 22 percent consist of land occupied by Israel since the 1967 Six-Day War (the so-called "occupied territories,") and the Gaza Strip, which consists of 141 square miles.

Judging by fossil remains that have been found in the area, this land, which has been variously called Israel and Palestine, has been lived in for tens of thousands of years. Jericho has been identified as one of the oldest sites of agricultural activity, based on archaeological findings of hybrid wheat dating back to 8000 B.C.E. According to anthropologists, Amorites, Canaanites, and other Semitic peoples entered the area about 2000 B.C.E. Subsequently, the area became known as the Land of Canaan.

Canaan Shmaanan

According to the Bible, Moses led the Israelites out of Egypt and into Canaan. King David of the Jews conquered Jerusalem around 1000 B.C.E. and established an Israelite kingdom over much of Canaan. The kingdom was later divided into Judah in the south and Israel in the north.

War thereafter became standard operating procedure in this part of the world:

◆ The Assyrians conquered Israel in 722 or 721 B.C.E.

◆ The Babylonians conquered Judah in 587 or 586 B.C.E., destroyed Solomon's Temple in Jerusalem, and exiled a large number of Jews.

◆ The Persians then conquered Babylonia about 50 years later, and they ruled the area from about 530 to 331 B.C.E.

◆ The Seleucids later ruled the area around 200 B.C.E.

When in Rome ...

About 61 B.C.E., Roman troops invaded Judah and destroyed Jerusalem, the land came under Roman control, and they began to call the area Judea. In 135 C.E., the Romans drove the Jews out of Jeru-salem, and then renamed the area "Palaestina," or Palestine.

Most of the Jews who continued to practice Judaism fled or were forcibly exiled from Palestine. In time, Christianity spread to most of Palestine, with the exception of its northernmost part, Galilee, where Jewish communities continued to carve out an existence for themselves. The rest of Palestine was now settled, according to Isseroff, by Jewish converts to Christianity and Paganism, peoples imported by the Romans, and others who had probably been long-time inhabitants of Palestine.

> **Reliable Resources**
>
> In Jerusalem today, about 450,000 Jews live with 200,000 Palestinians.

Enter the Muslims

Muslim Arab armies moved north from Arabia around 600 C.E. and conquered most of the Middle East, including Palestine. Muslim rule and influence continued thereafter, almost uninterrupted, until the early 1900s.

It is, therefore, important to understand a few things:

◆ Muslims allowed Christians and Jews to practice their religions, although most of the local population gradually converted to Islam.

- Both Jews and Palestinians can state that they have occupied the area for thousands of years based on their histories of settlement.

- Jews, Christians, and Muslims mostly lived in peace in the Middle East for more than a thousand years.

- Jerusalem became holy to Muslims as the site where Muhammad ascended to heaven. The al-Aqsa mosque was built on the site generally regarded as the area of the Jewish temples.

By 1880, according to Isseroff "only" about 24,000 Jews were living in Palestine, out of a population of about 400,000. However, because of increasing oppression of Jews in Eastern Europe, by the late 1800s, emigration of Jews to Palestine began to increase dramatically due to a fast-growing movement known as Zionism.

Zionism

Zionism is the national movement that calls for the return of the Jewish people to, and the resumption of Jewish sovereignty in, the Land of Israel. The term "Zionism" was coined in 1893 by Nathan Birnbaum. While a student at the University of Vienna in 1893, Birnbaum published a brochure entitled "The National Rebirth of the Jewish People in Its Homeland as a Means of Solving the Jewish Problem." As a result, Jews of all persuasions, left and right, religious and secular, joined to form the Zionist movement.

Reliable Resources

In 1975, the United Nations General Assembly passed a resolution equating Zionism with racism. In 1991, the resolution was rescinded.

Following the first Zionist congress organized by Theodore Herzl in 1897, the Zionist movement gained momentum as a formal organization. The Zionists' goal was to establish a "Jewish Homeland" in Palestine, and to that end Herzl and his followers began to help millions of European Jews immigrate to Palestine, which was not an independent country at the time. First establishing farms, and later, the new city of Tel Aviv, the Jews began to till the soil.

At the same time, as more and more Jews embarked on a journey home, Palestine's Arab population grew rapidly as well. By 1914, Palestine was home to about 700,000 people, of which about 600,000 were Arabs and 100,000 were Jews.

Birth of a Nation

In 1917, at the end of World War I, Britain issued the Balfour Declaration. In it, the British government proclaimed its support for the creation of a Jewish homeland in Palestine, without violating the rights of the existing communities.

Following World War I, the newly created League of Nations (precursor of the United Nations) divided much of the defeated Ottoman Empire into mandated territories, and in 1920, Britain received a mandate over Palestine—to help the Jews build a country.

British officials hoped to establish self-government in Palestine, but their proposals for such institutions fell on deaf ears because the Arabs wanted nothing to do with the Jews; thus they would not participate in municipal councils. Lord David Ormsby-Gore, under-secretary of state for the colonies stated that "Palestine is largely inhabited by unreasonable people" (Isseroff, 2001).

The Arabs hotly opposed the idea of a Jewish national home because they considered Palestine to be their land; thus they formed a national movement to combat the terms of the British Mandate. Tellingly, at hearings to determine how the Mandate was proceeding, Palestinian leader Aref Pasha Dajani said of the Jews, "Their history and their past proves that it is impossible to live with them. In all the countries where they are at present, they are not wanted ... because they always arrive to suck the blood of everybody ..." (Isseroff, 2001). Nevertheless, because of persecution in Eastern Europe and Nazi Germany, Jewish immigration in Palestine swelled in the 1930s. After World War II, the United Nations Special Commission on Palestine recommended that Palestine be divided into an Arab state and a Jewish state. Jerusalem was to be put under international control.

The Jews accepted the U.N. decision. The Arabs rejected it. On May 14, 1948, following an international legal mandate, the Jews proclaimed the independent State of Israel, and the British withdrew from Palestine. The next day, neighboring Arab nations attacked Israel. At the same time, about 700,000 Arabs voluntarily fled or were driven out of Israel, becoming refugees in neighboring Arab countries.

Landmine!

German concentration camps were responsible for the systematic deaths of more than six million Jews during World War II.

The United Nations created a series of cease-fires between the Arabs and the Jews in 1948 and into 1949. In the meantime, Palestinian attempts to set up a state were blocked by Egypt and Jordan. Finally, U.N. Resolution 194 called for a cessation of hostilities and a return of refugees who wanted to live in peace.

When the fighting ended, Israel held territories beyond the boundaries called for by the United Nations. Egypt owned the Gaza Strip and Jordan held the West Bank. Because the Arab countries refused to sign a permanent peace treaty with Israel, the borders of Israel established by the United Nations never received legal international recognition, and the refugee problem was never resolved.

The Suez War

Not only was Israel a new country, but so also were many of the Arab states, having gained independence from the colonial powers of Great Britain and France. So in 1956, as part of Egyptian President Gamel Nasser's new nationalist agenda, he seized control of the Suez Canal away from the British and French companies that owned it.

> ### Peacekeepers
>
> I am saying these words for history: Nasser was born in a poor family, and I promise that he will live and die a poor man.
>
> —Gamel Nasser, Egyptian President

According to historian Roger Lee, Nasser ordered his forces to block the Straits of Tiran, the thin strip of water that was Israel's only outlet to the Red Sea. Britain and France, in an effort to reassert control over this vital waterway, decided upon a joint invasion and occupation of the Suez Canal zone, and coordinated their invasion with Israel.

As Lee notes, on October 29, 1956, Israeli troops attacked and invaded the Sinai Peninsula in Egypt, overcame the opposition, and moved on towards the Suez Canal. The next day, France and Britain stated that they would agree to create a buffer zone between Egypt and Israel at the canal, but Egypt refused this premeditated offer. So on October 31, Egypt was attacked by Britain and France.

As with all things that happened in the world politically in the 1950s, the Cold War then intervened. The Soviet Union, which was having its own problems with Hungary at this time, nevertheless offered to help Egypt. A nervous President Eisenhower then successfully pressured Britain, France, and Israel into agreeing to a cease-fire and an eventual withdrawal from Egypt. Israel obtained guarantees from the United States that international waterways would remain open to Israeli shipping, and a U.N. force was stationed in Sinai.

The war lasted but a week, but the results were clear: Egypt was now part of the USSR's sphere of influence, and would arm Arab nations for years to come.

The Six-Day War

Over the ensuing years, doves in the region consistently expressed a desire to negotiate a peace, but hard-line elements across the board refused. Thus, for example, in an address to the United Nations General Assembly in 1960, Israeli Foreign Minister Golda Meir unsuccessfully challenged Arab leaders to negotiate a peace settlement.

The Arabs were adamant in their refusal to negotiate either a peace with Israel or a settlement for the Palestinian refugees. As Nasser told the United Arab Republic National Assembly March 26, 1964, "The danger of Israel lies in the very existence of Israel as it is in the present and in what she represents."

Reliable Resources

Golda Meir was born in Kiev, Russia, in 1898. In 1906, economic hardship forced her family to emigrate to the United States. In 1924, she emigrated to Israel. In 1948, Meir was appointed Israel's Ambassador to the Soviet Union. In 1956, she became Israel's Foreign Minister, a post she held until 1966. When Prime Minister Levi Eshkol died suddenly in early 1969, the 71 year old Meir became the world's second female Prime Minister (after Mrs. Bandaranaike of Sri Lanka).

In essence, the Arab states adopted a "kill two birds with one stone" policy: If they could rid the world of Israel, the Palestinian refugee problem would also be resolved in the process. So it was that in 1964 The Palestine Liberation Organization was formed. Its charter stated that its aim was to destroy Israel and allow Palestinians back into historical Palestine.

In the spring of 1967, the battle between Egypt and Israel erupted again when Nasser once again closed the Straits of Tiran to Israel, and then sent U.N. peacekeepers packing. The United States, which had pledged to keep the waterway open, failed to live up to its promises. And so, on June 5, 1967, Israel attacked the Egyptians. The Syrians and Jordanians then attacked Israel.

Six days later, the war was over. Israel had pummeled its enemies and now occupied the Gaza Strip, the West Bank, the Sinai Peninsula, and the Golan Heights.

Clearly the most enduring and disastrous result of the 1967 war for all concerned was that roughly one million Palestinians fell under Israeli rule as a result of Israel taking over the West Bank (of the Jordan River), as well as the Gaza Strip. So, whereas the conflict heretofore had mostly been about animus between Arab and Jew, after 1967, it took on the additional, and far more complex, issue of the fate of the Palestinians.

Problematically, although the Israeli government had declared that it was ready to return all the territories except Jerusalem in return for peace treaties with its Arab neighbors, religious and nationalist groups within Israel wanted to annex and settle the West Bank and Golan Heights. An increasing number of Jewish settlements began to sprout up, and settlement expansion became official Israeli policy after the opposition revisionist Likud party came to power in 1977.

 Landmine!

According to Ami Isseroff, "As of 2001, about 200,000 Israelis had settled in areas of the West Bank and Gaza, and an additional 200,000 were settled in areas of Jerusalem and the environs conquered in 1967. About 15,000 Jews were settled in the Golan Heights taken from Syria."

The Yom Kippur War

Yom Kippur is the holiest day of the year for Jews. Called the day of Atonement, it is the day that people of that faith ask God for forgiveness for their sins and pray to be a better person in the upcoming year.

In October 1973, on Yom Kippur, while the people of Israel were in synagogue, Egypt and Syria launched another war against the tiny Jewish state, catching the Israelis by surprise. Their goal was to regain control over Arab territory lost in preceding wars, which have left the entire Arab world frustrated and turned large groups of Palestinians into refugees. Although the war was technically fought between Israel on one side and Egypt and Syria on the other, Iraq, Jordan, and Saudi Arabia all supported their Arab brothers economically and militarily.

Syria made serious inroads in the Golan Heights, and Egyptians crossed the Suez Canal and retook a strip of the Sinai Peninsula. Israel then reconquered the Golan and advanced into Syria. In the Sinai, Israeli forces crossed the canal and cut off the entire Egyptian third army. The war was over in three weeks.

Peace in Our Time

Egyptian President Anwar Sadat had seen enough—enough war, enough bloodshed, enough hate. Something had to change, so, in 1977, he decided that he was the one who would have to change it.

Realizing that his path of action (as well as that of his predecessors) had brought neither peace nor prosperity, and realizing that his country would likely never defeat Israel, Sadat concluded that something new had to be done. So instead of listening to the worn-out tapes of advice he had received from Egyptian advisors, from other Arab leaders, from Washington, and from Moscow, he decided to do something altogether different— something that no one had ever dreamed of. He would go to Israel.

He did, and it was historic, but it did not bring about peace between the two countries. Would another war result? Not wanting to let this unique opportunity slip away, President Jimmy Carter summoned Sadat and Israeli Prime Minister Menachem Begin to the presidential retreat, Camp David.

After almost two weeks of intense, secret negotiations at Camp David, the Israeli-Egyptian negotiations resulted in two historic agreements. For the first time ever, Israel and one of her neighbors had agreed to live in peace.

The first agreement addressed the future of the Sinai and peace between Israel and Egypt. The second agreement provided a framework for the conduct of negotiations for the future of the West Bank and Gaza.

Reliable Resources

Camp David is located 70 miles from the White House in the Catoctin Mountains of Maryland. It was established in 1942 when President Franklin Delano Roosevelt needed to escape the summer heat of Washington, D.C., and the higher latitude of the camp provided cool breezes and good security. Named Shangri-La by Roosevelt, it was renamed Camp David in 1953 by President Eisenhower in honor of his grandson David Eisenhower. Guests at Camp David can enjoy a pool, putting green, driving range, tennis courts, and a gymnasium.

The Camp David Accords called for Israel to withdraw from the Sinai Peninsula and return it to Egypt. Egypt would agree to break with its Arab brothers and live in peace with its sworn enemy.

According to the preamble of the agreement, such sacrifices were necessary because

> After four wars during 30 years, despite intensive human efforts, the Middle East, which is the cradle of civilization and the birthplace of three great religions, does not enjoy the blessings of peace. The people of the Middle East yearn for peace so that the vast human and natural resources of the region can be turned to the pursuits of peace and so that this area can become a model for coexistence and cooperation among nations.

> The historic initiative of President Sadat in visiting Jerusalem and the reception accorded to him by the parliament, government and people of Israel, and the reciprocal visit of Prime Minister Begin to Ismailia, the peace proposals made by both leaders, as well as the warm reception of these missions by the peoples of both countries, have created an unprecedented opportunity for peace which must not be lost if this generation and future generations are to be spared the tragedies of war.

> Security is enhanced by a relationship of peace and by cooperation between nations which enjoy normal relations. In addition, under the terms of peace treaties, the parties can, on the basis of reciprocity, agree to special security arrangements such as demilitarized zones, limited armaments areas, early landmine stations, the presence of international forces, liaison, agreed measures for monitoring, and other arrangements that they agree are useful.

(It also didn't hurt that Egypt stood to obtain enormous financial assistance from the United States by opting for peace.)

Since the signing of the Camp David Accords on September 17, 1978, Egypt and Israel have not gone to war against each other again. For their heroic efforts, Sadat and Begin were awarded the Nobel Peace Prize in 1978.

The Campaign in Lebanon

Yet, while one border was finally secured, the same cannot be said for Israel's other borders. In March 1978, PLO terrorists killed an American tourist walking near an Israeli beach and hijacked a civilian bus—34 hostages died in the attack.

> **Landmine!**
>
> In 1983, terrorists killed 241 American Marines when a car bomb blew up next to the base where the Marines were stationed. Under pressure from Congress, President Reagan "redeployed" the marine contingent to the safety of ships off the coast.

In response, Israeli forces invaded Lebanon and attacked terrorist bases, in order to move the terrorists away from the border. Two months later, the Israeli forces withdrew and U.N. forces entered the region. By 1981, some 18,000 PLO members were encamped in scores of locations in Lebanon, and another 5,000 to 6,000 foreign mercenaries had joined them. Israeli strikes and commando raids were unable to stem the growth of this burgeoning army, and attacks by the PLO against Israel from Lebanon forced thousands of Israelis to flee their homes or to spend large amounts of time in bomb shelters.

Israel then invaded Lebanon again. The success of this second invasion forced Lebanon's President, Amin Gemayel, to sign a peace treaty with Israel, but only one year later, Gemayel reneged on the agreement under Syrian pressure.

The Lebanon war was very controversial in Israel. Prime Minister Begin eventually was forced to resign as demands to end the fighting intensified. By 1984, Israel withdrew from Lebanon.

Though Israel's primary mission—driving the PLO out of Lebanon—was successful, terrorist threats from Lebanon persisted. In all, 1,216 Israeli soldiers died in the campaign.

The Intifada

The Intifada ("insurrection" in Arabic) erupted in the Gaza Strip in 1987. It began as a general strike and grew rapidly thereafter. The Intifada was a watershed event that would transform Palestinian society and politics.

One of the essential elements was that the spontaneous revolt was led by Palestinian youths who had never known anything except the occupation and who took, at least during the first few years of the insurrection, the leadership of the uprising. Moreover, the images of Palestinian youth fighting Israeli tanks with little more than rocks proved to be a powerful image, strengthening their cause all the more. Indeed, the Intifada brought about an awareness of the Palestinian problem both by the Israeli people themselves and by the rest of the world.

Reliable Resources

Seeds of Peace is a group that tries to create friendships among children growing up in war zones. It is a nonprofit, nonpolitical organization that brings together young people from the Middle East as well as kids from other areas, such as Bosnia, Serbia, and U.S. inner cities. From May 1 to May 7, 1998, Seeds of Peace hosted the first 75 youths from Israel, Palestine, Jordan, Egypt, and the United States. Then, they drafted an Israeli-Palestinian peace treaty that was later presented to their leaders and U.N. Secretary General Kofi Annan.

Israel tried many things to suppress the uprising, including killing and injuring thousands of people, closing down the educational system, prohibiting alternative forms of teaching for two years, invading Palestinian towns, extending curfews, and imposing administrative detentions. Despite all that, the Intifada continued. It was becoming increasingly obvious to all concerned that a solution for the Palestinian refugee problem was now a necessity.

Onto Oslo

It is encouraging that although one constant in the Middle East has been incessant fighting, there has also been a constant search for answers. For every Intifada, there is an attempt at peace. So it was that in the early 1990s, Israeli and Palestinian negotiators met in secret in Oslo, Norway, in another attempt to bridge the gap.

These talks proved fruitful when, on September 19, 1993, Yasser Arafat, chairman of the Palestinian Liberation Organization and Israeli Prime Minister Yitzhak Rabin signed the Declaration of Principles, also known as the Oslo Accords, on the White House lawn under the endorsement of former President Bill Clinton. The Oslo agenda divided the peace process into an interim phase to establish limited Palestinian autonomy and a final status phase to discuss more explosive issues, including the Palestinian refugee problem.

As summarized by Global Exchange, the provisions of the Oslo Memorandum included the following:

♦ The creation of the Palestinian National Authority and future PNA democratic elections.

♦ Newly recognized Palestinian entities, that is the West Bank and Gaza Strip.

♦ A gradual withdrawal of Israeli troops from the Occupied Territories (OCT).

♦ The transfer of authority of the OCT from Israel to the PNA during a five-year period.

On September 28, 1995, the Israeli-Palestinian Interim Agreement on the West Bank and Gaza Strip was ratified. In addition to other provisions, including those outlined in the Oslo Accords, this document, commonly known as Oslo II, detailed the implementation of the second phase of Palestinian self-rule in the Occupied Territories, including …

♦ Elections for the Council of the Palestinian National Authority.

♦ A gradual withdrawal of Israeli forces from the centers of Palestinian populated areas.

♦ The establishment of Palestinian self-rule in the OCT.

♦ The transfer of planning and zoning authority in the West Bank and Gaza Strip from the Israeli Military Authorities to the PNA.

Landmine!

Fifty percent of the population of the Gaza Strip is younger than 16 years old.

In return, the Palestinians agreed to abandon the armed struggle against Israel and recognize the Jewish state. In exchange, they expected that Israel would recognize a Palestinian state in the Gaza Strip and the West Bank, including East Jerusalem, and acknowledge some measure of responsibility for the Palestinian refugees.

Although Oslo was good as far as it went, it is where it did not go that became the problem. Neither of the Oslo treaties satisfactorily addressed the most important issues of the region—the status of Jerusalem, the future of Palestinian refugees, and the right to and boundaries of a future Palestinian state. With enmity as high as it is in this part of the world, security always a concern, and attacks and counterattacks a way of life, it is not surprising that the parties had a difficult time implementing both the spirit and the letter of the Oslo Accords. Extremists on both sides tried to derail the process.

Death of a Statesman

On November 3, 1995, Israeli Prime Minister Yitzhak Rabin, a genuine war hero turned peacemaker, was assassinated by a right-wing Israeli opponent of the peace process, Yigal Amir. Rabin was then succeeded by his Foreign Minister, Shimon Peres, another proponent of the peace process. But in a subsequent election in May 1996, Peres was beaten by Benjamin Netanyahu of the opposition party which pledged to slow the peace process.

The War of the Roses

Yet the Israeli people longed for peace, and the Palestinians longed for a home. Neither side was yet ready to toss aside Oslo, despite the violence perpetrated by the extreme elements on both sides.

At the urging of new Israeli Prime Minister Barak, President Clinton invited Barak and Palestinian Authority Chairman Yasser Arafat to Camp David to continue their negotiations on the Middle East peace process.

On July 11, the Camp David 2000 Summit convened. The parties negotiated intensely for 15 days. Clinton tried to use his legendary personal charms and negotiation skills to cajole the parties into a final settlement, one that would address all the unresolved issues left for later by Oslo I and II. Later had finally arrived.

Israeli Prime Minister Barak pushed the limits of the possible, offering the Palestinians more than had ever been offered. Barak gambled that he could reverse his sagging political fortunes at home by bringing back a comprehensive peace deal, and then winning convincing endorsement for it in a popular referendum.

Specifically, Barak was prepared to make unprecedented concessions at Camp David. According to Stanford historian Joel Beinin, Barak was willing to recognize a Palestinian state on roughly 94 percent of the West Bank. Barak was also willing to trade land near the Gaza Strip for three Jewish settlements in the West Bank.

It may be that Barak's boldest move was to finally negotiate over Jerusalem, heretofore a taboo subject in Israeli politics. Barak offered Palestinians administrative autonomy over Arab East Jerusalem, as well as control over the Temple Mount. Under Barak's plan, Israel would retain actual sovereignty over the city. Finally, Barak agreed to the resettlement of about 100,000 Palestinian refugees inside Israel, as well as agreeing to participate in an international compensation fund for the four to five million other Palestinian refugees.

But in the end, as usual in this part of the world, old grievances triumphed over new solutions. The main sticking points were Jerusalem and the refugee question. Sharing Jerusalem was not good enough for the Palestinians, and Israel refused to address the refugee problem in a way that was acceptable to Arafat. The talks collapsed.

Israeli Prime Minister Barak and President Bill Clinton both blamed the Palestinian President Yasser Arafat for missing an historic opportunity to resolve the Arab-Israeli dispute. Barak was praised by Clinton for his courage for offering the Palestinians the best deal ever proposed by an Israeli leader, which included a hand-over of all Gaza and 90-odd percent of the West Bank, as well as "important concessions" in Jerusalem. It seems that Arafat wanted 100 percent or nothing, and the Israelis refused to budge on ultimate control of Jerusalem.

> ### Reliable Resources
>
> The Palestinian delegation worked hard, but it is fair to say that perhaps because they prepared more, perhaps because they thought about it more, the Israelis moved further relatively to their original positions compared to Arafat, especially on the issue of Jerusalem.
>
> —Bill Clinton

It was a tragic result, one that lead to much ensuing bloodshed. It is also a result that could have been avoided. One thing you will see consistently throughout this book is that peace usually only occurs when a leader emerges who is willing to buck conventional wisdom, take a big risk, and who is prepared to teach his or her people a new way. Although Barak seemed willing, Arafat was not, and, as they say, it takes two to tango.

In the black comedy *The War of the Roses*, Michael Douglas and Kathleen Turner play a married couple going though a nasty, bitter divorce. Fighting over everything from homes to forks, the couple simply cannot come to terms with the fact that they have to share. Consumed with hatred for one another, in the end they actually kill each other rather than agree to share anything.

After the collapse of the talks at Camp David, whatever power Oslo had left vanished. A new Palestinian Intifada erupted, the peace process died, Israeli hawk Ariel Sharon was swept into power, and the Middle East War of the Roses continued.

The Least You Need to Know

- Israelis and Palestinians have both lived in the Middle East for centuries.
- After years away, the Zionist movement brought Jews back.
- Wars have erupted every few years between Israel and her neighbors.
- The Oslo Accords put off the hard questions.
- The cycle of violence continues.

Chapter 4

A Wreck Called Iraq

In This Chapter

- ◆ Iraq: An ancient civilization
- ◆ The rise of Islam
- ◆ Saddam Hussein takes control
- ◆ The Iran-Iraq War
- ◆ The Gulf War

Home to humanity's first civilization, Sumer, the area around Iraq has been the backdrop to thousands of years of momentous human events.

In recent years, few countries have been more in the crossfire of human conflict than Iraq. In this chapter, I look at its war with Iran, the invasion of Kuwait, the subsequent Gulf War, and then the resulting intransigence of Saddam Hussein; all of which have created extreme hardship for Iraq's people and fear in an already volatile world.

Iraq: Two neighbors attacked (so far).

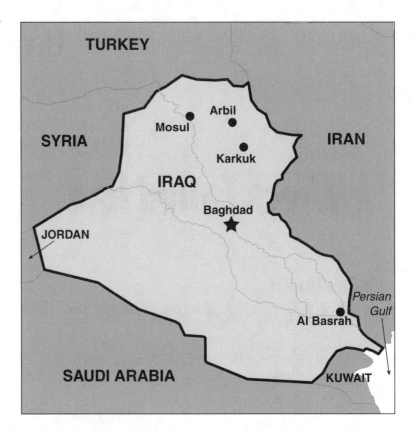

Don't Know Much About History

The Old Testament refers to modern Iraq as Mesopotamia—a land of lush vegetation, abundant wildlife, and copious, unpredictable water resources. By 6000 B.C.E., Mesopotamia had been settled, chiefly by migrants from the Turkish and Iranian highlands.

Sumer is the ancient name for southern Mesopotamia, and the people who populated it were known as Sumerians. Sumerian culture marks a watershed in human history.

To begin with, the Sumerians were the first people known to have devised a scheme of written representation. Called pictograms, these writings were created by scrawling pictures using reeds as a writing instrument on wet clay. The clay would then dry into stone-hard tablets. Through this method of writing, the Sumerians were able to pass on complex agricultural techniques.

Sumerians also recorded and preserved one of the oldest known pieces of literature, the story of Gilgamesh. Dated approximately 2700 B.C.E., it is the story of the king of the city-state of Uruk.

The Sumerians are also responsible for creating one of the world's first systems of monarchy. According to historian Richard Hooker, "the very first states in human history, the states of Sumer, were likely ruled by a type of priest-king whose duties included leading the military, administering trade, judging disputes, and engaging the most important religious ceremonies."

The most important and far-reaching of all Sumerian inventions, however, was their invention of law. Although little is known about Sumerian law, scholars agree that the Code of Hammurabi, written by a Babylonian monarch, reproduces Sumerian law almost exactly.

And so it is that modern Iraq has a rich history to live up to.

The Rise of Islam

The prophet Muhammed created Islam late in the sixth century, and as with much of the rest of the Arabian Peninsula, Islam was quickly adopted by ancient Iraq, although a schism that soon developed in Islam would affect Iraqi politics to this very day.

Sunni Versus Shiite

The most critical problem that faced the young Islamic community revolved around finding the rightful successor to the office of *caliph*, or successor to Muhammed, following the assassination of the second caliph of Islam, Umar of Arabia. The two contenders vying for the power and the glory were Uthman and Ali ibn Abu Talib (Ali), the prophet Muhammad's cousin and son-in-law. In the end, Uthman's conservatism, which promised continuity with the goals of the previous leadership, convinced the electorate to choose him over Ali as caliph—much to the disappointment of Ali's supporters, who opposed and never acknowledged Uthman's appointment.

Ultimately, this historical split between contenders and their supporters led to a division in Islam:

◆ Shia, or Shiites, are the party of Ali. Shiite Muslims are the smaller of the two parts of Islam. The Shias supported the claims of Ali and his line to presumptive right to the caliphate and to leadership of the Muslim community.

Diplomatic Dialogue

The person acting in Muhammad's place after his death, that is the leader of Islam, is called the **caliph**. Through history, there have been many caliphs, the last one however was removed by the Mongols when they conquered Baghdad in 1258. The term is seldom used for anything other than the leader of the entire Muslim community.

◆ Sunnis (from sunna, orthodox) are members of the larger of the two great divisions of Islam. The Sunnis supported the traditional method of election to the caliphate, and they accepted the Umayyad line that began with caliph Muawiyah in 661.

The politics and conflicts of Iraq are dominated by this split to this day. Saddam Hussein is a Sunni Muslim, but 80 percent of Iraq is not. Rather, it is made up of either Shiites or Kurds. As such, a large part of the problem in Iraq today is that Saddam Hussein continues to repress the Shiite majority in the southern part of his country, as well as the Kurds in the north (see Chapter 5 for more information.)

The British Mandate

What is now known as the modern state of Iraq resulted from the breakup of the Ottoman Empire after World War I. At the 1919 Paris Peace Conference, under Article 22 of the League of Nations, Britain was given a mandate over the so-called "Fertile Crescent," which included the areas known today as Iraq, Palestine, Kuwait, Jordan, and Egypt. Syria was placed under the French mandate.

Some of these territories had never been considered independent nations before; instead, previous conquerors had merely absorbed the lands and people of the Middle East into their own empires. Indeed, the borders of many modern Arab countries have no roots in history.

This time, however, the victors decided to carve the area into nation-states. The vast majority of nations that now occupy the Middle East were simply created out of whole cloth by France and Britain. And problematically, a basic lack of understanding of the history, geography, and religion of the area by these colonial powers would cause problems and conflicts for years to come.

> **CAUTION**
>
> **Landmine!**
>
> The vast majority of Syrians strongly opposed the French mandate and the French presence, even though it was to last 25 years. Maybe most of all, the Muslim population resented that France took considerable Muslim areas from Syria to form a new country—Lebanon.

The Creation of Modern Iraq

At the Cairo Conference of 1921, the British set the parameters for Iraqi political life that were to continue until 1958; choosing Faisal ibn Hussein, a member of the same family that continues to rule neighboring Jordan, as Iraq's first King. However, this British-created monarchy suffered from a legitimacy crisis, not only because the concept of a monarchy was foreign to Iraq, but also because Faisal wasn't even Iraqi! What's more, Iraq was almost too complex and too diverse a society to have any sort of peace for long. The country was beset by conflict from the moment the British set it free. Sunnis and

Shias, cities and tribes, sheiks and tribesmen, Assyrians and Kurds, all fought for places in the emerging state structure.

The longstanding Sunni-Shia conflict in particular continued to cause a rift in the country: Shias feared Sunni domination. Ultimately, lacking legitimacy and unable to establish deep roots, the British-imposed political system would be overwhelmed by these conflicts.

Faisal I died in 1933 and was succeeded by his 21-year-old son, Ghazi. King Ghazi then died in a tragic automobile accident six years later when he drove his car into a lamppost and died instantly in 1939. He left the crown to his only son, the three-year-old Faisal II who would "govern" for only a short while himself.

The lack of respect for the crown, combined with the quick lackluster succession of kings, fostered ferment among the masses. So it was that by 1958, Iraq was ready to rid itself of the British-imposed monarchy. Modern politics and the birth of modern Iraqi conflict occurred that year when the army murdered the young King in a bloody coup d'état, also killing the crown prince, several princesses, their relatives and servants, as well as the Prime Minister and most of the cabinet.

> **Reliable Resources**
>
> The Middle East is a land of deep interpersonal connections. One place that helps forge these connections is Victoria College in Alexandria, Egypt. Not only was this school attended by the bin Laden brothers, but their schoolmates also included the likes of King Hussein of Jordan and actor Omar Sharif.

The Times, They Are A-Changin'

The Republic of Iraq was then formed on July 14, 1958, with coup leader Abdul-Karim Qassem being the first prime minister of the newly formed government. The presidency of the country was entrusted to a three-member Sovereignty Council comprising a Sunni, a Shiite, and a Kurdish leader.

However, like the kings who preceded him, Qassem was to rule Iraq for only a short time. Five years after he took the reins of power, he was hoisted by his own petard—murdered on February 8, 1963, by members of the pan-Arab Baath (Renaissance) party in a successful coup against him and his government.

A succession of even more coups during the next few years left the country in disarray, and, as such, the time was ripe for the emergence of a strongman who could control the ever-fluctuating, volatile political situation. That man was Saddam Hussein.

> **CAUTION Landmine!**
>
> After his death, Qassem's corpse was strapped into a chair, and televised, while one of his executioners occasionally moved the head back and forth to convince viewers this was no manikin, but Qassem himself.

Saddam Hussein Emerges

Saddam Hussein joined the Arab Baath Socialist Party in 1957. Two years later, he was involved in an unsuccessful attempt to assassinate Prime Minister Qassem and was forced into exile. When Saddam returned, he was imprisoned; however, he escaped from jail, and in 1968, he helped lead the successful Baathist coup. As a result, control of the country landed in the hands of Saddam Hussein and General Ahmad Hassan al-Bakr, who became president and vice-president, respectively. From his new position of power, Saddam Hussein would build an elaborate network of secret police to root out dissidents.

Bakr, who had been a long-time defender of Arab nationalist causes, brought the party legitimacy and support from both Baathist and non-Baathist army officers. Saddam Hussein, by contrast, was the politician of the pair, adept at outmaneuvering (wink, wink) political opponents. Although Bakr started out as the more legitimate leader of the two, by 1969 Saddam Hussein clearly had become *the* major player in the Baath party.

This trend accelerated throughout the '70s, especially because Bakr was beset by illness and a series of family tragedies during this time. Disinclined in any case to share power, Saddam Hussein consolidated his base and began to view the Revolutionary Command Council (Iraq's highest executive body), as well as the cabinet as rubber stamps. On July 16, 1979, Saddam Hussein deposed Bakr and plastered the streets with portraits of himself.

Saddam Hussein came to full power. His titles included the following:

- President of the Republic
- Secretary General of the Baath Party Regional Command
- Chairman of the Revolutionary Command Council
- Commander in Chief of the Armed Forces

> **Reliable Resources**
>
> Economically, Iraq engages in extensive central planning and management of industrial production and foreign trade while leaving some small-scale industry and services and most agriculture to private enterprise. The economy has been dominated by the oil sector, which has traditionally provided about 95 percent of foreign exchange earnings.

So Just Who Is Saddam Hussein?

Summarily despised as the enemy of the Western world, Saddam Hussein is a ruthless dictator with a penchant for beating the odds against him. The son of poor farmers, Saddam Hussein grew up in Auja, a tiny village northwest of Baghdad. Inspired by his nationalistic uncle, an Iraqi army officer, Saddam Hussein gravitated to politics as a young man, immersing himself in the anti-British and anti-Western sentiments of the day.

His treatment of the Shiite majority in the south of his country has been equally repressive and violent. Shiites make up 60 percent of Iraq, and Iraq's fundamentalist neighbor Iran is a Shiite Muslim country. As such, the Sunni Saddam has reason to worry. It is his policy therefore to keep the Shiite population under tight control and scrutiny.

According to Middle-East analyst Gerald Butt, a former Iraqi diplomat living in exile summed up Saddam's rule in one sentence: "Saddam is a dictator who is ready to sacrifice his country, just so long as he can remain on his throne in Baghdad." Few people would disagree with this. In a region where despotic rule is the norm, he is more feared by his own people than any other head of state.

But maybe surprisingly, on the streets of other Arab cities, Saddam Hussein is often admired as a leader who has dared to defy and challenge Israel and the West. For many in the Middle East, he has become a symbol of Arab steadfastness in the face of Western influence.

That he is also a bold, possibly reckless, risk taker is similarly beyond doubt. Saddam Hussein endeavors to be more than a thug. Since the death of the greatest *pan-Arab* leader of the twentieth century, Gamal Abdul Nasser, in 1970, the Arab nationalist movement has been looking for a new leader, and Saddam Hussein has always longed to be that person. As Saddam Hussein saw it, when he took power in 1979, the time to fulfill that ambition had arrived, for several reasons.

Diplomatic Dialogue

Because the Ottoman Turks rose to power and conquered the Middle East in the fourteenth century, there have been stirrings among Arabs for reunification as a means of reestablishing Arab political power. **Pan-Arabism** is the modern movement calling for political unification among Arab states.

First of all, Saddam Hussein was a leader of a large industrious country that was benefiting from the 1970s oil boom. His country is situated on the edge of the Persian Gulf, one of the most strategically important regions in the world. And just when the Arab nationalist movement was looking for a new champion after the Camp David accords, Iraq found itself with the upper hand as the 1979 Iranian revolution weakened Iran, and made it an enemy of the United States. Finally, Saddam Hussein wielded a powerful army and large financial reserves.

So as the 1980s dawned, Saddam Hussein was poised and ready to make a name for himself. The question was—how? Unfortunately for his ambitions, Saddam Hussein is not the greatest strategist around. Rather than wait to exercise his power with some savvy, the void left by Nasser was too great a temptation for Saddam. He crassly concluded that if he could quickly defeat his neighbor Iran in war, he would emerge as the undisputed king of the Arab world.

That he had an ostensible reason to do so made the idea that much more palatable. Saddam Hussein feared that Iran's new Shiite leadership would threaten Iraq's delicate Sunni-Shiite balance. He was also concerned about a longstanding territorial dispute regarding access to the Persian Gulf. In this respect, Saddam Hussein's decision to invade Iran has historical precedent; the ancient rulers of Mesopotamia, fearing internal strife and foreign conquest, also engaged in frequent battles with the peoples of what is now Iran.

With both a political and a personal reason to attack, Saddam Hussein calculated that a war against Iran would be both quick and fruitful. So on September 22, 1980, Iraq launched a land and air invasion against Iran.

The Iran-Iraq War

Saddam Hussein has always held that his attack on Iran was the result of a legitimate dispute over the Shatt al Arab, a waterway in the Persian Gulf that forms the boundary between Iran and Iraq. But Saddam Hussein's reasons were not so pure as there was no legitimate dispute at all: The fact is that in 1975, Iraq had signed over to Iran partial control of that waterway. Sensing weakness in Iran after the fall of the Shah, Hussein concluded that the time was ripe to wipe out the treaty. That he thought he could also capture the western Iranian region of Khuzestan, an area with extensive oil fields, was further reason fueling the Iraqi invasion.

> **CAUTION**
>
> **Landmine!** _____
>
> An important part of the energy resources of the free world are under Iran's control. The free world cannot tolerate the loss of Iran, and there is no power in the world which can impose the smallest thing against Iran's national interests.
>
> —Mohammad Reza Pahlavi, Shah of Iran, 1976, three years before he was ousted by Ayatollah Khomeini's revolution

Although initially successful, the Iraqi invasion bogged down in 1982. Iranian resistance was stronger than Iraq had anticipated. Iran was backed by Syria, Libya, North Korea, and China. Iraq had much more support that included many western nations (including the United States!). What had begun as Saddam's attempt to quickly grab some oil fields and power had instead turned into a grudge match in which neither side could win, yet neither was willing to lose.

As the war dragged on into its seventh year, the United States and several Western European nations intervened after Iran started to attack oil tankers. These attacks greatly harmed Iran's reputation, making it difficult for Khomeini to obtain arms.

As this war of attrition dragged on into its eighth year, Iran was finally forced to accept a United Nations–mandated cease-fire. It is estimated that some 1.5 million died in the Iran-Iraq war. Amazingly, when it was all over, the conditions that existed at the beginning of the war remained virtually unchanged. Consequently, considerable potential exists for another war.

The Iran-Iraq War permanently altered the course of Iraqi history. It strained Iraqi political and social life, and led to severe economic dislocations. Saddam Hussein knew that he needed to do something to revive his, as well as his country's sagging fortunes, but what? Just as he had a decade earlier, Saddam Hussein concluded that war was his salvation. Again he would attack a neighbor—this time, Kuwait.

The Mother of All Battles

From its inception, Iraqis firmly believed that Kuwait was part of Iraq. In 1939, King Ghazi of Iraq mobilized his army to conquer what was then still a colony of Britain. Just before the army was ready to strike, however, King Ghazi died in a car crash, and the invasion was called off.

In 1961, when Kuwait finally gained its independence from Great Britain, Iraq again began preparations for an invasion of the tiny land and only backed down when Britain sent troops back into the region. Thereafter, relations between the two countries were never warm, but neither were they at war.

Reliable Resources

According to the Kuwait Information Office, much of Iraq's alleged claim to Kuwait is based on the Anglo-Ottoman Convention of 1913, an agreement signed between Britain and the Turks. In the Convention, Kuwait was named as "an autonomous qada (sub province, district) of the Ottoman Empire." Iraq therefore believes that Kuwait's status, as set forth in the Convention, makes it subordinate to Ottoman authorities that were based in Iraq. The problem is that the Convention was never ratified.

Countdown to War

Tensions began to rise, however, at the end of the Iran-Iraq War. That war had been largely financed by the oil-rich Gulf States, especially Kuwait, and once the war was over, Kuwait began to demand that its loans be paid back. Moreover, the price of oil, which had provided Iraq with most of its income, had dropped precipitously at the dawn of the '90s.

On July 17, 1990, Saddam accused Kuwait of deliberately flooding the oil market and stealing oil from the Rumailia Oil Field. On July 25, U.S. Ambassador to Iraq, April Galespie, told Saddam Hussein that the Iraq/Kuwait dispute was an Arab matter and did not affect the United States.

Saddam Hussein seems to have taken that to mean he had a free hand in dealing with his grievances, and on August 2, he invaded Kuwait. His troops easily overran the little country. Iraqi tanks were in Kuwait City before dawn, and by noon they had reached the Saudi frontier. The Kuwaiti emir and his cabinet fled to Saudi Arabia. On August 8, 1990, Iraq annexed the emirate.

The United Nations quickly passed a series of resolutions calling on Iraq to withdraw from Kuwait. The Iraqis responded with the claim that they had been invited in by a group of Kuwaiti rebels who had overthrown the emir.

> ### Peacekeepers
>
> It is not easy to vote in Kuwait. In fact, only 10 percent of all citizens are eligible to vote. Only adult males, who have been naturalized for 30 years or more or have resided in Kuwait since before 1920, and their male descendants can vote at age 21 or older.

As he did in the war with Iran, once again Saddam Hussein miscalculated the opponent. What he failed to realize was that by invading Kuwait, he seemed to be threatening the stability (such as it is) of the entire region. Whether Saddam Hussein had greater aims beyond Kuwait is another topic altogether, and it actually matters little. In politics, perception *is* reality, and the perception was that Saddam was in fact threatening the entire Persian Gulf region.

Oil fuels the American economy. The possibility that someone like Saddam Hussein could control much of the world's oil supply was seen as a direct threat to the interests of the United States, as well as other industrialized nations. Accordingly, President Bush (the first) began to forge a broad, international coalition to force Iraq out of Kuwait.

As Osama bin Laden would learn later, rousing the ire of the world's only remaining superpower is not smart. The United States is a country that is slow to anger, but lethal when provoked. As Japanese Admiral Yamamoto famously said after the attack on Pearl Harbor—"I fear we have aroused a sleeping giant." Saddam Hussein's invasion of Kuwait did the same thing.

The first order of business was to get the United Nations to permit an embargo on trade with Iraq. It did, and the world waited to see whether the embargo would work. At the end of November, the United States and Britain secured another U.N. resolution authorizing the use of force to drive Iraq out of Kuwait if the Iraqis did not leave voluntarily before January 15, 1991.

The United States took it from there. The Bush senior administration helped foster a multinational force composed of several NATO countries as well as neighboring Arab states. Even former Warsaw Pact countries sent in units to join this colorful international alliance.

Operation Desert Storm

The deadline passed, the Iraqis didn't budge, soon waves of Allied aircraft began a five-week bombing campaign of Iraq and Kuwait that marked the beginning of Operation Desert Storm. The American air forces employed their most advanced technologies, quickly destroyed Iraq's air defense network, and from then on owned the skies.

Compared to its airborne cousin, the ensuing ground offensive was anticlimactic—Iraq's army disintegrated in a mere 100 hours. At the end of February, Allied forces arrived at the gates of Kuwait City, which had been shrouded by clouds of acrid black smoke from the hundreds of oil wells the Iraqis had set afire during their hasty retreat.

Because the U.N. mandate was to excise Iraq from Kuwait, President George Bush decided not to invade Baghdad, nor to go after Saddam Hussein directly. The decision not to oust Saddam was augmented by a fear that Iran might overtake Iraq should Saddam fall, and that in any case, Saddam Hussein would likely be overthrown by his own people. As a result of this decision, the dictator remained in power, only to frustrate the West time and again.

Landmine!

In 1994, Kuwait convicted several Iraqis on charges of attempting to assassinate former President George Bush when he visited the emirate the previous year. The plot, according to the Kuwaitis, was uncovered and foiled at the last minute.

Postscript

After the war, the United States and United Kingdom were determined to clip Iraq's wings: They created two "no-fly" zones in the country, one north of the 36th parallel to protect the Kurds, and another below the 33rd parallel to protect the Shiites.

In addition, Saddam Hussein was also ordered to destroy all his weapons of mass destruction. After years of noncompliance and a cat-and-mouse inspection game with U.N. inspectors, Saddam finally kicked them out of his country in 1998, and his arsenal likely remains.

As reported by CNN's Special Report, "The Unfinished War: A Decade Since Desert Storm," the sanctions initially imposed before the war have never been lifted, a fact that has actually played into Saddam Hussein's hands. Says Sergey Lavrov, ambassador of the Russian Federation to the United Nations, "We never voted for making sanctions permanent. We never voted for a situation which would last for ten years, practically demolishing the Iraqi economy and the Iraqi civil society and bringing humanitarian catastrophe." According to Andrew Mack, director of strategic planning in the office of the U.N. secretary-general, "The human cost of the sanctions to the Iraqi people has been extraordinary."

The Border After the War

After the Gulf War, the international community moved to irrefutably reject Iraq's claims to Kuwait and to clearly demarcate the border. Following the conclusion of the ground war between the Coalition forces and Iraq, the United Nations adopted Security Council Resolution 687. This resolution called upon the Secretary-General to create a commission to assist Iraq and Kuwait to officially demarcate their common, international border, as agreed upon in a 1963 treaty between Iraq and Kuwait.

On May 20, 1993, the secretary-general of the United Nations released a letter stating that the commission had completed the demarcation of the Iraq-Kuwait Border. One week later, the Security Council passed Resolution 833, affirming the U.N. Demarcation Commission's work and calling upon Iraq and Kuwait to respect the "inviolability of the international boundary, as demarcated by the Commission."

On June 17, 1993, the Kuwait government sent a letter affirming the Security Council Resolution 833 and agreeing to the assigned border. On November 14, 1994, following 18 months of refusals and immediately after once again threatening Kuwait through massive troop deployments on the border, Iraq's permanent representative to the United Nations presented a letter from the Iraqi government containing a decree and declaration that Iraq affirmed "the sovereignty of the State of Kuwait, its territorial integrity and political independence and (Iraq's) respect for the inviolability of the said border."

> **CAUTION**
>
> ## Landmine!
>
> In official reports, the Pentagon stated that of the 148 American servicemen and women who perished on the battlefield in the Persian Gulf War, 31 percent of them were victims of friendly fire. Most soldiers said that the thousands of unexploded mines and bombs they encountered were more dangerous than enemy fire.

Iraq Since the Persian Gulf War

Despite Iraq's crushing military collapse and a decade of subsequent crippling sanctions, Saddam Hussein remained in power in Iraq, seemingly unshaken by plots to eliminate him. "I think Saddam as a person represents one of the darkest forces in modern Arab history," says former U.S. Assistant Secretary of State David Welch. "Here is a person who, for the sake of his own grasp for power and ambition, has been willing to execute hundreds, thousands, of his own citizens."

Former National Security Adviser Brent Scowcroft believes that Saddam Hussein is "one of the most ruthless people that the world has ever seen. One of the reasons he has been so successful," Scowcroft says, "is that he terrifies everyone who works for him—like personally executing people in front of his colleagues, or having somebody execute his best friend to show his loyalty."

In 1998, former U.S. President George Bush reflected on Saddam's staying power: "I thought when the war ended that he could not survive the humiliating defeat. And every single Gulf country told me the same thing. The British felt the same way, the French felt the same way, indeed our whole coalition did. We did not believe that he would stay in office," Bush said. "But you know something, we underestimated the brutality he would bring to bear on his own people to keep his own self, keep his own person, in office."

And stay in office he has. On the last day of the year 2000, Saddam Hussein presided over Iraq's largest military parade in a decade. Who knew what he would do next, after all, he still had four neighbors he had yet to attack.

The Least You Need to Know

- ◆ Iraq is an ancient culture with a rich history.
- ◆ The Sunni-Shiite rift in Islam affects Iraq to this day.
- ◆ Saddam Hussein is a ruthless dictator who suppresses the majority of his country.
- ◆ The Iran-Iraq war was a miscalculation on Saddam's part.
- ◆ The Gulf War was another miscalculation.

Chapter 5

Never-Never Land: Kurdistan

In This Chapter

- ◆ The history of the Kurds
- ◆ The Kurds' tragic life in Turkey
- ◆ The Kurds as terrorists
- ◆ The Kurds in Iraq and Iran
- ◆ What will the future hold?

As you might have gathered, the decision by the now-defunct League of Nations allowing the colonial powers of Great Britain and France to carve up the Middle East portion of the old Ottoman Empire into a series of new nation states has been nothing short of disastrous. Countries were created out of thin air; nations often contained peoples who had no business living together.

Another result of that awful decision is that some nations which actually did make some sense were eliminated. The ancient land of Kurdistan was one of those countries, erased from the world's maps after World War I. The problem is, although Kurdistan is gone, the Kurds are not. It is not unlike the Palestinians of today—Palestine might be gone, but they remain.

In recent years, the Kurdish question has reappeared on the international agenda. The crisis of the Kurds has been of fundamental concern to the countries of the region, and has led to extensive internal controversies and economic and social crises.

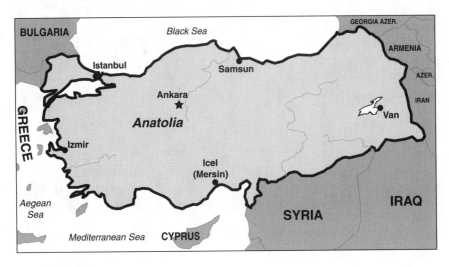

Kurdistan: Nowhere to be seen.

The Kurds of Kurdistan

The Kurds are the largest ethnic group in the world without their own country. There are 12 million Kurds living today in Turkey, 5 million in Iran, 4 million in Iraq, 500,000 in Syria, Azerbaijan, Armenia, and Georgia. Several million live elsewhere in Europe. As you might imagine, throughout the twentieth century, their struggles for political and cultural autonomy were opposed by countries they have been scattered to.

The Kurds are, together with the Arabs, Persians, and Armenians, one of the most ancient peoples of the Near East. The Greek historian Xenophon mentions Assyrian battles with the Kurds (circa 400 B.C.E.). After accepting the Islamic faith following persecution by the Arabs, they won a degree of autonomy that they retained for several hundred years. Literary works have been written in the Kurdish language since the tenth century. During the thirteenth century, Saladin, a Kurd, emerged as one of the foremost leaders in the struggle against the Crusades.

Peacekeepers

The vast traditional Kurdish homeland of Kurdistan is about 230,000 square miles. It would be about equal to the areas of Germany and Britain combined, or roughly the size of France or Texas.

The Kurds are predominantly shepherds and farmers, with a strong sense of family honor; feuding between rival families is not uncommon. Larger groups are brought together under an aga, or lord, who is usually a landowner. National dress is still worn in the more mountainous regions, and there is a strong tradition of poetry and music.

Despite their deep culture and having lived in the Middle East since antiquity, the volatile post-World War I world didn't know what to do with the Kurds.

Should Kurdistan remain an independent country? After the war, although the Ottoman Empire was history, it was decided that Kurdistan would not be. According to the Treaty of Sèvres, which was signed in 1920, the state of Kurdistan was to survive.

But the treaty was never ratified. Rather, in the Treaty of Lausanne, signed in three years later, that part of Kurdistan which had been part of the Ottoman Empire was carved up to be included in the British and French Mandates.

The largest part of Kurdistan became part of the Republic of Turkey, another country founded on the ruins of the Ottoman Empire. Yet the plan was that the Kurds would have a say in the new country. According to Ismet Pasha, the Turkish representative, "The Kurds and the Turks are the essential components of the Republic of Turkey. The Kurds are not a minority but a nation; the government in Ankara (the capital of Turkey) is the government of the Turks as well as of the Kurds."

> **Peacekeepers**
>
> The 1920 Treaty of Sèvres, which carved out Iraq, Syria, and Kuwait from the Ottoman Empire after World War I, promised the Kurds limited autonomy and recognized their right to form an independent Kurdish state. The treaty, though, was never ratified, partly because of the colonial powers' interest in the oil reserves in the region and nationalist desires of the Turks.

Should They Stay or Should They Go?

About 70 Kurdish Members of Parliament attended the first session of the Great National Assembly in Ankara, and were officially designated as the "MPs of Kurdistan." However, Ankara's policy rapidly changed. The structures of the new state were designed exclusively with Turkish interests in mind.

Turkish policy-makers attempted to create a unified nation, and to that extent, sought to melt other languages and cultures into the Turkish language and culture. They completely ignored Article 39 of the Treaty of Lausanne, which states that the citizens of Turkey have the right to freely use their respective languages in all areas of life. Instead …

> **Landmine!**
>
> Any language which is prohibited by law may not be used to express or distribute ideas. Printed matter, records, acoustic and video cassettes, or any other productions can be confiscated on the order of the authorities if they are in violation of this regulation.
> —Constitution of the Turkish Republic, Article 26

- ♦ The Kurdish language was totally forbidden in the educational system.

- ♦ Kurdish was also banned in the printed media.

- ♦ Speaking about the Kurds and criticizing their oppression became a crime.

- ♦ Even the concepts of Kurdish and Kurdistan were soon outlawed.

The Kurds Rebel

By 1925, it became apparent that the Kurds were not going to live as a recognized minority in Turkey, and would not enjoy the same rights as other minorities. The anger and humiliation, being too much to bear, led to calls for a rebellion. At this time, Sheikh Said was a religious nationalist figure who had a major influence among Kurds, thus enabling him to mobilize tribal chieftains against Turkish repression. So it was that the Kurds, led by Sheik Said, rose up against the discrimination that had been thrust upon them.

In February 1925, a minor clash occurred at the village of Piran between Sheikh Said's followers and the Turkish forces, but this local event struck a nerve, and a mass popular uprising by the Kurds against the Turks erupted:

- Kurds quickly took Turkish officials and officers prisoner.
- Tribes in nearby villages seized control of their own areas, driving out Turkish officials.
- The city of Diyarbekir was declared the capital of a revived Kurdistan.
- Within a month, Said's forces had seized control of about a third of Kurdistan in Turkey.

The initial success, rapidity, and sheer scale of the rebellion took the Turkish government by surprise. Turkey declared martial law in all Kurdish provinces and sent 50,000 armed men to the region. The power and size of the repression was more than the Kurds could handle, and Kurdish partisans were soon on the run. By March 1925, Diyarbekir had fallen, marking the beginning of the end of the "Sheikh Said Uprising."

Sheikh Said and 52 of his followers were caught and hung in Diyarbekir. Villages were burnt to the ground, and the inhabitants were massacred to teach the Kurds a lesson. Tens of thousands of Kurds were killed or driven into exile.

The Dersim Revolt

In June 1934, a new Turkish law abrogated recognition of Kurdish tribes, their chiefs, and sheiks, effectively giving Turkish authorities the right to demolish villages or towns where Turkish was not the mother tongue, and relocating their inhabitants to Turkish-speaking areas.

In 1936, 60,000 Turkish soldiers participated in an attempt to uproot the population of the Dersim area. Until then, the Dersim region had kept out of all conflicts. But in August 1937, Turkish forces began to destroy villages in Dersim. This was too much. Dersim rebelled.

In the spring of 1938, aerial bombing and artillery barrages battered the Kurdish rebels. But, refusing to quit, the rebels fought back, only to witness the destruction of even more villages. By August, Turkish forces had control over Dersim, rounding up rebels, burning villages, and declaring the Dersim area an uninhabitable zone.

According to estimates, as many as 40,000 Kurds perished in Dersim. Those who survived the massacre were put under the supervision of the local army.

Dersim marked the end of the tribal revolts against the Turkish state. However, it probably isn't surprising that the Kurds—who had few rights and were being subjected to oppression, who were forced into poverty, and who thought that all peaceful and legal avenues of political struggle had been closed off to them—once again began to arm themselves against the Turkish state.

> **Reliable Resources**
>
> A key feature of Kurdish society since medieval times has been its strong tribal associations. Tribes are the highest form of social organization, and the political process is tribal to a large degree. Today, in the absence of a Kurdish nation state and government, tribes are where Kurd allegiances remain.

The Birth of Modern Conflict

Out of the ashes left behind by Turkish aggressors rose the Kurdish Workers' Party (PKK). The name is somewhat a misnomer if there ever was one, given that PKK members are about as interested in the plight of workers as are conservatives who claim to be compassionate citizens. The true aim of the party has been the rebirth of a Kurdistan to be carved out of Turkey.

> **Reliable Resources**
>
> Since World War I, Kurdistan has been administered by five states: Turkey (43 percent of old Kurdistan), Iran (31 percent), Iraq (18 percent), Syria (6 percent), and the former Soviet Union (2 percent).

Founded in 1978, the PKK began as a Marxist-Leninist political party by Abdullah Ocalan. It emphasized freedom from colonialism and class divisions, thus opposing both Turkish government oppression and the traditional tribal hierarchy of Kurdish society. The PKK has widespread support among Kurds, in part because of its lack of allegiance to any particular tribal faction.

The Turkish government fought the PKK to the brink of obliteration during the early 1980s, but Ocalan then fled to Syria, where, in 1984, he and his supporters regrouped and declared war on the Turkish government.

The PKK had become a terrorist organization. It launched a fierce campaign against Turkey, seemingly following the example of Peru's Shining Path and Cambodia's Khmer

Rouge. PKK rebels have reportedly slaughtered tens of thousands of Kurdish villagers who refused to support their nationalist cause and have claimed responsibility for numerous bombings across the country.

Politically, the group is based in Brussels and calls itself the National Liberation Front of Kurdistan, which includes a self-proclaimed Kurdistan parliament. Although most European Union nations at least pay lip service to the rights of Kurds, they don't want to offend their NATO partner Turkey. Even so, the group was eventually outlawed in Germany and France after attacks on Turkish sites in those countries.

Say Uncle

According to *Time Magazine* journalist Ron Usher, the PKK is quite well organized. Aside from its strong propaganda arm (including a television station), its most important asset has been its charismatic leader, Abdullah Ocalan, a hated terrorist to Turks, but a hero to stateless Kurds who call him Apo ("uncle").

Usher notes that as a teenager, Ocalan was moved by the plight of his poor, illiterate farming parents. He rose from those paltry beginnings to become a cult figure.

Wheras Turkey blames Ocalan for thousands of deaths, the PKK counters that their tactics pale in comparison to the state-sponsored terrorism of Turkey, who, the PKK claims, has engaged in a scorched-earth war against Kurds.

The problem for the PKK is that the Kurds are neither united by a single religion or language, and are dispersed among many different countries. This is quite different than say, more homogenous nation seekers like the Palestinians.

Initially, the group aimed to secure an independent Kurdish state, but has since modified its demands, indicating a willingness to accept autonomy, if not nationhood. However, despite the softening of the PKK's hard-line stance, Ocalan remained Turkey's most wanted man.

Reliable Resources

In 1991, the Turkish government announced a review of laws that forbade the use of languages other than Turkish and passed a law that allowed the Kurds to celebrate the Kurdish New Year for the first time. The same year, the government also proposed to relax restrictions on the use of Kurdish by the national media. But the PKK's armed campaign and the government's military retaliation continued, and in 1993, the reforms were dropped.

Apo on the Run

Another *Time* journalist, Thomas Sancton, has noted that Ocalan has actually spent most of his time in Syria. It is there that Ocalan directed his terror campaign against Turkey.

But by 1998, Turkey had had enough—it told Syria that it would invade unless Ocalan was handed over. In response, the Syrians deported Ocalan. He went to Greece, and then Moscow. Unable to find sanctuary anywhere, Ocalan eventually flew to Nairobi, Kenya, hoping to find a safe harbor there.

The day after Ocalan's arrival, Kenyan officials demanded that he leave. Ocalan had agreed, with the understanding that he would be safely transported to the Netherlands under Greek protection.

But it was not to be. While getting ready to leave, Ocalan was nabbed by 20 Turkish undercover policemen. A blindfolded, handcuffed, and drugged Ocalan was flown back to Turkey.

Your Terrorist Is My Freedom Fighter

Following Ocalan's arrest on February 15, 1999, by Turkish secret police, Turkey rejoiced. However, Kurdish uprisings across Europe quickly subdued the festive mood. Almost immediately, Europeans, who have a history of criticizing Turkey for its human rights record, issued calls for a fair trial.

But as Ocalan's trial commenced, Turkey confirmed European skepticism about the trial by barring international observers from the courtroom. Limiting Ocalan's access to his legal team, Turkish authorities announced that he would be tried not by a criminal tribunal, but by a State Security Court—a panel usually convened to hear cases dealing with national security.

At trial, where he could have been given the death penalty, Ocalan warned that if he is executed "thousands of people will start the terror machine for me." Nevertheless, in June 1999, the Turkish court sentenced Abdullah Ocalan to death, holding him responsible for almost 40,000 deaths.

CAUTION

Landmine!

Anyone who writes or publishes news items or texts which threaten the ... indivisible unity of the state's territory or people, or which incite people to commit crimes or launch an uprising or rebellion, or anyone who writes or prints news items or texts with a similar purpose or who distributes them, must answer for such criminal conduct.

—Constitution of the Turkish Republic, Article 28, Section 7

As the judge read the verdict, Ocalan stood inside a bombproof glass case. Outside, Turkish soldiers were on guard, and Turkish police were prepared for potential plane hijackings or attacks at embassies and airports. As far away as Berlin, police were preparing for the possibility of violent demonstrations like the ones that erupted after Ocalan's capture.

After the verdict was read, families of Turkish soldiers killed in the fighting began to sing the Turkish national anthem. As he was escorted from the courtroom, the terrorist/freedom fighter waved to the gallery before leaving the glass box.

The verdict created new obstacles in the path of reconciliation between Kurdish separatists and the Turkish government. If there is one lingering certainty in this outcome, it is that the long-running dispute over Kurdish rights in Turkey has not ended with the trial of Abdullah Ocalan.

The Kurds of Iraq

Life has been no easier for the Kurds of Iraq. With the overthrow of the Iraqi monarchy in 1958, the Kurds there hoped for greater administration and autonomy. The first Iraqi constitution of 1958, names the Kurds as part of the new state, and guarantees their rights. Kurds were allowed to broadcast in their language, as well as to publish books and periodicals. Kurdish was the language of instruction in elementary schools in Kurdish-speaking areas, and Kurdish departments were established in some of the Iraqi universities.

Landmine!
Today, Kurds are the fourth largest ethnic group in the Middle East, after the Arabs, Persians, and Turks.

By 1960, however, Kurds had been stripped of their constitutional rights, and for the next 15 years the Iraqi government carried out an extended campaign of "Arabization" of the Kurdish areas, using armed warfare to destroy Kurdish villages and deport their inhabitants while moving Arabs into Kurdish areas, among other measures designed to weaken and demoralize the Kurds.

In 1980, when Iraq and Iran went to war, the Iraqi Kurds saw an opportunity and decided to support the Iranians. But Saddam Hussein is a man who does not forget, and is given to revenge, and so decided that the time to strike back was at hand near the end of the war in 1988. Over a six month period, hundreds of Kurdish villages were totally destroyed, and as many as 200,000 Kurds were murdered. Among the weapons used by Saddam Hussein against his own people: chemical weapons.

The Gulf War Aftermath

Following the Gulf War cease-fire on March 2, 1991, the Iraqi government experienced an uprising of the dissident Shiite Arabs in the southern parts of Iraq. The Kurds in the north, sensing an opportunity, took advantage of the situation. Encouraged by American radio broadcasts to take up arms against their "dictator," the Kurds of northern Iraq rebelled against a defeated and certainly weakened Saddam Hussein.

Within three weeks, all Kurdish areas in northern Iraq were in revolt. However, fear of being drawn into an Iraqi civil war and possible diplomatic repercussions precluded President Bush from committing U.S. forces to come to the aid of the Kurds. As such, Saddam Hussein was able to regroup his Republican Guard, and within a week had crushed the rebellion.

Over a million Iraqi Kurds fled to the Turkish and Iranian borders. Although Iran accepted the Kurdish refugees, Turkey did not. As such, the refugees on the Turkish border were in a very bad situation. Unable to return home, stranded on mountainsides exposed to the cold, thousands of the refugees began to die. In response, western governments decided to create a U.N.-protected Kurdish region in northern Iraq.

> **Peacekeepers**
>
> Sanctions and war have had a devastating effect on the Iraqi economy. According to the Iraq Action Coalition, Iraq's total Gross Domestic Product has fallen to just $5.7 billion, down from $60 billion before the Gulf War. The average annual salary has declined from $335 in 1988 to $24 in 1999. Average shop prices for essential commodities in 1995 stood at 850 times the 1990 level.

Operation Provide Comfort

Allied troops set up camps with relief supplies at the base of the mountains, the Kurds descended, and Operation Provide Comfort began. Thirty-thousand military personnel and 50 NGOs (nongovernmental organizations) aided in the efforts to end what had become almost 1,000 deaths a day. This was the largest airdrop since the Berlin airlift in the 1950s.

Allied troops also went into Dahuk in order to allow Kurdish refugees the chance to go back to their homes in safety. The area of Iraq above the 36th parallel became a so-called "no-fly zone." Iraq was forbidden to fly there and would be subject to military action if it did. In July of 1991, Western troops began to withdraw. The no-fly zone remained in effect. The bad news is that Operation Provide Comfort never challenged Saddam Hussein's claims to northern Iraq. Accordingly, in 1996, Hussein was able to attack the Kurds in the north again, kidnapping and killing scores of them. Although the United States

> **Reliable Resources**
>
> Operation Provide Comfort (OPC) had two goals: To provide relief to the refugees and enforce the security of the refugees and the humanitarian effort. From April to September of 1991, allied forces in support of OPC flew over 40,000 sorties, relocated more than 700,000 refugees, and restored 70 to 80 percent of villages destroyed by the Iraqis.

evacuated some of the threatened, in actuality, Operation Provide Comfort did little to protect the Kurds from the Iraqi war machine.

Iran and the Kurds

Not only does historic Kurdistan lie in parts of Turkey and Iraq, but also it covers parts of Iran. And like the others, the state of Iran, after the war, has practiced a policy of oppression against the Kurds as well.

However, in the 1970s, the Shah of Iran adopted a policy of assimilation, hoping to make the Kurds part of Iranian culture. As such, Iranian Kurds enjoyed more prosperity in the 1970s than at any other time. They were allowed to hold positions of high power in the military as well as participate in the parliament—but they were not granted autonomy.

Things were looking up as the Iranian Islamic revolution neared at the end of the decade. Khomeini and his followers promised the Kurds autonomy in return for support against the Shah. The Kurds agreed, but Khomeini's promises were never kept. In fact, soon after the revolution, when the Kurds made moves toward autonomy, Khomeini declared a jihad against them.

As for now, neither the Kurds nor any other ethnic minority in Iran can hope to gain autonomy from the government. Such nationalistic aspirations run counter to the Islamic ideals of the government. According to Kurdistanweb.org, it was Ayatollah Khomeini himself who claimed that "there is no room in Islam and Islamic countries for such divisive ideas, which aim at weakening the unity of the Islamic community."

What's Gone Wrong?

Why have the Kurds not gained a homeland? There are many reasons. First, as already noted, Kurdish society is fragmented; the Kurds live in many lands and have different religions and languages. Also, the Kurdish tribal structure creates obstacles to unification.

Reliable Resources
The first ruler of the Ottoman empire was Osman, hence the Anglicized name, Ottoman. Descendents from the Osmanali family ruled the the Ottoman Empire for seven centuries, from thirteenth to the twentieth centuries.

But these are not the main reasons. There are two main reasons. First, the Kurds have few real supporters. The Kurds have no powerful countries who are committed to the vision of a Kurdish state.

Indeed, countries not involved in the issue see no benefit in taking a stand in opposition to the four established states who are involved (Turkey, Iraq, Iran, and Syria).

The second reason is that the aspirations of the Kurds require some country to give up land. Kurdistan, if it is ever to be, would be carved from Turkey, Iraq, Iran, or Syria. Countries simply do not give up land very easily, and almost never without a fight. Re-establishing Kurdistan therefore is a monumental task.

Is There a Solution?

Oppressing the Kurds has certainly been costly for Turkey. Undoubtedly, continual war waged against the Kurdish people has consumed vast national resources; Turkey's direct expenditures for the war amount to $10 billion annually. If there is going to be a solution, it will be when Turkey finally realizes that the cost of conflict is higher than the price of peace.

The Least You Need to Know

- The Kurds have been around for eons.
- The Kurds live a tragic life of oppression in Turkey.
- The PKK has taken up armed resistance to Turkey.
- Saddam Hussein and Iraq have oppressed the Kurds as well.
- The Kurds in Iran have it no better.
- These policies of oppression are costly.

Chapter 6

Hotspots in Northern Africa

In This Chapter

- ◆ Sudan: A land divided
- ◆ Terrorists and slaves
- ◆ Egypt at war
- ◆ The rise of Gamal Nasser
- ◆ Egyptian Islamic Fundamentalism
- ◆ Muslims in Algeria

Geopolitically speaking, when one thinks of the Middle East and Northern Africa, Israel, the Palestinians, Osama bin Laden, and Saddam Hussein come to mind. But sadly, these are not the only conflicts that affect this troubled region. More than probably any other place in the world, conflict runs rampant and hatred deep throughout this region.

Egypt and Sudan have been the subject of probably just as many conflicts as have any other country in the area. The difference is they don't get as much attention from the press; probably a bad thing because the watchful eye of the world can have a deterring effect on mayhem. It is simply amazing what people can do to each other when they think no one is noticing.

Egypt got the Sinai back in exchange for peace.

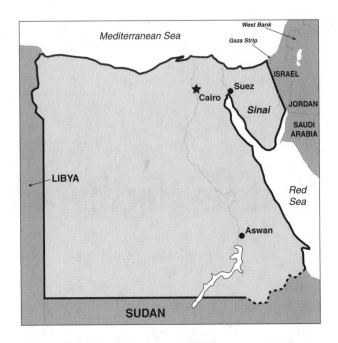

Sudan should probably be divided in half.

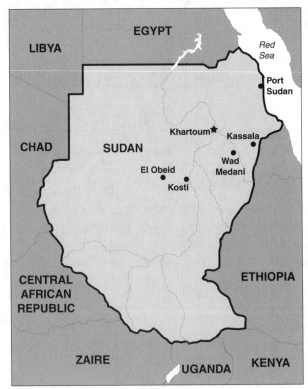

A Sudan Divided Against Itself Cannot Stand

Military dictatorships promoting an extreme Islamic government have mostly run Sudan since independence from Great Britain in 1956. Over the past two decades, at least 1.5 million lives were lost in a vicious civil war pitting black Christians and animists in the south against Arab Muslims in the north.

Sudan Backgrounder

Sudan is the largest country in Africa. It has been populated for over 9 million years, and the ox-driven water wheel, introduced to the region some 2,500 years ago, still plays a vital role in the economy today.

For as long as Sudan has been around, Egypt has seemed to control it. Egyptian dominance in this region probably began 2500 B.C.E. when Sudan was known as Nubia, with ruined temples and monuments a sure sign of ancient Egyptian influence.

A succession of foreign invaders followed the independence that Nubia had attained in the eighth century B.C.E. The Romans invaded Nubia around the time of Christ, and Christian Ethiopia overtook the country 300 years later, resulting in the conversion of most of the population to Christianity.

> **Peacekeepers**
>
> At its peak, the British Empire was the largest formal empire the world had ever known. After successful wars with the Dutch, the French, and the Spanish in the seventeenth century, Britain managed to acquire most of the eastern coast of North America, most of Canada, territories in the Caribbean, India, Australia, and stations in Africa.

> **Reliable Resources**
>
> The modern inhabitants of southern Egypt and Sudan still refer to themselves as Nubians. They speak the Nubian language as well as Arabic.

Sudan Piques Their Interest

In 1854, by a French initiative, the viceroy of Egypt decided that it was technically feasible to build a canal that would connect the Mediterranean to the Red Sea. In 1858, a company was formed to construct and administer the Suez Canal. Both French and Egyptian interests owned the company, and it was decided that they would administer the canal for 99 years.

The canal project proved to be a very expensive proposition, and as a result, Egypt found itself heavily in debt to foreign powers. As such, in 1873, the British were able to get one of their own, General Charles George Gordon, appointed governor of Egyptian Sudan.

And that is how it came to be that Sudan would be governed by Egypt through Egypt's British colonial master. It was this dichotomy—Egyptian Muslims and British Christians controlling the Sudanese populace in a joint, and often conflicting, manner—that would eventually shape all contours of Sudan.

The Dichotomy Emerges

Because of their differences, and because they mutually needed each other if they were to control the vast Sudan, British and Egyptian forces made the fateful decision to jointly administer Sudan as two regions. In the north, the Egyptians would run the country. Islam became the main religion. In the British-controlled south, Christianity became the dominant religious and moral influence.

By the turn of the twentieth century, the British colonies were growing restless. In 1924, the British governor-general of Sudan was assassinated in Cairo. In retaliation, Britain expelled all Egyptian officials from Sudan. Sudan was their puppet.

By 1936, Britain and Egypt had ended hostilities, but the signing of their 1936 peace agreement only served to stimulate Sudanese nationalists who were clamoring for independence.

Independence Day

Finally, on February 2, 1953, Britain and Egypt agreed to grant Sudan self-government within three years, and also provided for a Senate, a Council of Ministers, and a House of Representatives. Elections were to be supervised by an international commission.

> **Reliable Resources**
>
> Bartleby.com describes Sudan as an overwhelmingly agricultural country. However, although agriculture in the late 1990s occupied some 80 percent of the workforce, it contributed only 33 percent of the GDP. In general, agricultural production varies from year to year because of intermittent droughts that cause widespread famine.

The elections were held during November and December 1953, and Ismail al-Aihari became Sudan's first prime minister in January 1954.

Despite this rosy beginning, the problems caused by jointly administering Sudan and essentially running it for years as two very different countries soon came home to roost. The Muslim-Christian division was just too much for the country to understand, absorb, and deal with.

In 1955, fighting broke out between the northern Islamic Arabs and the southern Christian and animist blacks. In 1957, all Christian schools in the south were closed and Christian missionaries were kicked out of the country. Things worsened when, on November 17, 1958, a coup led by General Ibrahim Abboud took power. General Abboud explained to the population that he would rule through an army junta and that democracy had to be suspended in Sudan.

Southern Christians and Animists, alarmed by the coup, began a rebellion, demanding more and more autonomy from their Muslim brothers in the north. Although successive prime ministers visited the south, nothing stopped the rebels. Civil war was on, and would continue for 17 years, misusing national resources by diverting them from development and services to the purchase of war machinery.

The Civil War Era

Another coup in 1969, led this time by Colonel Jafaar Mohammed al-Nimeiry, set up government under another revolutionary council. But in 1972, having consolidated his hold on power, Nimeiry held elections and became the Sudan's first elected president. Wanting to end the strife between north and south, Nimeiry worked with combatants in the south to forge some sort of peace for the impoverished, war-torn country.

The Addis Ababa Agreement finally brought the war to a halt in 1972. An uneasy peace was maintained for almost a decade and in 1983, Nimeiry was reelected for a third term of office.

Emboldened by his success, Nimeiry decided to make Sudan into an Islamic fundamentalist country. Coming on the heels of the 1979 Iranian

> **Reliable Resources**
>
> Nimeiry was temporarily expelled from high school in 1948 after leading a student strike against British rule.

Islamic revolution, this desire to create an Islamic state in Sudan, although not surprising, made much less sense given the demographics of the country. Nevertheless, on September 8, 1983, Nimeiry instituted Islamic Law.

The Koran became the rule of law—and alcohol and gambling were now prohibited for starters. The southern Christians, already feeling like a minority in their own country, refused to acknowledge the change in the law. A new round of violence began.

Here's a pop quiz! What do people do in Sudan when they are unhappy with the government? Altogether now: They stage a bloodless coup! Nimeiry was deposed in April 1985. A year of military rule followed before the rise of new leaders and more coups.

The new rulers were neither able to unify the country nor instill Islamic law on the south. Civil war had become a way of life.

Osama bin Laden in Sudan

Osama bin Laden first came to Sudan from Afghanistan in 1991. Although al-Qaeda had been formed three years before, the United States did not yet realize the threat he posed. Yet, by 1998, he was a wanted man. Obviously then, bin Laden's years in Sudan were critical in the development of his terrorist network. So just what was he up to while he was there? Bin Laden seemed like just another businessman. He had recently inherited as much as $300 million (though estimates vary). Accordingly, bin Laden was a most welcome addition to the poor country when he arrived. He started several businesses in Sudan, the biggest being a construction company and a giant farming operation.

Landmine!

Other bin Laden companies included an import-export concern, a currency trading company, and a farm that grew sesame, peanuts, and corn.

Bin Laden opened his first office in Khartoum (the capital), and then moved it to an affluent suburb where he bought a farmhouse. Most often, he could be found at his farm just outside Khartoum. The farmhouse was a single-story building, with no furniture. The floor was the dirt, covered with woolen rugs.

According to a report in the *Guardian Newspaper* out of London, "His men all had nice air-conditioned flats in the city but bin Laden preferred to live simply with his horses and wives. He was just another Saudi investor. Said one associate, 'If there is nothing between you, he is very kind. He smiles a lot. I never considered him dangerous.'"

Meanwhile, according to the *Guardian*, the Sudanese government was augmenting the army with Islamist militias. Bin Laden was rumored to have been assisting the Islamists far more than running his businesses.

This was confirmed by the trial testimony of a former al-Qaeda member, Jamal Ahmed Fadl, a 38-year-old Sudanese man who worked as a general laborer for bin Laden in Khartoum before running off with $100,000 in 1994. He says the businesses were all a front for al-Qaeda. At his trial, Fadl described a web of worldwide Islamist terrorism groups that were supplied by al-Qaeda with guns, money, and expertise.

Fadl said that he smuggled crates of explosives to rebels which he had transported from a stockpile at bin Laden's farm. Fadl also described how he had delivered $100,000 to an opponent of King Hussein of Jordan. He also explained how he had once led a caravan of 50 camels loaded with weapons to Islamic terrorists in Egypt. Fadl concluded his trial testimony describing how, while in Sudan, al-Qaeda supported Islamic terrorists in Saudi Arabia, Algeria, Syria, Chechnya, Turkey, Eritrea, Tajikistan, the Philippines, and Lebanon.

Landmine!

Like any business, al-Qaeda, too, had its experts. Abu Anas al-Liby was the computer wizard and Abu Khalid el-Masry maintained the tanks.

In 1996, the United States government was demanding that Sudan expel all its suspected terrorists, including bin Laden.

According to Donald Petterson, the American ambassador to Sudan throughout most of bin Laden's stay, "There was an awareness that he was tagged a dangerous figure, but we didn't have a handle on him as I recall." Sudanese officials actually offered to hand bin

Laden over to America, says el-Mahdi, the Sudan's spy chief. "If America had had something against him, we would have looked at extraditing him to America, but they had not."

The Slave Trade

If all this were not enough, consider that in Sudan a massive slave trade flourishes. The reasons are varied, but, in essence, the government's civil war requires the assistance of local, unpaid, militias. In return, Sudan's Islamic leaders encourage soldiers to take slaves as reward.

As reported by Associated Press writer Karen Davis, according to Christian Solidarity International (CSI), a humanitarian group that buys slaves and sets them free, young women and children are the most valuable sorts of slaves in Sudan. Old people are old, and young men cannot be trained into useful, harmless slaves. Says John Eibner of CSI: "According to the Khartoum's regime ideology of jihad, members of the resistant black African community—be they men, women or children—are infidels, and may be arbitrarily killed, enslaved, looted, or otherwise abused."

Interestingly, some groups—including UNICEF—oppose the work of CSI, believing that buying slaves, CSI is contributing to the slave trade and driving up demand.

Yet the Sudanese government denies condoning slavery, and insists that slavery persists because holding prisoners for ransom is a tradition rooted in tribal disputes. As Davis reports, however, according to Gaspar Biro, a researcher for the U.N. Commission on Human Rights for Sudan, there has been an "alarming increase in cases of slavery, servitude, slave trade and forced labor" since February 1994. "The total passivity of the government can only be regarded as tacit political approval and support of the institution of slavery," he said. A U.S. State Department report said accounts it received on the taking of slaves in the south "indicates the direct and general involvement" of Sudan's army and militias "backed by the government."

> ### Reliable Resources
>
> CSI estimates that thousands of children and adults have been stolen from their homes in southern Sudan by suspected members of the militias. CSI buys the freedom of slaves for about $100 each, or three cows per person.

What Now?

Does it matter to any of the participants in this long civil war that the country has been wracked by drought and famine, slavery and terrorists, and that cooperation might ease some of the suffering? Judging by their action, the answer, sadly, is no.

Although it is not difficult to see how tensions between north and south began, it is almost inexplicable that they continue. Poor African countries like Sudan have had a

Landmine!

An estimated one million Sudanese died as a result of either war or starvation during the past decade. Three million people have been displaced by the fighting, and the capital, Khartoum, has been inundated with poor, sick, homeless refugees.

difficult time shaking the shackles of European colonial rule. These powers often went into poor third world countries and shipped many of the best resources back home.

By the time Britain (for example) was finally kicked out or "voluntarily" left, these countries had little in the way of natural resources with which to start over. So it is easy to understand why indigenous people often hate their former colonial rulers. What is more difficult to understand is why they hate each other so much.

It is hard to see a peaceful resolution to this conflict as long as the government tries to impose religious dogma on its own people, as long as it tolerates its children being taken into slavery, and as long as terrorists are given refuge. Indeed, it might be that the gulf between north and south is so wide as to warrant dividing the country in two.

Egypt's Troubles

Egypt had always been an important route to the east. And so in 1798, the French, led by Napoleon Bonaparte, invaded Egypt in an effort to control trade with the East.

Reliable Resources

Napoleon's invasion included many people interested in recording Egypt's past. Artists drew pictures of the flora, fauna, and the ruins. Their combined efforts were published in 1801 in a work called *The Description of Egypt*, a series that is still a standard reference work on Egypt.

Diplomatic Dialogue

A **protectorate** is a relationship in which one state surrenders (or is forced to surrender) much of its sovereignty to a stronger nation.

Napoleon had many problems in Egypt. Grain supply was difficult to control, and the British ships occupied ports in the north. So, although Napoleon tried to export numerous antiquities back to France, his ships were captured by the British (which is one reason why the British Museum now has one of the most extraordinary collections of Egyptian antiquities in the world). Napoleon and his French army eventually were forced to evacuate Egypt. The vacuum left by Napoleon was filled by the British, soon declaring that Egypt had become a *protectorate*.

The British were eventually forced to respond to Egypt's desire to become independent and in 1922 gave them sovereignty, but not independence. Faud was made king, and he was replaced by King Faruq in 1936.

Egyptian nationalism continued to grow, and the king and his wealth drew increased criticism. In 1952, mobs rioted in Cairo as the Egyptian army officers seized control. On July 25, King Faruq abdicated the throne and Egypt was under Egyptian control for the first time in more than 2,600 years.

One of the young Egyptians who had fought against British rule for years was Gamal Abdel Nasser. In 1942, Nasser founded the secret Society of Free Officers, a group which fought for independence.

In July 1952, it was Nasser who led the army coup that deposed the king. Although General Muhammad Naguib became the head of the government, in 1954 Nasser arrested Naguib and became premier of Egypt. Nasser would lead Egypt through some of its most bitter conflicts.

The Nasser Years

Nasser would turn out to be one of the most important Arab leaders of the twentieth century. Advocating Arab unity, he undertook a series of actions to increase power to both his country and his cause.

July 26, 1956, was the fourth anniversary of King Faruk's abdication. That day, Nasser appeared in Muhammad Ali Square in Alexandria. With a huge crowd in attendance, Nasser began a three-hour speech. When he said the code word, "de Lesseps," it was the signal for Egyptian engineers and the army to take over the Suez Canal.

At this time, the canal was still owned by the Suez Canal Company, a foreign company with headquarters in Europe. The British prime minister called Nasser's actions theft.

Nasser's nationalization of the canal precipitated a short-lived, abortive invasion by Great Britain, France, and Israel. The Soviet Union, its allies, and many third world countries supported Egypt. Afraid of further escalating an already cold Cold War, the United States stated that although it opposed the nationalization of the canal, it was against the further use of force. In the end, Nasser kept the canal and promised to guarantee right of access to all ships.

Peacekeepers

Ferdinand de Lesseps came from a family that was long distinguished in the French diplomatic service. In 1832, he moved to Egypt, where he befriended the new Egyptian Viceroy. When the time came to build the Suez Canal, de Lesseps was tapped to oversee its construction. He was, therefore, a symbol of colonial rule in Egypt.

Under Nasser's leadership, Egypt helped ferment pro-Arab, anti-Western feelings throughout the Arab world.

◆ In 1958, Egypt and Syria formed the United Arab Republic, with Nasser as its president. He hoped this would be the first step toward Arab unity. But although the alliance with Syria ended after only three years, Nasser kept the name United Arab Republic. (The name was changed back in 1970.)

◆ In 1967, he precipitated Egypt's third war with Israel by dissolving U.N. peacekeeping forces in the Sinai (see Chapter 3). The quick war, which ended in a massive defeat for Egypt, was nothing short of a personal disaster for Nasser, and, in humiliation, he offered to resign from office.

It says much about what a beloved figure he was that the Egyptian people refused to let him quit. Massive demonstrations of support forced him to stay.

Nasser died on September 28, 1970, of a heart attack while still in office. Nasser is probably best remembered for leading a resurgence in Arab nationalism.

Sadat Takes Over

After Nasser's death, his vice president, Anwar al-Sadat, was elected president. Although he had been one of Nasser's closest associates, Sadat set a new, independent, course. Whereas Nasser had oriented Egypt away from the West and aligned his country with the Soviet Union, Sadat kicked 20,000 Soviet military personnel out of the country two years after taking power.

In Egypt, if there has been one constant up until this time, it was a hatred of Israel. Sadat was no different. In 1973, he was one of the instigators of the Yom Kippur war. The war demonstrated Arab military strength, and helped boost Sadat's image in the Arab world.

> **Reliable Resources**
>
> The Begin-Sadat Center for Strategic Studies in Israel is dedicated to the study of Middle East peace and security.

> **Peacekeepers**
>
> Nineteen eighty-one was a big year for attempted assassinations. Not only was Sadat killed, but also John Hinckley shot President Reagan near the chest outside the Washington Hilton Hotel, and Pope John Paul II was struck by two bullets and wounded in the abdomen, right arm, and left hand by Mehmet Ali Agca (both men survived their attacks).

So it was a huge surprise when Sadat visited Israel in 1977. This visit was motivated by the economic problems Egypt faced after so many wars with Israel. The price of conflict, as Egypt had learned, is a high one. Sadat spoke of peace before the national assembly of Israel, the Knesset. This overture resulted in a peace agreement between the countries—the Camp David Accords (see Chapter 3).

Although he was rewarded with the Nobel Peace Prize in 1978 (together with Menachem Begin), the treaty with Israel isolated Egypt from the rest of the Arab world. Sadat was condemned by the Arabs for making peace with Israel, and Egypt was expelled from the Arab League.

More ominously, the rise of Islamic fundamentalism had begun to take root in Egypt, and the Islamists detested what they considered to be Sadat's capitulation. Aware of this growing threat, in September 1981, Sadat arrested almost 2,000 dissidents, Islamists, and Communists. Not coincidentally, a month later he was assassinated at a military parade in Cairo.

The Rise of Islamic Fundamentalism

After Sadat's death, his successor, Hosni Mubarak, was elected president. Under his direction, Egypt endeavored to become a moderate Arab nation. But the rise of Islamic fundamentalism was impossible to root out because its roots run deep.

Islamic fundamentalism began in Egypt in 1928 when the Muslim Brotherhood was formed. Preaching a return to Islamic values, the group developed a huge following in the 1940s when it committed a series of political assassinations. There was a brief respite from the government after the new regime of the charismatic Nasser took power.

But in 1954, Nasser became the next target while speaking to a crowd in the Mediterranean city of Alexandria. The assassination attempt failed, Nasser had hundreds of Muslim Brothers arrested, and the movement was crushed for another 20 years. After Nasser's death, Sadat decided to let the leaders out of prison in an amnesty effort. But he had opened Pandora's Box; it was an Islamic fundamentalist who plotted Sadat's killing.

Islamic groups were then repressed again by Mubarak. But in the 1980s, they slowly regained strength. They took control of many powerful unions and professional associations, set up numerous charities, enjoyed growing support, and established a network of schools and hospitals in an effort to gain legitimacy.

But the government fought back. New laws were introduced to reverse their power in the unions, and the government began to keep a tight watch on all charitable institutions. Nevertheless, by the early 1990s, two organizations, Islamic Jihad and the Islamic Group, continued to flourish. How serious is this threat? Consider that Egypt's Islamic Jihad is headed by Ayman al-Zawahiri, Osama bin Laden's right-hand man.

The problem for modern Egypt is that corruption and poverty help foster huge slums around the country, and that in turn fosters the desire for something different, something better. As in other countries in this region, Islamic fundamentalism offers that something. Until those problems are addressed, Islamic fundamentalists are likely to remain a fact of life in Egypt.

Algeria Has Its Own Problems

The rise of Islam has also affected that other large country in northern Africa, Algeria. And Algeria, with its strong French influence, has endeavored to remain a secular country, even if that requires implementing martial law.

Reliable Resources

The French Foreign Legion is a volunteer armed force composed chiefly of foreigners. Its international character and the tradition of not revealing enlistees' backgrounds have helped to surround the Foreign Legion with an aura of mystery and romance. The Legion was stationed in Algeria until 1962.

The French conquered Algeria in 1830 and ruled it for more than 100 years. Pressure for independence began in the early 1950s with the formation of the Front de Libération Nationale (FLN). The Algerian war for independence resulted from French resistance to Algerian desires for freedom.

The Algerian war for independence was more brutal than most; it is estimated to have led to one million casualties. Independence was finally achieved in 1962, bringing to power an FLN-controlled government under Ahmed Ben Bella. Ben Bella was subsequently deposed by Houari Boumedienne, who ruled until his death in December 1978.

In 1990, local elections were held. Although the FLN secured another majority, Islamic parties made a surprisingly strong showing, frightening the ruling FLN party officials. The most prominent of these new Islamic parties was the Islamic Salvation Front (FIS). So strong were they, and so strong was the growing Islamist movement, that in January 1992, FIS won a resounding victory in national elections.

The Algerian government proved itself to be a repressive regime when it immediately annulled the election results and declared a state of emergency. The military took over complete control of the country, with the support and collaboration of civil servants and intelligence officials.

A brutal civil war was the inevitable result. In 1994, the government distributed arms to villagers. This was necessary because 400 villagers had just been killed by machete-wielding Islamic rebels.

So far, since the outbreak of violence, some 80,000 people have been killed in Algeria. The police arrest leaders of the Islamic movement one day, and the next day they kill others. Islamists then retaliate. The cycle of violence continues, and war goes on.

The Least You Need to Know

- Sudan is a land divided between the north and south, and between Animists and Christians, and Muslims.
- In some parts of Sudan, civil war has become a way of life.
- The rise of Gamal Nasser fostered Arab nationalism.
- Egypt has its own Islamic terrorist problem.
- The Algerian civil war pits Muslims against a repressive government.

Part 2

Central and Southern Africa

In terms of conflict, Africa can be proud that the most intransigent of conflicts—the one between Africans and Afrikaners in South Africa—was peacefully resolved, with nary a shot being fired.

But on the rest of the continent, the brutality and mayhem that are part of everyday life are almost too horrific to believe. It is simply shocking what Africans do to one another.

Chapter 7

Death Around the Horn

In This Chapter

- ◆ Ethiopian civil war
- ◆ Ethiopian famine
- ◆ Eritrea wants independence
- ◆ Somalia falls to pieces

No continent on Earth is more wracked with mindless violence, conflict, and bloodshed than Africa. Military dictators readily steal money and goods intended for their country, callous to the desperate blight that daily surrounds them. This senseless greed and need for power, when combined with famine and poverty, has become a recipe for unimaginable disaster.

This is especially true on the Horn of Africa. On the Horn, only Libya has any economic prosperity at all because of its oil reserves. The other countries in the region, especially Ethiopia, Somalia, and Eritrea, have been victims of drought, corruption, poverty, and war.

The Horn of Africa is a dangerous place.

Ethiopia

Ethiopia is a country that prides itself on its independence, yet even so, in 1896, Italy attempted to invade Ethiopia, but was rebuffed. However, in 1935, Italy was finally able to invade the country, and Ethiopian King Haile Selassie was forced to flee to British protection. However, in 1940, Italy entered World War II and was preoccupied with other matters, so Selassie was able to return to Africa, and in 1941, he reentered Ethiopia and regained his throne.

Despite financial support from the United States, Ethiopia remained an underdeveloped, undemocratic country. In 1960, although Selassie was able to crush a revolt by a group of young army officers who were demanding an end to oppression and poverty, dissatisfaction with the Ethiopian monarchy only grew.

By 1974, the desire for reform had hit a crescendo, and the army was able to seize more and more control from

Reliable Resources

Jamaican Black Nationalist Marcus Garvey said in 1920, "Look to Africa, for when a black king shall be crowned, the day of deliverance is at hand." The prophesy was to be fulfilled in 1930 when Ras Tafari, who claimed to be a direct descendant of King David, was crowned emperor Haile Selassie 1 of Ethiopia.

the king. Haile Selassie was slowly stripped of his powers and finally, on September 12, 1974, deposed in a palace coup. He was murdered in prison at the orders of the coup leaders in 1975.

Is This Place Coup Coup or What?

In Africa it seems, the only thing worse than your present leader is the next one. The Ethiopian coup leaders suspended the constitution, parliament was dissolved, a Marxist-Leninist course was plotted, and Colonel Haile Mengistu became head of the government. Under his regime, thousands of political opponents were crushed, property was confiscated, and defense spending was greatly increased. Soon enough, Mengistu wielded absolute power.

In 1976, Mengistu began a campaign that he officially dubbed the "Red Terror." At a rally in the capital of Addis Ababa, he threw to the ground before a huge crowd bottles filled with a red substance representing the blood of enemies of the revolution. The time was now, he told his audience, to root them out. In particular, the campaign targeted students and young people suspected of membership in the Ethiopian People's Revolutionary Party, a group opposed to the petit dictator.

Thousands of young men and women turned up dead in the streets of Ethiopia in the next two years. Not only were they murdered by roaming militias, but what's worse is that these students were fingered by local neighborhood watch committees who served during this period as security surveillance units for the militias.

The process of elimination was well organized. Neighborhood committees met and discussed potential suspects. Once a decision had been

> **Landmine!**
> When victims families attempted to reclaim their loved ones bodies for burial, the watch committees required the families to reimburse the committee for the price of the bullets used to kill the victims.

made, each member of the committee would then sign documents to confirm the decision that had been reached at the meeting. These decisions were then sent on to the party which would in turn condemn the suspected counterrevolutionaries to death, thus leaving a huge paper trail of murder. The Mengistu regime was able to pay for its mass murder with help from the Soviet Union. The USSR, caught up as it was in its own Cold War, saw Mengistu as a potential ally. Because the Horn of Africa borders the Red Sea, and because Ethiopia had been an American puppet during the Selassie years, the strategic importance of the country was obvious. Pouring weapons and money into the corrupt Mengistu regime, as well as Cuban troops and "special advisers," Moscow gained itself a puppet and helped fuel the fire that would engulf the region for decades.

However, even as he was murdering his own people, Mengistu faced two other problems. On one hand, a longstanding dispute with Somalia regarding the border erupted anew.

Similarly, another longstanding dispute with Eritrea was revived when the Ethiopian province began its war of liberation. With the Eritreans attacking in the north, Somalis in the south, and counter-revolutionaries to kill in the middle, the Mengistu regime diverted all monies to the army to fight its many enemies, both real and perceived.

War and Famine

As a result of all this incessant warfare, the Ethiopian people had one of the lowest standards of living in the world. Then, in 1984, things got worse. A famine hit; the Ethiopian harvest looked likely to be very poor that year.

In March, according to BBC Online's Kate Milner, the Ethiopian government stated that five million people were at risk of starvation. Aid agencies put the number at six million.

Despite the very real threat of mass starvation, Western governments were hesitant to get involved. As the BBC has noted, the West feared the military government of Mengistu might steal and spend the incoming aid money. And yet, the specter of starvation forced their hand; food and aid began to pour into the country.

The fears turned out to be prophetic:

- Delivery by the Mengistu government of incoming aid to the needy was sporadic at best.
- Food for civilian famine victims was diverted to feed troops.

With the situation as dire as it was, relief organizations appealed for more help anyway, but Western governments balked. Aid agencies were forced to buy grain on the open market. By October 1984, eight million people were in danger of starvation.

What fended off this potential disaster was a wave of increased television and newspaper coverage throughout Western Europe and the United States. Public donations flooded in; the U.K. public alone gave $8 million in one three-day period. With Western awareness now high, people wanted to help, including musicians. Two Live Aid concerts and the hit single "Do They Know It's Christmas?" alone provided millions of dollars for relief efforts.

The worst was over. Unfortunately, drought and famine are recurrent problems in Ethiopia.

Is This the End of Mengistu?

The end of the Cold War meant that Ethiopia would have to face its wars, insurgents, and drought by itself without Soviet aid. That it could not do. After the 17 years of Mengistu's dictatorship, the economy was in shambles, and civil unrest had grown beyond the control of the military.

In May 1991, two secessionist forces closed in on Addis Ababa, and Mengistu fled the country. He was eventually granted asylum in Zimbabwe. A transitional government consisting of a coalition of 27 political organizations came to power, and set out to transform Ethiopia into a free and democratic nation.

The new government inherited six million people facing famine, a shattered economy, and no funds. Despite all the problems, the new government steered the country toward democracy, giving Eritrea its freedom and establishing a commission to prosecute war crimes. May 1995 saw the first parliamentary elections, and Meles Zenawi was confirmed as prime minister.

In 1995, Mengistu was tried *in absentia* and found guilty on charges of mass murder, relating to the assassination of Emperor Selassie and the deaths of thousands of his political opponents during the Red Terror period.

> **Reliable Resources**
>
> Threatened by the turmoil surrounding the famine and the impending collapse of the Mengistu regime were some 14,000 Ethiopian Jews. Rather than let them die, Israel sent in relief planes, airlifted them out of chaos, and brought them to Israel to be resettled.

> **Diplomatic Dialogue**
>
> When a person who is on trial is not present for the proceedings, he is **in absentia**; literally, he is absent.

Eritrea Fights for Freedom

Eritrea lies next door to Ethiopia, separating that country from the Red Sea. Like so many other African countries, Eritreans, long part of other countries and empires, also wanted their freedom.

Italy ruled Eritrea since the end of the nineteenth century, but in 1941, Allied forces forced Italy out of the country. Thereafter, it was administered by the British military. Set to divide the country along religious lines, Britain decided to give the coast and highland areas to Eritrea's next-door neighbor Ethiopia, and the Muslim-inhabited northern and western lowlands to British-ruled Sudan.

But the Eritreans wanted independence, and so, in 1952, the United Nations created the Eritrean-Ethiopian federation. But in 1962, Haile Selassie ended the federation. A civil war ensued and lasted for the better part of 30 years. Finally, with the overthrow of the Mengistu regime, Eritrea was finally given its independence.

> **Peacekeepers**
>
> Isaias Afwerki was the first president of Eritrea, elected in 1993. In 1970, Afwerki founded the Eritrean Popular Liberation Front, one of several Marxist groups that overthrew the government and helped Eritrea gain independence.

For a while, Ethiopia and Eritrea got along well. Ethiopia no longer had a border along the Red Sea and therefore had to go through Eritrea in order to ship and trade goods. Eritrea introduced its own currency in 1997, which destabilized the Ethiopian economy, such as it was. As a result, tensions rose. In 1998, of course, these two neighbors, who had once been part of the same country, decided war was the way to resolve their differences.

The war between Eritrea and Ethiopia has been brutal. 100,000 people have been killed, probably one million have been displaced, and hundreds of millions of dollars has been diverted into war instead of development.

> **Peacekeepers**
>
> U.N. Secretary General Kofi Annan said the agreement represents "victory for the voice of reason, for power of diplomacy and for the recognition that neither one of these countries—nor the continent as a whole—can afford another decade, another year, another day of conflict."

Both Ethiopia and Eritrea have since been accused of gross human rights violations. Amnesty International reports that the Ethiopian authorities detain a large number of Eritreans simply because of their Eritrean heritage, while also recruiting child soldiers for the front lines.

And, as if this were not enough turmoil, severe drought threatened both Eritrea and Ethiopia. On the Horn of Africa, some places had gone without enough rain for up to two or three years.

On December 12, 2000, the two countries ended hostilities (for now) by signing an internationally brokered peace agreement. Whether it will hold is only as predictable as the rains.

Somalia

Americans know of Somalia because of a failed rescue mission in 1993. But that is only a small slice of the sorrow that is Somalia. Like so many countries in Africa, Somalia was devastated by colonial rule and has yet to resolve the conflicts that resulted.

During the colonial era, the British were able to control the northern part of Somalia. In southern Somalia, Italy was the main colonizer, acquiring its first possession in 1888 when the Sultan of Hobyo agreed to Italian "protection."

Following Italy's defeat in World War II, the British established military administrations in what had been Italian Somaliland; almost all Somali-inhabited territories were now under British rule.

Political protests and a desire for independence in 1956 forced Britain to introduce representative government in its Somali protectorate. Accordingly, in 1957, the Legislative Council was established, composed of six members appointed by the governor to represent the principal clan-families that make up Somalia.

Although unified as a single nation at independence, the south and the north were, in actuality, two separate countries. Italian and British rule had left the country divided, with separate administrative, legal, and education systems in which affairs were conducted in different languages. Police, taxes, and even the currencies differed. Educated elites had different interests, and economic contacts between the two regions were virtually nonexistent. Somalia was one country in name only.

Nevertheless, in 1960 the first elections were held. Muhammad Igaal was chosen as prime minister. During the nine-year period of parliamentary democracy and stability that followed Somali independence, politics was a rambunctious, open, heated affair, and freedom of expression was widely accepted.

Peacekeepers

Women have long had political rights in Somalia. They have voted in Italian Somaliland elections since 1958, and suffrage was extended to women in former British Somaliland as well in 1963.

All Good Things Must Come to an End

As it is throughout the African continent, paramilitary groups run roughshod over civilians when they don't like what is happening in the country. On October 15, 1969, a bodyguard killed the Somali president while Prime Minister Igaal was out of the country. Igaal returned to the capital of Mogadishu to arrange for the selection of a new president. His choice was a member of the Daarood clan-family, even though Igaal was of the Isaaq clan.

Army officers, unhappy with the choice, decided to take matters into their own hands. Capturing strategic points around Mogadishu and rounding up government officials and other prominent political figures, the military staged a coup. With the help of local police, who supported the coup, army commander Major General Muhammad Siad Barre assumed leadership of Somalia.

Of course, one of Siad Barre's first acts was to prohibit the existence of any political association. He then plotted a socialist course for the country, despite the fact that Somalia had no history of class conflict. To be more precise, Siad Barre explained that his official ideology consisted of three elements, which he called "scientific socialism":

Peacekeepers

One of the principal objectives of the revolutionary regime was the official adoption of a standard of orthography of the Somali language for administration of the country and as the principal language to be used in the schools (instead of Italian and English).

- Community development based on self-reliance
- Marxist socialism
- Islam

Siad Barre was a dictator, like so many dictators who ran rampant through the world in the 1960s and 1970s. Clearly enamored of the cult of personality that Mao Tse Tung had fostered in China, Siad Barre soon began to call himself Somalia's "Victorious Leader." Portraits of him in the company of Marx and Lenin littered the streets. Advice from this paternalistic leader, who claimed he had found a uniquely Somali path to socialist revolution, were widely distributed in Siad Barre's little blue-and-white book.

But power corrupts, and absolute power corrupts absolutely. Siad Barre became a tyrant, and by the early '80s, his grip on power was slipping as criticism of his repressive regime came from both inside and outside the country. Faced with shrinking popularity and an armed and organized domestic resistance, Siad Barre did what all dictators do—he unleashed his private army on his enemies, mainly the three clans who opposed him: the Majeerteen, the Hawiye, and the Isaaq.

Things Get Worse

In November 1986, Siad Barre's elite and dreaded Red Berets began to terrorize Somalia's citizens. While the people were distracted, government ministers and bureaucrats plundered what was left of the national treasury. Chaos reigned.

Clans were systematically targeted and murdered. These genocidal actions were waged first against the Majeerteen clan, then against the Isaaq clans of the north, and finally against the Hawiye, who occupied the strategic central area of the country, including the capital of Mogadishu.

The powerful Hawiye clan organized an armed resistance. Faced with increasing opposition, Siad Barre finally ordered his Red Berets to kill ordinary civilians who seemed to oppose him, regardless of their clan affiliation. By 1989, torture and murder had become commonplace in Mogadishu.

On July 9, 1989, Somalia's Italian-born Roman Catholic bishop was gunned down by an unknown assassin in his church in Mogadishu. It was a widely held belief that Siad Barre ordered the hit.

Soon thereafter, the Red Berets killed 450 Muslims who were demonstrating against the treatment of the leaders. Then, on July 15, 47 more people were executed.

> **Landmine!**
>
> The arsenal in the streets is awesome. I went to the main arms market—the baqara market. Everything is on sale here including anti-aircraft missiles. The only restriction to the sale is that you must belong to the Hawiye clan.
>
> —Hussein Ali Soke, correspondent for *Africa Conflict Journal*

The regime grew desperate. At an anti-Siad Barre demonstration, people began to riot, causing army officials to panic and open fire on the demonstrators, killing almost 100 people. A week later came the Stadia Corna Affair, when Siad Barre sentenced to death 46 prominent intellectuals who had been calling for elections and improved human rights.

Things came to a head when, on July 13, a besieged Siad Barre dropped the charges. As the city celebrated, the president was forced to retreat into his bunker in his military barracks to save himself.

After Siad Barre was deposed in January 1991, anarchy ensued. The people of the northern regions declared the independent state of Somaliland. Political leaders in the southern regions refused to acknowledge this. Power throughout the land was contested by heavily armed guerrilla movements based on clan loyalties. Savage struggles for economic assets by the various factions led to anarchy and famine.

Black Hawk Down

Somalia was now without a central government. As warlords gained hold, stealing food and money wherever they went, famine and poverty spread rapidly. The subsequent fighting among rival faction leaders resulted in the killing, dislocation, and starvation of thousands of Somalis.

In 1992 the United Nations decided to intervene militarily. As part of this effort, the United States created Operation Restore Hope. 1,800 American Marines landed in Mogadishu on December 9, 1992: The first of nearly 30,000 troops to arrive with the mission of restoring some semblance of order.

Over the next two years, about 50,000 Somalis were killed in factional fighting, and an estimated 200,000 died of starvation. It became impossible to transport relief supplies through the war-torn country without rebels killing the messenger and stealing food intended for the starving. Mogadishu had become the most dangerous city in the world, and 14 armed factions, each led by its own warlord, were fighting to dominate Somalia.

On August 26, 1993, a U.S. Army task force flew into Mogadishu. The Rangers' mission was to capture a local warlord named Mohammed Aidid, a man thought to be the most successful of the many warlords vying for power. Aidid's authority was absolute and feudal within his main power base in south Mogadishu.

October 3, 1993, was a Sunday. Seventeen helicopters took off from their base at the airport. This raid would take the Rangers into the heart of Aidid's territory. Intelligence had it that Aidid was meeting with his associates. According to Ranger Jason Moore, as the helicopters came in to where Aidid was supposed to be, "We heard a loud explosion, and the whole helicopter shook. And

Peacekeepers

Every American has seen the shocking images from Somalia. The scope of suffering there is hard to imagine. Only the United States has the global reach to place a large security force on the ground in such a distant place quickly and efficiently, and thus save thousands of innocents from death.

—President George Bush, Oval Office address, December 1992

the two door gunners just started screaming, 'Go! Go! Go! We're taking fire! Get out of the bird.'"

The next morning, Somalis celebrated the downing of not one but two American helicopters. Eighteen Americans were dead. More than 80 were wounded. One was being held prisoner. U.S. troops had come to help feed a starving Somalia. Now Somalis dragged an American soldier's body through the streets.

Terrorists in Somalia

It shouldn't be surprising that, given the lawlessness that is Somalia, as well as it being a Muslim country, Osama bin Laden's al-Qaeda terrorists have found it to be both a perfect breeding ground as well as a great hiding place. "Somalia has been a place that has harbored al Qaeda and, to my knowledge, still is," said the U.S. Defense Secretary, Donald Rumsfeld in 2002.

Since 1995, the United States had gathered intelligence about terrorist cells in Somalia through its embassies in Nairobi and Addis Ababa. Renewed U.S. interest in Somalia began within days after the September 11 attacks, when a Somali group, Al Ittihaad Al Islamiya (Islamic Unity), appeared on the U.S. hit list of foreign terrorist organizations. The United States claimed that Islamic Unity had links with Osama bin Laden. It also believed that al Qaeda fighters helped in the 1993 killings of those 18 American servicemen, and that Somalia subsequently hosted terrorist training camps.

Once the American War on Terror began, the United States also decided to freeze the assets of al-Barakaat, a money-transfer company based in Somalia, saying it had evidence that Barakaat funneled millions of dollars to al Qaeda.

As the American hunt for bin Laden escalated, some speculated that the terrorist might have been hiding in Somalia. But by and large, Somalis thought that bin Laden would be stupid to hide out there: The $25 million on bin Laden's head would be too great a temptation.

"We would hand him over to the international court and claim the money," said Mogadishu Police Chief Hassan Awaale. "We have enough problems of our own without more from this man."

The Least You Need to Know

- ◆ The Ethiopian civil war has killed or displaced millions.
- ◆ Relief efforts to help the Ethiopian famine were thwarted by the government and the military.
- ◆ Eritrea fought for independence for 30 years, and then went to war against Ethiopia.
- ◆ Somalia is a ruined country.

Chapter 8

Insanity in West Africa

In This Chapter

- ◆ European domination
- ◆ Sierra Leone scrapes the bottom of the barrel
- ◆ Liberia's wacky dictator
- ◆ Senegal's secession
- ◆ Nigeria: Oil and politics don't mix

Although nomadic tribes have lived in West Africa for thousands of years, the first permanent settlements did not exist until about 800 B.C.E. These tribes settled in the rain forests along the coast and in the river basins to the north. They were hunters and gatherers, thriving on the plentiful animal and vegetable populations in the area. The religion of these early tribes was based on mythology and magic and often involved sun worship.

Although several empires rose and fell, none of these centers of influence was prepared for what came next: the power of Allah in the seventh century. Many tribes throughout West Africa converted to Islam. In the sixteenth century, European explorers arrived, and it was this clash of values and power—European versus Islamic—that would affect West Africa for the next 400 years.

West Africa is awash in blood.

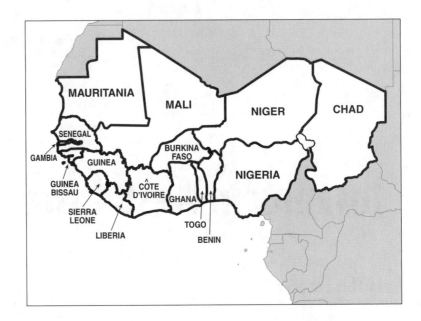

Take, Rattle, and Roll

Led by promises of the untold wealth that lay in the inner kingdoms of West Africa, several European nations soon had outposts in the area. Before long, the regions of the continent were renamed to reflect the products that were being taken: Ivory Coast, Gold Coast, Slave Coast.

> **Reliable Resources**
>
> How big was the slave trade? Between 11 and 20 million people were stolen and sent across the Atlantic Ocean.

> **Reliable Resources**
>
> The European colonial empires are said to have held sway over more than 85 percent of the rest of the globe by the advent of World War I.

Colonialism in this part of Africa reached its peak in 1895 with the establishment of French West Africa. Thereafter, the French dominated the region for several decades. England dominated along the Gambia River, and down the coast in Ghana, Portugal kept its colony in present-day Guinea-Bissau until the 1970s.

After World War II, European colonists began to lose influence as a pan-African movement toward independence emerged. For most countries, this culminated with independence around 1960. But because the goal of colonialism was to plunder the natural resources of a country for the good of the empire, and keeping people poor and uneducated supported that goal, the newly freed countries of Africa had a difficult time making the transition from feudal colony to free society.

Underdeveloped, stricken by poverty, torn between western ways and Muslim values, uneducated for the most part, with few resources to export and little industry, these countries started down the road to freedom with more than their share of problems. The brutal conflicts that followed were ample evidence of this.

Sierra Leone: Making Kosovo Look Good

How bad have things been in Sierra Leone? According to Amnesty International, civilians continued to be deliberately and arbitrarily killed, mutilated, raped, and abducted a year *after* the peace agreement between the government of Sierra Leone and the Revolutionary United Front (RUF) was signed.

In 1991, a little known corporal, Foday Sankoh, declared to the one-party government of the then-President Joseph Saidu Momoh that unless multi-party elections were held within 90 days, the RUF would launch an armed campaign to overthrow the government. The rebels were embittered over what they saw as a corrupt elite that took over following the end of British rule in 1961. Poor rural people increasingly resented the richer ruling class of Freetown (the capital) while battles to control the wealth of the country's lucrative diamond mines further fanned the flames of conflict.

Unwilling to cede power, President Sankoh was ready to fight. The rebels in turn knew that alone their forces would have a hard time displacing the powers that be, so they formed an alliance with Liberian rebel leader Charles Taylor. Together, they launched a war against the Sierra Leone government.

It first seemed that the rebels were nothing but a puppet movement; an offshoot of Liberian fighting factions. But the Sierra Leone rebellion soon took on a life of its own, attracting disaffected young men from the country's impoverished countryside. A gun gave these fighters power and the chance to avenge themselves on a society that often offered them little.

Peacekeepers

Sierra Leone was founded by repatriated slaves. In 1789, the first freed slaves arrived from Great Britain. In 1792, more came from Nova Scotia, and in 1800, even more came from Jamaica. In 1808, Sierra became a British colony.

As the rebellion got underway, a group of army soldiers arrived in the capital of Freetown in 1992, ostensibly to demand better pay and conditions. In actuality, their mission was to overthrow the government. Due to rapidly deteriorating social conditions, the coup was extremely popular.

The RUF, struggling as it was to make headway, decided to attack economic targets, focusing on the diamond-rich Kono district. It worked, and by 1994, the military situation had tilted in their direction, depriving the government of its major source of revenue, the diamond trade. Bolstered by its success, the RUF overran titanium and bauxite mines in 1995, two of the biggest employers in the country and major sources of state income.

A Campaign of Systematic Torture

Although the rebel RUF has called the various governments corrupt and accused them of mismanagement of diamond and mineral resources, which might well be true, the fact is, the rebels are a heartless, ruthless band of animals.

Unlike most wars—where civilian causalities are an unfortunate by-product of the fighting between the combatants—the RUF stands out for its policy of deliberately *targeting* civilians. Human Rights Watch took testimony from dozens of survivors and witnesses of gross violations of human rights committed by the RUF on Sierra Leonean civilians. They included the following:

- Machete lacerations to the head, neck, arms, legs, feet, and torso
- The gouging out of one or both eyes
- Rape
- Gunshot wounds to the head, torso, and limbs
- Burns from explosives and other devices
- Injections with acid
- Genital mutilation

> **Landmine!**
>
> An often cited U.N. report describes an incident in which a rebel commander ordered that all virgin girls report for a physical examination. Those who passed a virginity test were dispersed among the RUF soldiers. Most of the girls were younger than 15. The United Nations says it presumes that every abducted girl was sexually assaulted.

> **Reliable Resources**
>
> When the rebels reached the city, in a matter of days they are said to have amputated the limbs of around 1,500 people.
>
> —Jeremy Vine of Freetown

The RUF also introduced a particularly new phenomenon to civil conflicts: the amputation of limbs as a tool of terror. The RUF uses two types of amputation: The "shirt sleeve," where the arm is amputated close to the shoulder, and the "long sleeve," where the arm is amputated at the wrist. Human Rights Watch found ample machete amputation evidence among civilians of one or both hands, arms, feet, legs, ears, and buttocks as well as one or more fingers.

Sending Children to War

Both sides have also used a large number of child soldiers. The United Nations estimates that of those that fought with Sierra Leone government forces, a quarter are teenagers below the age of 18.

Children have told Human Rights Watch they were forced to kill and commit atrocities. A teenager described removing the heart and liver from his victims for food. He decided to join the rebels only after discovering that his pregnant mother had been murdered. He wanted revenge.

According to Human Rights Watch, "Many children describe witnessing atrocities against civilians, in some cases against their own parents. Almost all underwent military training. Some describe being coerced into taking drugs to make them "fearless" in combat. One boy described how a "doctor" would inject a large group of children with drugs using a single needle for all. They said they were physically abused by rebels charged with caring for them, and the girls were sexually abused."

Human Rights watch also has described how RUF rebels would inscribe "AFRC" (for Armed Forces Revolutionary Council) on children's chests with a razor blade after kidnapping them.

UNICEF says that many of the children who have been released are "malnourished, haggard, and in tattered clothing." Many of the girls were pregnant, and most of the children suffered from various ailments.

> **Landmine!** _____
>
> A young girl's report: "We went to find wood in a village, and one of the rebels grabbed me. He made me pound rice and wash his clothes, and he was the one who had sex with me. I begged him to let me go, but he said "I'm going to have sex with you until they disarm us." I wanted so much to escape, but he kept saying he'd kill me if I ever tried to get away. Some days I complained to his wife. She was so nice. She sympathized and said she too had been abducted. I'm only 11 years old."

Is Peace Possible?

Practically half the country's 4.5 million inhabitants were displaced by the war. Another half million became refugees in neighboring countries, and at least 50,000 people died in the fighting while there are an estimated 100,000 mutilation victims. The economy is in ruins while the national infrastructure needed to run the country has effectively collapsed.

The cost of conflict is higher than the price of peace.

In 1999, the United Nations brokered a peace deal. The so-called Lomé Peace Accord was characterized by a British diplomat as "a very dirty deal, but unfortunately the only one available." It was dirty because, although it did require the rebels to disarm, it also provides amnesty for the rebels. Their years of mayhem would go unpunished, and many believed the agreement therefore tacitly, if unwittingly, condoned their actions. Yet almost as soon as it was signed, the agreement was being violated by the rebels.

The United Nations then sent in peacekeepers to oversee RUF disarmament, troops eventually numbering some 13,000. British military support for the peacekeepers and the

Sierra Leone government army finally helped to stabilize the situation. With the help of British troops who were providing security, Sierra Leone was better able to contain the rebels.

Peacekeepers

Diamonds were discovered in Sierra Leone in 1930. In 1998, the international diamond industry produced an estimated 115 million carats, which, at the end of the diamond chain, is worth close to $50 billion.

The United Nations has especially tried to enforce the disarmament of the rebels near various diamond-rich areas that the rebels controlled. The RUF used the diamonds to fund their atrocities and so the U.N. Security Council imposed an 18-month ban on diamond exports from Sierra Leone.

With the help of the international community, Sierra Leone began to return to a bit of normalcy. The disarmament campaign became a main priority and successfully took weapons out of the hands of perpetrators. In fact, early in 2002, the last remaining 11 rebel commanders handed their guns to United Nations peacekeepers, which it is hoped will end one of Africa's most brutal wars. Peace was finally at hand.

The irony is that Sierra Leone remains one of the poorest countries in the world, despite its vast set of natural resources and minerals, including one of the world's great caches of diamonds.

Liberia

Founded in 1822 by freed African American slaves, Liberia became a republic in 1847. After a military coup in 1980, Samuel Doe became Liberia's President in 1986. Doe was pro-Western but his regime was unstable. The Doe government adopted ever-increasing repressive measures to maintain control, but even so, in 1989, violence erupted after another failed coup. Civil war ensued as three factions fought for power: troops loyal to Doe and two rebel groups. One of them was led by Charles Taylor. The other was led by Prince Yormie Johnson.

Reliable Resources

According to the BBC News, "Charles Taylor was born in Liberia in 1948 to a Liberian mother and an American father. He was educated in the United States. When Tolbert was ousted in 1980, Taylor joined Samuel Doe's government, but was soon charged with fraud and fled to the United States, where he was arrested. He escaped custody, returning to Liberia to lead the National Patriotic Front."

In 1990 Doe was deposed and shot. Although Johnson became president, he would last only a short time. The presidency passed through several hands, settling soon with Amos Sawyer, who managed to pacify some parts of the country.

Taylor and his guerrillas nevertheless kept up the fight. To complicate matters further, even more guerrilla groups formed and fought in the war. Two hundred fifty thousand people had died, and more than a million people were either internally displaced or had become refugees in other parts of the world.

Yet in August 1995, to the surprise of many, six years of brutal civil war came to an end as the main factions signed a peace agreement. A six-person ruling council took control of the country, and elections were scheduled for 1997. When the elections were finally held, the overwhelming winner was the former warlord, half-American, fugitive from justice, and now politician, Charles Taylor, with 75 percent of the vote.

Although it seemed that Liberia might finally be on the road to peace, it was not. By 2001, rebels now opposing the Taylor government attacked. In May that year, Taylor remobilized the army.

Taylor also called on his old friends, the rebels in neighboring Sierra Leone, for support. Yet he got little help because Taylor has few actual friends in West Africa. In Sierra Leone for example, they resent his support of the RUF terrorists.

His other neighbor, Guinea, similarly despises the man, for several reasons. First, during Liberia's civil war years, thousands of Liberians fled next door to Guinea, causing a refugee crisis in that country. Then, when fighting broke out again in 2000 in Liberia, the violence spread to Guinea. At first Liberian attackers came across the border, burned villages and killed civilians, and then retreated back across the border. Soon all Guinea became fair game for the rebels.

The spread of the war to Guinea has caused potential problems throughout the region. If Guinea falls into the hands of President Taylor and his friends—perhaps as the result of a coup d'etat precipitated by the fighting—it can only further destabilize the entire West African region.

> **Peacekeepers**
>
> The state-owned Liberian Broadcasting System can hardly compete against Charles Taylor-owned Liberian Communication Network (LCN). LCN owns a television station, two radios stations, and two newspapers.

> **Landmine!**
>
> In a statement on Liberian Radio and TV that caused a local uproar, President Taylor said "I cannot compromise God even with Jesus Christ. ... I put my trust in God. ... There are beliefs that there is one God, that Jesus is not God, [but] that he's God's son .... I don't equate God with anyone."

Senegal

In Senegal's southern Casamance province, the Movement of Democratic Forces in the Casamance (MFDC) are waging a bloody independence campaign. Due to flaws in recent elections, the government has had much difficulty defusing the MFDC secessionist rebellion.

Reliable Resources

Senegal joined with Gambia to form Senegambia in 1982. It was dissolved in 1989.

Peacekeepers

Roughly 700 million people live in Africa: about 10 percent of the total world population.

In 1997, an escalation of fighting in Casamance between the government and the rebels caused many civilians to flee their villages. Rebel forces reportedly were responsible for, as is their wont in Africa, killings, disappearances, and torture.

MFDC rebels have reportedly used land mines in the Casamance in an effort to terrorize. It is estimated that up to 80 percent of the usable land in some areas has been rendered unusable because of the mines.

The government is no better. In a February 1998 report, Amnesty International alleged that numerous Senegalese civilians have been killed by the government. AI further charges that the victims were buried in secret in hidden mass graves.

Government forces were also suspected of the August 1997 death of a leader of the MFDC who was found murdered. Although no group claimed responsibility for the killing and no direct proof of guilt has emerged, Amnesty International attributed responsibility for the death to the government.

In 1999, the government and the rebels met and began negotiations on the future of the Casamance. An immediate cease-fire was agreed to. Although they also agreed to meet at least once a month, little progress has been made. (Despite the truce, the MFDC's armed wing continues to fight.)

Nigeria

It seems that no matter which country you pick in Africa, the recipe is almost always the same, give or take an ingredient or two:

- A government is elected.
- A rebel group opposes it.
- The government's leader is ousted by a coup.
- Civil war breaks out.
- Atrocities occur.
- The United Nations intervenes.
- Peace is restored (at least until the next coup!).

And so it is in Nigeria. Nigeria is a country that seemingly should have little to fight over. Rich in oil as it is, poverty should be low, education high, and the need to murder nonexistent. But that is not the case. Nigeria is torn by divisions.

Since its independence, Nigerians have experienced more than 25 years of military rule, with only short periods of civilian administration. In the early 1970s, Nigeria became OPEC's fourth largest producer. This oil wealth was both a blessing and a curse—although it was the basis of the country's rapid economic growth, it was also the cause of much corruption and political turmoil.

The unequal distribution of wealth, too, has caused much violence. Very little of the oil wealth has found its way to the poor tribes who work the wells whereas billions of dollars have been paid to the military (dominated by the Hausa tribe).

To make matters worse, according to Human Rights Watch, "multinational oil companies are complicit in abuses committed by the Nigerian military and police." Exploited by international oil corporations, plundered by ruthless dictators, Nigeria has become a country of immense poverty and environmental destruction.

Indeed, the oil companies have been accused of plundering the environment and ignoring the local communities. Oil spills threaten the rich Niger Delta, industrial waste continues to be dumped there, and development projects are never built.

Landmine!

A report titled *Oil For Nothing* by Essential Action and Global Exchange states: "While the story told to consumers in the United States is that oil companies are a positive force in Nigeria, the reality that confronted our delegation was quite the opposite. Our delegates observed inadequate environmental standards, public health standards, human rights standards, and ruptured relations with affected communities. Far from being a positive force, these oil companies act as a destabilizing force."

In 1995, eager to keep some of this oil wealth for himself, military leader Sani Abacha seized power. Since then, he ruled the country with an iron and corrupt hand.

For example, in 1995, Nigeria's military government hung nine political activists, including the well-known playwright Ken Saro-Wiwa. As a result, the British Commonwealth suspended Nigeria and threatened its military rulers with expulsion unless they restored democracy. The 52-member organization of Britain and its former colonies chose this unprecedented penalty to evidence their deep concern over Nigeria's horrific human rights record.

Abacha's abuses were so obvious that they caught the attention of the U.N. Human Rights Committee. In 1996, the Committee stated that it was concerned about the "high number of extra judicial and summary executions, disappearances, cases of torture, ill-treatment, and arbitrary arrest and detention by members of the army and security forces and by the failure of the government to investigate fully these cases, to prosecute alleged offences, to punish those found guilty and provide compensation to the victims or their families."

The expulsion from the Commonwealth and a reprimand from the United Nations forced Abacha to promise that he would hand over power to a civilian government. To that end, he began a circuitous transition process toward elections, forcing each of the country's five political parties (the only ones he would allow) to nominate him for the presidency. But before his plan could work, Abacha died of a heart attack.

Thereafter, Nigeria's new military government said that they intend to release the country's political prisoners, and promised that free elections would be held in 1999. In February of that year, for the first time in many years, Nigerians got to vote for a civilian president.

Post script: The election was marred by claims of voter fraud and irregularities. Two days later, Nigeria's election commission confirmed the winner: former military ruler Olusegun Obasanjo.

The Least You Need to Know

- ◆ Sierra Leone's war atrocities are almost incomprehensible.
- ◆ Liberia spreads dissent throughout the region.
- ◆ Secessionist forces are still alive in Senegal.
- ◆ Nigerian oil makes for a lot of corruption.

Chapter 9

Struggles in Central Africa

In This Chapter

- ◆ The Angolan civil war
- ◆ The Rwandan genocide
- ◆ Hutus and Tutsis in Burundi
- ◆ The Democratic Republic of Congo is a dictatorship

European colonial rule was based on the overwhelming military superiority it held over its subjugated populations. Resistance was futile and dealt with harshly. This was a lesson that subsequent African leaders apparently learned far too well. The modern history of Africa is the history of men blinded by power, succumbing to greed, killing indiscriminately, and caring little for the consequences. This is but one reason why there has been so much bloodshed in the Central African republics of Angola, Rwanda, and Burundi.

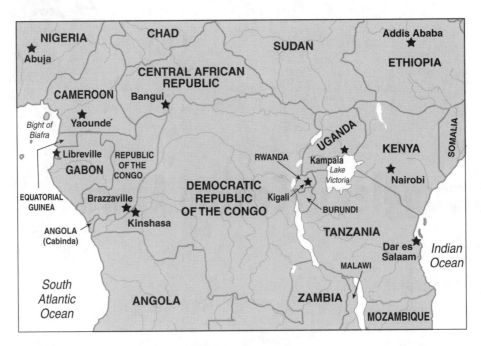

Central Africa used to be a mystery, now it is just a misery.

The Neverending Angolan Civil War

The Portuguese arrived in Angola in 1483, establishing colonies and developing a lucrative slave trade. When locals resisted, the Portuguese clamped down by killing, capturing, and exporting even more slaves. Colonial exploitation continued until the mid-twentieth century.

The Portuguese resisted attempts for peaceful decolonization. In 1956, a Marxist group emerged, the Popular Movement for the Liberation of Angola (MPLA), demanding independence.

In the northern part of the country, a rival group also emerged: the National Liberation Front (FNLA), supported by the large Bakongo tribe. In southern Angola, another group became engaged in the effort to oust Portugal. Dr. Jonas Savimbi's National Union for Independence (UNITA) found support among the country's largest tribe, the Ovimbundu.

Reliable Resources

According to Worldatlas.com, "Angola is located on the southwestern coast of Africa and is home to 11.5 million people. The capital city is Luanda, and the official language is Portuguese. Although blessed with some of the greatest oil deposits on the continent of Africa, output per capita is still among the world's lowest. Other resources include gold, diamonds, extensive forests, fisheries, and useable farmland."

Each rebel group attracted support from outside Angola as well:

- The United States and Zaire supported the FNLA.
- South Africa backed UNITA.
- Communist nations helped the MPLA, which had the greatest popular support.

So it came to be that even after the Portuguese were tossed out of the country in 1974, Angola became a Cold War proxy combatant. As a result of meddling by the United States, South Africa, and Cuba upward of one million people have been killed in the Angolan civil war.

When the Cold War ended, however, Cuba could no longer afford to make mischief in Africa and disengaged from the continent. Around the same time, South Africa became focused on its transition away from *apartheid* and needed to withdraw from Angola as well. And the United States, no longer concerned about the Soviet menace, also had no reason to stay.

Diplomatic Dialogue

Apartheid was the official state policy of South Africa that forcefully subjugated the African majority to the will of the European minority.

With their state sponsors gone, it became much more difficult for the combatants to continue killing each other. Elections were scheduled.

And so, in 1992, United Nations–monitored elections were held, and the MPLA won 58 percent of the vote. Savimbi, though, refused to accept the results, and his well-equipped guerrillas resumed the civil war.

In 1994, the United Nations decided to send in peacekeeping forces, and another peace deal was struck. Under this agreement, Savimbi was made the vice president of Angola, and his UNITA forces were allowed to join the Angolan army. Despite the concessions to UNITA, divisions remained and trouble festered. Accordingly, the United Nations left in 1997, and Savimbi refused any further participation in negotiations. Angola's civil war has the dubious distinction of being the longest in African history.

Landmine!

Angola is a land replete with landmines. Indeed, it has the greatest concentration of landmines in the world. It is estimated that about 70,000 Angolans have lost limbs because of landmine explosions.

For whatever reason, in Africa, differences cannot be smoothed over; they must be fought over. Compromise is a lost art; murder and mayhem the required skill.

Genocide in Rwanda

The atrocities that occurred in Rwanda in 1994 might be the worst thing you will read about in this book. They make Angola look like a vacation spot. To understand what happened and how genocide became public policy, you need to know a bit about the two main tribes in this part of the world—the Hutus and the Tutsis.

Tu-Tu-Tutsi, Goodbye

According to a 1999 report by Human Rights Watch, over the last 2,000 years, the people who are now known as Hutus and Tutsis developed a single language, crafted a common set of religious beliefs, and created a common culture that valued song, dance, and poetry.

How then did the Tutsis and Hutus come to be two separate peoples? When Rwanda emerged as a major state in the eighteenth century, its rulers counted both their power and their wealth in the number of cattle they owned. The word "Tutsi" first referred to an elite group of people who were rich in cattle. "Hutu" meant a subordinate or follower of a more powerful person.

Most people married within their own tribe. This practice created a shared gene pool within each group, which meant that over many generations, Tutsis came to share several characteristics: tall, thin, and narrow-featured. Hutus were shorter, stronger, and with broader features.

Peacekeepers

According to the CIA, "Rwanda is a rural country with about 90 percent of the population engaged in agriculture. It is the most densely populated country in Africa, is landlocked, and has few natural resources and minimal industry."

As Belgium ran its colony, it obviously needed assistance from the locals, and thus tapped the wealthier and better educated Tutsis for the job. As a result, the Tutsis had a virtual monopoly on public life. Unfortunately, Hutus far outnumbered Tutsis. So, in the 1961 independence election, some 80 percent of Rwandans voted the Hutu-dominated Parmehutu party into power. This became known as the "Hutu Revolution."

The ensuing years brought Rwanda the usual mishmash of success followed by corruption and rebellion. Drought and a fall in international coffee prices in the late 1980s made matters worse, and by the late 1980s, the Rwandan community in exile had grown to approximately 600,000 people, mostly Tutsis.

Confronted by economic problems and the evidence of increasing corruption on the part of the government, political leaders, intellectuals, and journalists began demanding reforms, including a return of the refugees. But Hutu authorities declared that the country was too overpopulated to permit their return.

Rwandan Tutsi opposition forces, called the RPF, decided to go home on their own terms, proclaiming its goals not only to be just the return of the refugees, but also the establishment of a more democratic government. On October 1, 1990, the RPF crossed the border from Uganda and headed for the capital.

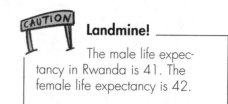

Landmine!

The male life expectancy in Rwanda is 41. The female life expectancy is 42.

In response to the news, the great majority of people, Tutsis and Hutus alike, came to the support of the government. But President Juvenal Habyarimana thought that the Tutsi attack might embolden the Tutsi opposition within the country. He decided to sacrifice the Tutsi minority in his country for his own political gain.

Setting the Stage for Slaughter

As the Human Rights Watch report points out, once the RPF made advances and civil war erupted, the government was forced to make concessions to the rebels.

If Habyarimana was to stay in power, he had to do something. He decided to redefine "the enemy." On September 21, 1992, Colonel Déogratias Nsabimana, Habyarimana's chief of staff, sent a top-secret memorandum to his commanders, identifying and defining "the enemy."

The report declared that the principal enemy of Rwanda was "the Tutsis inside or outside the country, extremist (as they are) and nostalgic for power, who have NEVER recognized and will NEVER recognize the realities of the 1959 social revolution and who wish to reconquer power." The RPF rebels were no longer the country's enemy; rather, its own Tutsi minority had officially become "the enemy."

The Stage Is Set

The president and his closest colleagues began portraying Tutsis inside Rwanda as RPF collaborators, even though it was essentially untrue. For three and a half years, the government elite worked to turn the Hutu against the Tutsi by redefining the population of Rwanda into "Rwandans" (those who backed the president), and the "accomplices of the enemy" (the Tutsi minority).

In the government campaign to foster hatred and fear of the Tutsis, Habyarimana and his cronies reminded the Hutus of the Tutsi legacy of domination.

But destroying the bonds between Hutus and Tutsis would not prove to be easy. For years, the

Reliable Resources

Rwanda is home to some of the world's last remaining mountain gorillas, featured in the movie *Gorillas in the Mist*.

two people had mostly lived in peace. They shared a common language, history, religion, and cultural practices. They were neighbors and friends, they went to the same schools and churches, and they worked and played with one another. And not a few Rwandans were of mixed parentage.

Nevertheless, in a campaign that mostly utilized propaganda, the Habyarimana gang was able to increase the divisions between the two peoples. Then, in 1993, a military victory by the RPF and a subsequent peace agreement that was favorable to the Tutsi rebels left Habyarimana and his supporters facing the imminent loss of power. They decided that the brainwashing had to increase.

So, by late March 1994, Hutu leaders had decided that the solution lay in murdering mass numbers of Tutsis, in order to shatter the peace process and retain power. In the center of the country, they successfully disseminated the doctrine of "Hutu Power." Hitler would have been proud.

Firearms and machetes were freely distributed to the Hutu population. The genocide would actually occur mostly by machete.

It Begins

On April 6, the plane carrying President Habyarimana crashed, killing him. The ensuing crisis convinced a small group of his close associates that the time was right to execute the planned extermination.

> ### Reliable Resources
>
> BBC News Online pointed out that the Canadian daily, *The National Post*, said it had obtained a confidential U.N. report that provided detailed testimony from Tutsi RPF informants explaining how they shot down the president's plane.

By April 20, the organizers of the genocide had gained control of the state political apparatus. The murder would be well organized if nothing else. Finally, orders from the prime minister began to be handed down, all the way to the local level. The enemies had to be killed, now!

Human Rights Watch points out that Rwandan authorities used the media to spread propaganda and lies so as to convince Hutus that their Tutsi neighbors were actually dangerous RPF agents and sympathizers who had to be killed. Meetings were held where community leaders and even the local clergy told the assembled Hutus that they were justified in attacking Tutsis in the name of "self-defense." And so the genocide began.

This was to be genocide in the truest sense of the word, a word that is far too often misused these days. In Rwanda, the Hutus planned a real genocide—the intentional, systematic, premeditated murder of a distinct group (although many moderate Hutus were also killed in the process).

Government officials drove Tutsis to various places to be murdered. They also were in charge of recruiting murderers and giving them the weapons they needed to do their "work." And, of course, the corpses had to be disposed of.

By using the Rwandan military, administrative, and political systems, the leaders of the Tutsi genocide were able to kill huge numbers of Tutsis very quickly and efficiently.

Mass murder was also fostered by rewarding the participants. The greater the commitment to the genocide, the greater the rewards. Food, drink, liquor, and promotions were given to wiling participants.

Authorities encouraged people to steal Tutsi farm animals and crops. Tutsi farms, homes, cars, businesses, and such goods as television sets and computers were given to murderous thugs. And don't think that not participating in mass murder was an option. The military, when faced with reluctance to act, forced citizens and local administrators to attack.

Landmine!

BBC News Online, April 17, 2001: "Two Roman Catholic nuns from Rwanda have gone on trial in Belgium charged with aiding and abetting the murder of Tutsis as part of the genocide that swept the Central African nation in 1994. The two nuns, Consolata Mukangango, or Sister Gertrude, and Julienne Mukabutera, known as Sister Julienne Kisito, are expected to plead not guilty to charges of helping Hutu soldiers to massacre 6,000 Tutsis."

The Rwandan genocide was unique in that rather than hiding their objective, the murderers were quite open in their goal of exterminating their Tutsi brethren. Using the print and electronic media, they encouraged Hutus to join the campaign, insisting that it "concerned everyone." And so, amazingly, the worst massacres often occurred in broad daylight. The dead, too, were usually left out in full view for everyone to see.

When all was said and too much done, between 800,000 and 1 million Rwandans were murdered by their fellow citizens during the course of 100 days.

Afterward, the International Criminal Tribunal for Rwanda held investigations into the political, military, and church leaders connected with the genocide. The investigations were expected to end in 2004, and the court was to conclude its work by 2008.

Burundi

As indicated, many countries that make up Africa were, by and large, created by European colonialists with often little regard for the people who lived there. As such, for example, the Hutus and Tutsis also make up large portions of Burundi, just as they do in Rwanda.

Belgium took control of Burundi during World War I. After 1948, Belgian officials began to move toward creating a democracy in the country. As that happened, two parties surfaced: the Tutsi party (UPRONA) and the opposition Hutu party (PDC).

In January 1962, in preparation for independence, elections were held between UPRONA and the PDC. The Tutsis dominated UPRONA party won 58 of the 64 seats in the national assembly, and Luis Rwagasore became prime minister. Thereafter, even through coup after coup, the Tutsis would dominate public life in Burundi.

> **Landmine!**
>
> Malaria, tuberculosis, cholera, hepatitis A, meningitis, typhoid fever, yellow fever, and schistosomiasis can be contracted while traveling in Burundi.

Two weeks after being elected, Rwagasore was assassinated by members of the Hutu-dominated PDC. This event was both monumental and detrimental to the future of Burundi, setting the stage as it did for years of civil unrest and instability. Open conflict between the Hutus and Tutsis began.

The subsequent government knew that it had to include Hutus as part of the ruling body or be deemed irrelevant, so a Hutu was named prime minister. In January 1965, he was assassinated. A political crisis was averted, however, when the Hutus procured a majority of the seats in the parliamentary election that May.

Chaos did erupt, though, in October after a Tutsi prince became prime minister and a Hutu group tried to overthrow his government. The Tutsis retaliated, and many Hutu politicians were killed, along with thousands of common Hutus who had supported the attempted coup.

What followed was a series of coups and countercoups. In September 1987, Major Pierre Buyoya seized control of the country. In August 1988, ethnic conflict resulted in 20,000 Hutu deaths and 60,000 refugees escaping to Rwanda. (You know things are bad when you have to escape to Rwanda!)

In an effort of reconciliation, the progressive Buyoya appointed a Hutu as prime minister, and his council of ministers contained equal numbers of Hutus and Tutsis. In 1991, Buyoya called for a new constitution, a new form of government, human rights, and regulations requiring parties to accept a charter on national unity. This new constitution became official on March 13, 1992, and presidential and legislative elections were to follow in June 1993.

Different from past elections, there were few electoral abuses on either side. Although the Tutsi party had ruled for the previous 30 years, it only got 32 percent of the vote. Melchior Ndadaye, a Hutu, won the election with 64 percent. This election made Ndadaye the first civilian, the first Hutu-elected president of Burundi.

> **Landmine!**
>
> AIDS kills some 6,000 people each day in Africa—more than wars, famines, and floods.

Probably the best part of the election was how peacefully it occurred. Ndadaye assumed power, and no shots were fired. Were the days of ethnic violence finally over?

Unfortunately, this being Africa, three months later a coup was led by former president Jean-Baptiste Bagaza. Following the coup, 700,000 refugees fled the country, prompting the new government to call a national emergency and seal off the country's borders.

Following the coup, roughly 100,000 people were killed in ethnic fighting, most being Hutus. In response, there was a Hutu-led massacre in which whole families of Tutsis were killed. Thus began a cycle of retaliatory violence because the deaths of people in one tribe led to deaths of people in the other tribe. All-out civil war was on.

In 2000, South African President Nelson Mandela brokered a peace deal that created an interim government in which power would be shared between Hutus and Tutsis. A cease-fire resulted, and South African peacekeepers were sent in during 2001, begging the question—how long would it last?

The Democratic Republic of Congo

Once known as Zaire, the Democratic Republic of Congo (DRC) is the third largest country in Africa, the location for "Heart of Darkness," and the inspiration for movies such as *Apocalypse Now*. It is comprised of four major ethnic groups and more than 200 smaller groups. Many of these tribal groups have home territories that extend beyond the national borders but were divided into separate countries by colonial mapmakers.

Since independence in 1960, the DRC has been ravaged by near continuous inter-ethnic and civil strife, claiming untold lives, plunging the country into chaos and poverty.

> **Reliable Resources**
>
> The DRC includes the greater part of the Congo River Basin, which covers an area of almost 400,000 square miles. The country's only outlet to the Atlantic Ocean is a narrow strip of land on the north bank of the Congo River.

Enter the Colonists

Belgium conquered the DRC (soon to be known as the Belgian Congo) in the late nineteenth century and stayed for 150 years. Yet, as suddenly as they arrived, they left, voluntarily relinquishing power in 1960. Elections were held and Patrice Lumumba was made prime minister.

Problematically for Lumumba, the United States was opposed to his nonaligned policies, seeing him as an extension of the Soviet Union. While serving as Lumumba's army chief-of-staff, Mobutu Sese Seko carried out a CIA-backed coup d'état a few weeks after the election, on September 5, 1960. By 1965, Mobutu had consolidated his power, beginning his 30-year reign as one of the most autocratic and corrupt dictators in the world, as well as a crook, siphoning literally billions of dollars from the national treasury.

Mobutu the Corrupt

The new president was a repressive despot. He supported rebels in Angola, allied himself with racist South Africa, crushed opposition in his own country, and began amassing personal wealth through his corrupt rule. It was the Mobutu regime that gave rise to the term "kleptocracy"—rule by thieves.

As Mobutu stashed much of the country's economic output in European banks, the newly renamed Zaire became the most notorious example of a country in which state institutions came to be little more than a way of delivering money to the ruling elite.

And there was certainly a lot to steal. The DRC is, in fact, one of the most richly endowed countries in the world in terms of natural resources, including (but not limited to) …

- Water
- Diamonds
- Coltan
- Cassiterite
- Tin
- Copper
- Timber

Despite Mobutu's corrupt regime, he continued to receive U.S. and World Bank support because he was aligned with the West during the Cold War. Yet pressure to institute democratic reforms increased through the years as word about Mobutu's theft spread. Finally, in 1991, Mobutu adopted a new constitution and scheduled multi-party elections.

> **Reliable Resources**
>
> As explained in a 2001 NPR Radio Expeditions episode, Coltan, a contraction of the actual ore name coloumbo-tantalite, is a source of the element tantalum, and tantalum is an essential coating for components found in many modern electronic devices, especially cell phones and computers.

As usually occurs in elections, opposition parties emerged, and they called for Mobutu to resign. He responded by killing 100 student demonstrators at Lubumbashi University. This event provoked international outrage, opposition leaders called for Mobutu's resignation again, and uprisings spread throughout the country.

The election was held anyway, amid this continuing political turmoil. Mobutu was unhappy with the result and fired the new prime minister. Now even the West was outraged, demanding that Mobutu honor the prime minister's election. He refused.

Mobutu had dominated the country for three decades, and he succeeded in staying there by successfully playing rival army factions against one another. He thought he could do it again, but he thought wrong. Events beyond his control would soon bring Mobutu down.

At this time, the Tutsi-led Rwandan government, which took over after the genocide, was concerned that perpetrators and supporters of the mass killing were living with impunity in Zaire. So tiny Rwanda invaded its vast neighbor to try to flush out the Hutu extremists who had committed the genocide.

The corrupt and disorganized Zaire army fled, and the Rwandan army, along with anti-Mobutu rebels, then pushed all the way to the Zairian capital of Kinshasa. Mobutu's army backers had seen enough, and in 1997 removed him from office. At the time of his death, Mobutu was one of the richest men in the world.

The Kabila Era

Lawrence Kabila assumed power after Mobutu left, amid hopes of reform. Kabila changed the name from Zaire to the Democratic Republic of the Congo (DRC) and promised elections.

Soon enough however, Kabila began to act like every other African dictator. He ...

- ◆ Banned opposition parties.
- ◆ Arrested the former elected prime minister.
- ◆ Alienated and angered his allies.

Most tellingly, despite naming the country the Democratic Republic, Kabila never held a single election.

War

Kabila was quickly challenged by a Rwandan and Ugandan-backed rebellion in August 1998. Troops from Zimbabwe, Angola, Namibia, Chad, and Sudan intervened in support of Kabila, and a massive seven-country war was underway in the DRC.

In July 1999, a cease-fire agreement was signed by all countries involved, but it did not hold. Further complicating the situation, the rebel forces split in 1999 and have at times fought against each other. The struggle eventually degenerated into a series of petty isolated conflicts in which the participants were principally concerned with securing access to the country's still substantial mineral resources.

Reliable Resources
During the war, there were an estimated 50,000 foreign troops in the DRC.

Then, in January 2001, Kabila was assassinated, allegedly by one of his own bodyguards, although not a few DRC watchers believe that it was his son, Joseph, the new president, who orchestrated the assassination. In February that year, the U.N. Security Council approved a plan for the withdrawal of all fighting factions to be replaced by U.N. peace-keepers throughout the country.

Peacekeepers _____

Reuters, May 21, 2001: "President Joseph Kabila expressed disappointment on Monday with the United Nations' peace effort in the Democratic Republic of Congo and said the world body should send 20,000 peacekeepers. Speaking to Reuters and CNN, the 29-year-old president said the United Nations should do for the former Zaire what it did for Kosovo. 'Their commitment is not what we really expected,' he said."

The Least You Need to Know

- The Angolan civil war is the longest in Africa.
- The Rwandan genocide is unfathomable.
- Burundi Hutus and Tutsis also kill each other.
- The DRC continues to be embroiled in turmoil.

Part  3

Asia and the Pacific

In the coming century, it is not inconceivable to imagine that the largest conflicts will begin in Asia. North and South Korea have been estranged for more than 50 years. China and Taiwan have been at odds for just as long. And of course, we cannot forget India and Pakistan, countries that hate each other and who now have nuclear capabilities.

Yet even beyond these obvious examples, several smaller conflicts also continue to brew just under the radar, any one of which could start a major conflagration.

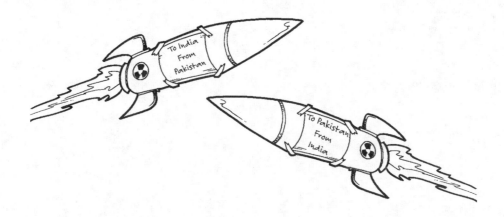

All in the Family: North and South Korea

In This Chapter

♦ The Korean Peninsula

♦ The Korean War

♦ Subsequent skirmishes

♦ The need for new blood

♦ Prospects for unification

No part of the world today is more divided than Korea. Fought over for centuries by China and Japan, its unity and independence have always been fragile. Now the 70 million people of the peninsula, who speak the same language and have the same history, live in two utterly different countries.

The heavily fortified border dividing north from south is one of the last remnants of the Cold War. Tensions between the two countries run the gamut. At times, peace seems imminent, at others, annihilation does. One thing is for certain: Should war ever erupt again, millions of people could die. As related by the U.S. Army Center of Military History, the history of conflict between North and South Korea is frightening indeed.

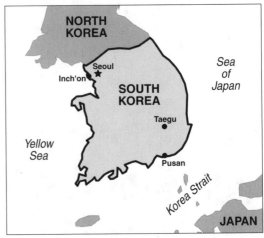

North and South Korea long for reconciliation.

The Korean Conundrum

The Korean peninsula resembles Florida in its shape, and in total area it is about the size of Tennessee and Kentucky combined, covering about 85,000 square miles. It is a mountainous land where roads and railways climb up vast hillsides only to then wind down through twisting valleys.

China, Japan, and Russia, because of their proximity to Korea, have played important roles in its history. Various invasions by each have made Korea a battleground time and again. Accordingly, Korea rarely has been completely free of conflict with one of its stronger neighbors.

Korea's Conflicted History

China, Korea's huge neighbor to the north, has long influenced Korean thought, customs, and cultures. By the seventh century, Korea had become a virtual Chinese satellite. And, like China, Korea endured the Mongol armies in the thirteenth century. Thereafter, for nearly a hundred years, the Mongols ruled and ravaged Korea.

In the late nineteenth century, China and Japan had designs on Korea. Japan fought the Sino-Japanese War of 1894, in part, to prevent Korea from invasion. The treaty of Shimonoseki terminated the war in Japan's favor. Thereafter, the Japanese integrated Korea's industry into its own economy and Korea became dependent, economically and otherwise, upon Japan.

As the U.S. Center for Military History points out, the Japanese came to control key governmental and economic functions by banning Koreans from responsible positions and from educational opportunities. Comprising only 3 percent of the population of Korea, the 750,000 Japanese residents ran the country. Nearly 80 percent of the Korean people were illiterate.

Despite the heavy-handed Japanese rule, the spirit of independence remained strong in Korea. When World War II broke out, Korea was regarded by the Allies as a victim of, and not a party to, Japanese aggression.

> **Reliable Resources**
>
> One sign that the Allied Powers were concerned about Korea appeared in a joint statement by the United States, China, and Great Britain in December 1943, after the Cairo Conference: "The aforesaid three great powers, mindful of the enslavement of the people of Korea, are determined that in due course, Korea shall become free and independent."

Korea Is Divided

As the war wound down and it became apparent that the Allies would win, plans were being made for how and where the Japanese surrender would be taken, detailed in what was known as General Order No. 1. In mid-August of 1945, copies of the draft order were sent to the White House. President Truman gave his approval to the plan, and General Order No. 1 became official U.S. policy.

The essence of the order was that Japanese forces north of the 38th Parallel in Korea would surrender to the Russians and those south of that line would surrender to U.S. forces. That dividing line, the 38th Parallel, was an arbitrarily chosen line, which sliced across Korea.

At the time, North and South Korea were two parts of the same country, economically, agriculturally, and industrially interdependent. For instance, North Korea furnished the fertilizer for the south, from whom it got many of its crops.

> **Landmine!**
>
> According to the U.S. Army Center of Military History: "The 38th Parallel cut through more than 75 streams and 12 rivers, intersected many high ridges at variant angles, and at that time, divided 181 small cart roads, 104 country roads, 15 all-weather roads, 8 highways, and 6 north-south rail lines."

Now, it is true that differences between North and South had always been part of the Korean scene. While South Koreans considered their Northern neighbors backward, North Koreans dismissed their Southern cousins as lazy. Yet they also knew they were one people.

Even so, the country was divided at the end of the war, and the Russians moved into the North to take the Japanese surrender and the Americans moved into the South.

Afterward, neither was willing to move out. South of the 38th Parallel, the American zone held an estimated 21 million people. North of the line, the Soviet zone contained about 9 million people. Of the 20 largest Korean cities, 12 were inside the American zone, including Seoul, with a population of nearly two million. The American zone included six of Korea's 13 provinces in their entirety, the major part of two more, and a small part of one other.

By 1948, the emerging split in the country, exacerbated by the arbitrariness of the 38th Parallel and the heat of the Cold War, led both areas to adopt different forms of government as the time for actual liberation drew near.

On August 15, 1948, the Republic of Korea was established south of the 38th Parallel, and on September 9, 1948, the inappropriately named Democratic People's Republic of Korea was established in the north. From this moment on, the one people were divided into two countries, with two different agendas, two different value systems, two different economies, and two different paths. Like any bad divorce, anger and tensions ran high.

The two governments could not have been more different. North Korea became a communist state in the Soviet mold. There were no free elections, no privately owned land, and few consumer goods. South Korea became a capitalist country and soon would have one of the strongest economies in the world.

The Korean War

After partition, North Korea was determined to conquer South Korea and make it a communist state. In the 1950s, communism was on the rise, and the North Koreans saw it as their historical duty to indoctrinate their one-time countrymen. To this end, agents and terrorists from North Korea began to infiltrate the South and carry out subversive actions. Border incidents occurred time and again. By 1950, the North Korean military machine was ready, and the people had been psychologically prepared for war.

Invasion

According to the war history provided by the U.S. Army Center of Military History, North Korea invaded South Korea at 4:00 A.M. on June 25, 1950. Striking without warning, northern units "gained complete tactical surprise as they swiftly burst across the 38th Parallel in numbers. Coordinated columns of Soviet-made tanks and Soviet-trained infantry followed."

Whole units of South Korean defenders were destroyed as the North Koreans invaded in a well-conceived and carefully prepared all-out assault. North Korean planes, giving tactical support, went virtually unchallenged.

What North Korea did not anticipate was the swift decision by the United States to commit forces in support of South Korea. The United States, worried about the *domino theory*, and fearing that inaction in Korea might be interpreted as appeasement of communist aggression elsewhere, was determined that South Korea would not fall. Truman ordered the use of U.S. planes, naval vessels, and ground troops in support of the South Koreans.

The United States also asked the United Nations to intervene. When the Soviets made the mistake of walking out of the Security Council emergency session, that body decided that the United Nations would send troops to South Korea. This was the first collective action for the newly formed United Nations, and 16 member nations sent troops and assistance to South Korea.

China then got involved. Mao Tse Tung feared that the West might not stop in Korea, but would continue across the Yalu River into China and attempt to overthrow his communist regime on the mainland. He therefore dispatched some 850,000 troops to China's Korean border.

> **Reliable Resources**
>
> Washington learned of the attack six hours after the first North Korean troops crossed into South Korea. The telegram bearing the news said: "Fighting with great intensity started at 0400, 25 June on the Ongjin Peninsula, moving eastwardly taking six major points; city of Kaesong fell to North Koreans at 0900; Comment: No evidence of panic among South Korean troops."

> **Diplomatic Dialogue**
>
> During the Cold War, it was the conventional wisdom that if one democratic state in a region fell to communism, all other democracies might fall, too, like so many dominos; hence the name **domino theory**.

In the second phase of the war, the North Koreans suffered a complete reversal of fortune due to major advances by the U.N. forces. China then assisted North Korea, marking the third phase of the war.

The last phase was a stalemate, during which neither side would risk vast casualties in an attempt to gain a complete victory. By the end of May 1951, the battle lines had been established and set. Fighting continued, but there would be no more large advances and withdrawals up and down the peninsula.

Truce talks began in 1951, but the fighting continued until 1953, when the conflict ended with a cease-fire agreement.

Aftermath

The war left long-term marks on the Korean Peninsula and the world. The Korean peninsula was ruined, and roughly 180,000 South Korean and United Nations troops died. The number of communist soldiers estimated killed range as high as 500,000 North Koreans and 900,000 Chinese.

Peacekeepers

"It is a landscape of nightmare, this wasteland of the demilitarized zone: artillery craters, barbed wire, minefields, graveyards, the skeletons of villages, and the remains of rice paddies. The earth has been shelled, mined, overgrown, booby-trapped, burned, and abandoned to grow wild yet another time," William Holinger in *The Fence Walker*.

Fifty years later, in June of 2000, the U.S. Department of Defense said that it was revising the number of Americans killed in the Korean conflict. Dramatically dropping the number of dead from 54,246 to 36,940, the DOD declared that it had mistakenly included 20,617 nonbattlefield U.S. military deaths that had occurred worldwide during the three years of the conflict as part of the Korean dead number.

The cease-fire took effect on July 27, 1953, but no peace treaty was ever signed. Technically, the two countries are still at war. The dividing line now is the Demilitarized Zone (DMZ), today the most heavily fortified border on the planet, with more than a million soldiers on both sides.

Subsequent Skirmishes

The end of the war did not end the conflict. Through the years, countless small battles and several large ones have erupted between the now virulent enemies.

The Blue House Incident

On January 21, 1968, 31 commandos from a North Korean Special Forces unit made a bold incursion across the border and into Seoul. Their destination: The presidential residence, also known as the Blue House. Their aim: To kill key government officials, including the South Korean president.

The commandos, outfitted in South Korean military uniform, were armed with submachine guns and hand grenades. They got within 500 meters of the Blue House before being detected. South Korean military units killed them all.

The *Pueblo* Incident

Two days later, on January 23, 1968, North Korean patrol boats seized the U.S.S. *Pueblo*, a Navy intelligence-gathering vessel that was sailing in international waters. One U.S.S. *Pueblo* crewmember died during the siege and 82 others were taken hostage. This was the first U.S. Navy ship to be hijacked on the high seas by a foreign military force in more than 150 years.

The *Pueblo* crew was taken to North Korea and held in two different compounds, one in Pyongyang, the other in the nearby countryside. The North Koreans pressured the crew to write letters home telling of the humane treatment they were receiving and asking that the United States apologize for spying and for its intrusions into Korea's waters. The crew members were also forced to give rehearsed presentations at two different press conferences.

The crew was held by North Korea for 11 months while negotiations continued. Upon the United States admitting to espionage in the coastal waters of the Sea of Japan, the 82 prisoners were freed. The crew was released on December 28, 1968. The ship remains in Wonson Harbor, North Korea to this day.

> **Reliable Resources**
>
> The crew tried to signal to the people at home that their "confessions" were in fact false by using innuendo, lacing their letters with obviously false information, and displaying obscene gestures in photographs and movies. During the press conferences, they also used slang and corny and archaic language.

The Tunnels Incident

On November 15, 1974, a joint Korea/U.S. military team in South Korea discovered an underground tunnel that seemed to extend into North Korea. Upon further examination, the team found several Soviet-made items and a North Korean-made telephone, as well as traces indicating that the tunnel had been dug by the North Korean army.

Apparently, North Korea had built the tunnel to infiltrate, and invade, South Korea. According to South Korean armed services, the tunnel was wide enough to handle the passage of 15,000 soldiers per hour. On March 19, 1975, a second tunnel was discovered. North Korea denied involvement.

Based on information revealed by defector Kim Bu-song, the Korean army was then able to detect the presence of a third tunnel on October 17, 1978. This tunnel's exit was discovered to be but a few miles from the South Korean capital of Seoul.

Kim Bu-song testified that the orders to build the tunnels came from North Korean dictator Kim Il-sung, who is alleged to have said at the time, "blitz tactics are the only means to enable North Korea to liberate South Korea, and one tunnel must be regarded as effective as 10 nuclear weapons."

On March 3, 1990, a fourth tunnel was discovered. It is estimated that there might be more than 20 such tunnels and that North Korea is still digging tunnels under the DMZ.

> **Landmine!**
>
> World Tribune, Monday, October 16, 2001. "WASHINGTON—North Korea has built a network of tunnels in several countries in the Middle East designed to conceal weapons of mass destruction and ballistic missiles. One unnamed U.S. official said that North Korea is regarded as a leader in the construction of tunnels, adding that Pyongyang has equipment and know-how to quickly build tunnels."

The Tree Incident

Near the Bridge of No Return in the DMZ sits a row of poplar trees, one of which would always grow and block a line of sight at checkpoint 3. The trimming of the poplar tree each summer had become a routine procedure. However, in early August 1976, a South Korean work force was threatened with death by North Korean troops if they tried to trim the tree.

The work force returned later with American troops at their side. The North Koreans, true to their word, attacked. Among the victims were two American officers beaten to death with the blunt end of axes after they ignored the North Koreans' order to halt.

After a mobilization on both sides, President Ford decided the appropriate response would be to chop down the tree. On the morning of August 31, 1976, a joint mission involving South Korean and U.N.–supported American troops began "Operation Paul Bunyon." Supported by an armed platoon, 27 helicopters, and B-52 bombers, the troops chopped down the tree, proving that conflict can take you from the sublime to the ridiculous in short order.

Are Things Getting Warmer or Colder?

As the Cold War was ending with the demise of the Soviet Union, the client states of that superpower were being squeezed. Money was drying up. In January 1991, the Soviet Union demanded that North Korea begin to pay for its goods with hard currency. This only exacerbated the worsening economic conditions that were occurring throughout the communist regime, including food and power shortages.

Although peace is sometimes the result of brave men taking bold action, just as often, it is the result of calculating men deciding that it is the lesser of two evils. So, with the Cold War ending, times being tough, and maybe a realization that overthrowing the South was not going to happen, North Korea's leadership decided that the time for rapprochement was at hand.

This was even truer given that, despite their many differences and conflicts, North and South Koreans were one people, sharing a common ancestry, gene pool, and history, if not ideology. The arbitrary split at the 38th Parallel, exacerbated by the Cod War, did not change the fact that South Koreans had family members they hadn't seen in 40 years living in North Korea, and vice versa. If peace didn't happen soon, generations would die without ever seeing their loved ones again.

The Reconciliation Agreement

Negotiations had been an on-again, off-again affair for some time, but in the early 1990s they were on again. In late 1991, North and South Korea signed an "Agreement on

Reconciliation, Non-aggression, Exchanges and Cooperation and the Joint Declaration on the Denuclearization of the Korean Peninsula."

The Declaration, which came into force on February 19, 1992, stated that the two sides "shall not test, manufacture, produce, receive, possess, store, deployed use nuclear weapons," and that they "shall not possess nuclear reprocessing and uranium enrichment facilities." This was important because the international community feared that North Korea had in fact begun a nuclear weapons program, and the West was demanding access to various sites within North Korea, who had so far refused.

In recognition of the Reconciliation Agreement, and as a gesture of goodwill, President George Herbert Walker Bush pulled all American tactical nuclear weapons off the Korean Peninsula, hoping to get North Korea to open up its nuclear program for inspection. But it didn't work.

The implementation of the reconciliation accords ground to a halt almost immediately after they were signed because of the nuclear issue. The United States and South Korea insisted that North Korea live up to the Joint Declaration and open a suspected nuclear plant to inspections.

On February 10, 1993, North Korea refused to permit the International Atomic Energy Agency (IAEA) to conduct inspections as permitted under the terms of the Treaty on the Non-Proliferation of Nuclear Weapons (NPT). In March 1993, unable to shake off a persistent IAEA insisting on exercising inspection rights under the NPT, North Korea announced its intention to withdraw from the NPT because of the insistence of the IAEA.

The West threatened sanctions against North Korea if they wouldn't comply, and North Korea threatened to go to war if sanctions were imposed. A nuclear crisis had begun.

Landmine!

In mid-May 1994, U.S. Defense Secretary Perry said that "The North Koreans have stated that they would consider the imposition of sanctions to be equivalent to a declaration of war. We may believe, and I do believe, that this is rhetoric on their part, but we cannot act on that belief. We have to act on the prudent assumption that there will be some increase in the risk of war if we go to sanctions."

After a period of high tension brought on by failure to resolve the nuclear issue, the Clinton Administration decided to send former President Jimmy Carter to Pyongyang in June 1994 to see whether he could help defuse tensions. Just days later, Carter successfully obtained Kim Il-sung's pledge to freeze North Korea's nuclear program. Kim also said that he would allow nuclear inspectors into his country and would agree to high-level talks with the United States for the first time in 40 years.

This opening foreshadowed that the time was coming for serious reconciliation discussions. Leaders on both sides of the DMZ seemed ready for change.

New Blood

Kim Dae-jung began experimenting with anti-establishment politics in South Korea while working in the shipping industry. In 1961, after his fifth run for office, Kim was elected to the National Assembly. One month after Kim's election, General Park Chung-hee organized a military coup and seized control of the government, forcing Kim to step down. The authoritarian Park, however, became the perfect foil for the charismatic Kim.

The more Park persecuted Kim, the more Kim grew in popularity. In 1971, when Kim called for the reunification of North and South Korea, Park branded him a communist. He ran for president and won 46 percent of the vote against Park. Kim was headed to a rally in Seoul a month after the election when a truck forced him off the road; an event widely believed to have been an assassination attempt.

Park tightened his hold on the country in 1972 when he scrapped the constitution. In 1979, with people angry over his autocratic rule, Park was assassinated by the head of the Korean Central Intelligence Agency. Another general imposed martial law as Kim and other leading opposition figures were arrested when tens of thousands of South Koreans protested.

After two more failed attempts for the presidency, in 1987 and 1992, Kim decided to retire his political aspirations. His retirement did not last long though. In 1997, he joined forces with another opposition leader and was finally elected president on his fourth try.

According to CNN News, shortly after winning the presidency Kim told *Time Magazine*, "Throughout my life I have faced death five times. For six years I was in prisons, and for 10 years I was in exile or under house arrest … I never lost hope that someday there would be something like this."

Kim's election set in motion a major thaw in relations between Seoul and Pyongyang, culminating in an historic North Korean-South Korean Summit in 2000, an unprecedented achievement that brought Kim accolades from around the world and won him the label, "visionary."

While Up North …

At the same time, new blood was also emerging in North Korea. Kim Il-sung had run North Korea since its inception in 1948. He had taken the country down a Soviet-style path, complete with Soviet-style purges, Soviet-style gulags, and even a Soviet-style Kim personality cult. But Kim knew as he got older that he would need a successor. And who better than his own son?

Kim Jong-il is that son, and after a period of grooming for leadership, was officially designated successor to his father in 1980; power in title only. The South Korea media portrayed Kim as a playboy, with permed hair, lifts in his shoes, and a penchant for foreign liquor. In addition, journalists reported rumors of young women being kidnapped to be his courtesans in a string of luxury villas.

Kim didn't hold any positions of real power until 1991, when he took control of the armed forces despite his lack of military experience. Some analysts also believe the younger Kim was responsible for developing North Korea's suspected nuclear weapons program. He finally took over the country upon his father's death in 1994.

Before his death in 1994, Kim Il-sung surprised everyone by announcing that he would meet with South Korea's President Kim for a summit. The summit never happened because Kim Il-sung died on July 8, 1994.

> **Landmine!**
>
> In early 2002, North Korean defectors testified before a U.S. congressional delegation. The eight defectors said North Korean women who attempted to flee their country were raped, kidnapped, and sold to human traffickers.

> **Reliable Resources**
>
> In 1998, North Korea called Kim Il-sung (dead, at this point, for more than four years) their "Eternal President."

Summit

Things brightened, though, in 1997 with the election of opposition leader Kim in South Korea. At the same time, Kim Jong-il in the North seemed ready to shed his secretive ways. For years, North Korea had been one of the world's most enigmatic, secretive societies, but there were clear signs that decades of rigid isolation might be coming to an end.

Once suspicious of all contact with the outside world, Pyongyang went on the diplomatic offensive, meeting with leaders in the United States, China, and Japan. Most importantly, Kim was ready to meet his counterpart in the South.

In June 2000, a joint summit between the two Kims was held in North Korea. By all accounts, it was a jubilant affair, and the once reclusive North Korean leader turned out to be an affable host. It was, for most, their first glimpse inside North Korea in more than half a century.

The summit ended with the two Koreas signing a five-point accord that was to open up the insular Stalinist state to capitalist development. In the months since, the ice continued to melt between the two sides:

◆ Following the summit, North Korea stopped propaganda radio broadcasts against the South.

- ◆ In July, high-level officials from the two sides met in Seoul to find ways to implement agreements made in the June summit, including improving economic and military ties. They also agreed to reopen border liaison offices.

- ◆ In August came the most dramatic action: 100 North Koreans met their relatives in the South in a highly charged, emotional reunion. The meeting was followed by a group of 100 South Koreans visiting relatives in the North.

On October 13, 2000, the once ostracized South Korean President Kim Dae-jung won the Nobel Peace Prize for his efforts toward reconciliation with North Korea.

Said Kim, "I thank all the citizens who love democracy and human rights, who have supported these efforts with our people. I will keep up my efforts for human rights, democracy, and peace on the Korean peninsula, Asia, and the world."

Postscript: After September 11, President George W. Bush said that North Korea was part of an "axis of evil." That speech, and that declaration, did much to chill the then-warming relations between North and South Korea.

South Korea, unwilling and afraid to offend its American protectors, did not publicly dispute the characterization. North Korea in turn was offended that its newfound "friends" in the south did not speak up on its behalf.

And so it goes on the Korean peninsula.

The Least You Need to Know

- ◆ The Korean Peninsula was divided after World War II.
- ◆ The Korean War ended in a stalemate.
- ◆ Subsequent skirmishes erupted over the years.
- ◆ New leaders brought in new ideas.

Chapter 11

Enter the Dragon: China

In This Chapter

- ◆ The Communist revolution
- ◆ China and Taiwan
- ◆ China and Tibet
- ◆ The Xinjiang province
- ◆ China and Russia
- ◆ China and the United States
- ◆ Old guard versus the new guard

The twentieth century has often been called the American Century. It is not inconceivable that the twenty-first century will come to be known as the Chinese Century. Although China has long been considered a third world country, the economic boom unleashed by the relaxing of communist ideology in the 1980s, combined with a population of more than one billion and a resurgent military, might well propel the country into the forefront of nations.

Certainly the economic changes wrought by abandoning orthodox Communism raised the country's standard of living, but it also has created a potentially troubling resurgence in Chinese nationalism. The question now is whether the powers that be—the controlling, rigid, Communist party—will be able to retain control in light of the country's economic liberalization and newfound prosperity.

China may yet need more room.

Who Lost China?

Chinese society has developed out of some 5,000 years of recorded history. The so-called Middle Kingdom was marked by the cyclical rise and fall of imperial dynasties. An ethical system of relations also developed during this time, governed by rules of propriety (known as the Confucian school), which defined each person's place in society. In this system, harmony of social relations, much more than the rights of the individual, was the ideal.

You Say You Want a Revolution?

Despite its ancient creed of harmony, China has long been a target of foreign interest and invaders. The Middle Kingdom, so secret and intriguing, made for many alien incursions. First from Mongolia, then from Japan, and later from Great Britain, these invasions often found China being dominated by stronger countries. In 1895 for example, the Chinese lost another war, the first of two Sino (Chinese)-Japanese wars.

Burdened with the legacy of thousands of years of imperial rule and nearly a century of humiliations at foreign hands, China was ready for a revolution as the twentieth century dawned. The imperial dynasty system was overthrown in favor of a republic in 1911, but civil war continued for nearly forty more years, accompanied by war with Japan (again) between 1937 and 1945.

The real revolution came with the Chinese Civil War of 1945, which was won by the Chinese Communist Party in 1949. Except for the island of Taiwan (which became the home of those who lost the civil war, see the next section), the new government unified the nation and achieved a stability China had not experienced for generations. However, eagerness on the part of its new leader, Mao Tse Tung, resulted in some horrific social and public policy blunders, including

♦ The Great Leap Forward (1958–60): A program that attempted rapid economic modernization but proved disastrous.

♦ The Cultural Revolution (1966–76): An amazing time of upheaval, whereby Mao attempted to keep the revolution "alive" via radical experimentation and political chaos that brought the educational system to a halt and severely disrupted attempts at rational economic planning. When Mao Tse Tung died in 1976, the Cultural Revolution era came to an end.

On his deathbed, Mao anointed Hua Guofeng, a former party secretary, as his successor. Hua survived Mao, but National Defense Minister Ye Jianying led a coup that eventually put the country in the hands of Mao's one-time foe, the diminutive (five feet tall) Deng Xiaoping.

The Capitalist Revolution

Deng created a second revolution, one possibly more powerful than the first. When he became head of the Chinese state in 1978, Deng realized that China's economic problems stemmed from state control of the economy. He decided to challenge the very precepts of *Karl Marx* and Communism itself by adopting a hybrid system not quite like anything seen before. Outside analysts often call it "market socialism," Deng called it "socialism with Chinese characteristics." Whatever you call it, the fact is that it was capitalism.

Deng decided to liberate the energies of the individual, a daring concept not just for a Marxist but for a Chinese. (The concept of individualism can have a negative connotation in Chinese society.) He began with agriculture, which had been collectivized by Mao. The land was worked by communes that grew what the state directed and turned over all food produced to the state for distribution.

Deng's reforms slowly abolished the communes and replaced them with a contract system. Although the state continued to own the land,

Diplomatic Dialogue

Karl Marx was a German social philosopher and the chief theorist of modern socialism and communism. His book, *Das Capital*, laid out his ideas for a world controlled by the working class in which people worked—not for the good of themselves, but for the good of the whole community.

families were allowed to grow anything they wanted and sell it for profit. Farmers were encouraged to build privately owned houses. The results were phenomenal. Chinese farmers increased food production around 8 percent beginning in 1978; about 2½ times the rate over the preceding 26 years.

The success of the agricultural reforms expanded into all kinds of businesses—small businesses like hotels, restaurants, stores, tailor shops, beauty parlors, as well as larger businesses like manufacturing, oil exploration, and technology companies. All were all given the right to compete.

Diplomatic Dialogue

A country's **gross domestic product** is the value of all goods and services provided within the borders of a nation.

Output quadrupled over the ensuing 20 years, and China now has the world's second largest *gross domestic product* in the world. China's economy grew by an astounding 7.9 percent in the first half of 2001, compared with the same period in 2000.

This unprecedented growth has made China a much stronger country, and now a much more formidable foe. In 2000, China stood as the second largest economy in the world after the United States. No longer forced to be anyone's whipping boy, China has emerged as one of the strongest countries in the world, buoyed by its 1.2 billion people. To wit,

- China's People's Liberation Army is the largest in the world, with 3 million soldiers.
- China's soldiers directly supervise and control more than 15,000 business enterprises and 50,000 factories. They operate shipping companies, airlines, arms exporters, factories, telephone companies, and toy companies. The military reinvests its profits back into feeding troops and modernizing its military capabilities.

With this newfound economic prosperity and military might has come a greater willingness to deal with several conflicts that have been on the backburner for years.

China and Taiwan

In 1895, China lost the first Sino-Japanese war. In article 2 of the Treaty of Shimonoseki, which ended that war, China ceded Taiwan (then called Formosa) to Japan in "perpetuity and full sovereignty." Japan's sovereignty over the island would not be disputed by China or any other state for the next 50 years.

During World War II, in paragraph 3 of the Cairo Declaration (1943), the United States, Great Britain, and China declared that Japan would be stripped of all the islands in the Pacific the country had seized or occupied since the beginning of World War I in 1914. In the same vein, the Declaration demanded that all the territories Japan has taken from the Chinese, such as Manchuria, Formosa, and the Pescadores, would be restored to the Republic of China.

In accordance with this sentiment, Taiwan was returned to China as a province after the war. But after the war, in 1945, the Chinese were in the middle of their own civil war. There really was no one to give Taiwan back to because no one controlled the country.

As the civil war wound down in 1949, Nationalist leader Chiang Kai-shek and his forces withdrew to Taiwan, vowing to reclaim the mainland. Since then, China has considered Taiwan to be a renegade, runaway province that must someday be reunited with the mainland.

The Renegade Province

Following the outbreak of the Korean War in 1950, U.S. President Harry S. Truman hoped to prevent a possible Chinese attack on the island by sending the 7th Fleet into the Taiwan Strait. For Truman, Taiwan came to represent a buffer against communist expansion in Asia, and to guarantee its safety, he sent money and military supplies to the island. Although this was the first time the United States had intervened in the conflict between Taiwan and China, it would not be the last.

During the following 20 years, from 1952 to 1972, Taiwan grew economically. But on the diplomatic front, they lost ground. As China also grew, it became more and more difficult for countries to choose Taiwan over the mainland. The Chinese Market, with its one billion people, was simply irresistible.

In 1972, President Richard Nixon made an historic trip to Beijing, opening up China to the West. China and the United States then signed the Shanghai Communiqué, which "acknowledged" the Chinese position that there is but one China and that Taiwan is part of China.

Nixon's trip, and the Shanghai Communiqué, reinforced a growing belief in the international community that, 20 years after the Chinese Civil War, there was one China and that the Communists ruled it, despite Taiwan's protestations to the contrary. The United Nations expelled Taiwan in favor of the Communist China.

Eight years later, the United States formally recognized the People's Republic of China, severing official diplomatic relations with Taiwan. The U.S. move meant that America accepted Beijing's "one China" claim (stating that there is but one

Peacekeepers

Richard Nixon was the most intense, feared anti-communist of his day. In fact, he made his name by trying to root out "Red" spies in the government. Thus, when he went to China, no one could accuse him of being soft on Communism. That is why people now say, when a politician does something unexpectedly against the grain, that "only Nixon could go to China."

China, and Communist China is it). Within months though, the U.S. Congress reinstated unofficial economic ties with Taiwan, including the sale of arms.

Taiwan Becomes a Democracy

Although international relations were not going Taiwan's way, it still was not part of the mainland and was still a thorn in China's side. But, like China, it too was a dictatorship.

That began to change in 1979 when police crushed a rally in the southern city of Kaohsiung that had turned violent. The leaders were jailed and later defended by a then little known, yet successful, maritime commerce lawyer named Chen Shui-bian. Twenty years later, Chen would become the first non-Nationalist party president elected into office.

In 1996, contemporaneous with the first ever direct presidential election in Taiwan, China decided to conduct missile tests and concurrent joint military exercises close to Taiwan. China admitted the drills were meant to intimidate Taipei into dropping any pretensions toward full independence.

The United States responded by sending warships to the Straits of Taiwan, the tiny slip of water that separates China from Taiwan. This became the largest show of naval force for America since the Vietnam War. President Clinton ordered two aircraft carrier battle groups to the straits.

The elections went forward as planned, and Lee Teng-hui was elected president. It was the first time voters had elected their own president in 5,000 years of Chinese history.

Tensions increased dramatically during the 2000 election when, for the first time, the opposition party called for full independence from China. According to a PBS Online News Hour report, "Chinese Premier Zhu Rongji threatened 'bloodshed' if the Taiwanese voters 'acted on impulse.' The statement was pointed at supporters of Chen."

> **Landmine!**
>
> It's becoming ever more clear to people that the divisive policy of Taiwan's leader Lee Teng-hui has been pushing Taiwan's people to an abyss of misery.
>
> —Commentary published in the *People's Daily*, as reported by Reuters (1996)

Despite the veiled threats, for the first time in 50 years, a non-Nationalist party leader took control in Taiwan. The former defense attorney, Chen Shui-bi an was elected president. During his inaugural speech, Chen backed off a bit, saying that as long as China refrained from using military means to take control of Taiwan, he would not push for independence from Beijing.

Given that China could overrun Taiwan in a matter of hours and has remained steadfast in its insistence that the province return to the fold, the likelihood of this conflict turning violent is not remote by any means.

How the United States Fits In

Any war between China and Taiwan could easily involve the United States. Under the 1979 Taiwan Relations Act, American law says that the United States would view any conflict over Taiwan with "grave concern."

The United States takes this matter very seriously. Aside from the naval showing in 1996, a similar show of force occurred in 1995. That year, Taiwanese President Lee went to visit his alma mater, Cornell University. China responded by conducting military exercises near Taiwan, leading the United States to send an aircraft carrier through the straits for the first time in 17 years.

If China ever did invade, the United States might be forced to intervene. And if that were to happen, all bets are off.

> **Peacekeepers**
>
> Although it may be difficult to understand China's position, consider the following analogy presented by the Cox News Service: "Imagine how Americans might feel if the Civil War had ended just 50 years ago and the Confederates escaped to Florida. Americans might demand that Florida be repatriated." Many Chinese, for the same reason, want Taiwan back.

China and Tibet

Tibet lies at the center of Asia. The earth's highest mountains, as well as a vast arid plateau and great river valleys make up the physical homeland of six million Tibetans, a land traditionally free and independent.

In 1950, Radio Beijing announced that "The task of the People's Liberation Army for 1950 is to liberate Tibet." China then invaded Tibet, saying that Tibet historically was part of China."

The facts are these: At the time of China's invasion, Tibet was essentially an independent country. It had a defined territory, system of government, tax base, currency, its own postal system, and its own army.

Nevertheless, the invasion occurred, Tibet fell to the Chinese, and two years later, a 17-point agreement was imposed on the Tibetan Government by the Communists. The Chinese maintained that the Dalai Lama supported China's actions in Tibet and "acknowledged" that Tibet was in fact part of China.

Yet eight years later, in 1959, after a Tibetan uprising at Lhasa and its savage suppression by the Chinese, the Dalai Lama and 100,000 followers fled for refuge in India. After his escape, the Dalai Lama repudiated the 17-point agreement, stating it was forced upon the "Tibetan Government and people by the threat of arms."

Since then, the Dalai Lama has become an international symbol of peace, and his intent to reclaim a free Tibet a cause for many.

Despite the efforts of the Dalai Lama, since its invasion, China has sought to re-create Tibet in its own image, by force if necessary. According to FreeTibet.org …

♦ It is estimated that since 1950, 1.2 million Tibetans have been killed by the Chinese.

♦ Long-term Chinese settlement in Tibet has been encouraged, with the result that Tibetans are in the minority in many areas.

♦ The Chinese have replaced Tibetan as the official language.

♦ Young Tibetans are being re-educated about their cultural past, with references to an independent Tibet being omitted.

♦ Mining and mineral extraction have become among the largest economic activities in much of Tibet, and at least one half of Tibet's forests have been logged since Chinese occupation.

In 1988, The Dalai Lama put forward the "Strasbourg proposal," which called for autonomy for Tibet rather than independence. Although it was rejected by the Chinese, the following year the Dalai Lama received the Nobel Peace Prize.

Tibet remains an occupied country and liberation but a dim hope. As the Swedish Human Rights Delegation to China and Tibet said in October 1994, "Since the Chinese Government perceives demands for independence as a formidable threat to national unity, it sees repression as the only means of dealing with (the problem)."

The Xinjiang Province

Xinjiang covers fully one sixth of China's total land mass. It became a Chinese province in 1881, but even as late as the establishment of the Chinese republic in 1912, Xinjiang remained more or less independent of the central government. Rebellions in 1936, 1937, and 1944 further lessened Chinese rule. Late in 1949 though, Xinjiang capitulated to the Chinese Communists invasion without a struggle.

As it did with Tibet, China sent native Chinese to Xinjiang in order to reinvent the population in the Chinese mold. In the 1950s and 1960s, the central government sent massive numbers of Chinese to Xinjiang, drastically altering the population balance; the Chinese are now approaching numerical parity in the region. The percentage of ethnic Chinese in the population has grown from 6 percent in 1949 to 40 percent at present.

Beijing has long claimed to be confronted with "religious extremist forces" and "violent terrorists" in Xinjiang, a largely Muslim area. It is true that much like Tibetans, the Uighurs in Xinjiang have struggled for religious and cultural survival in the face of the mass influx of Chinese immigrants, as well as the harsh repression of political dissent. Some have resorted to violence in a struggle for independence.

Nevertheless, according to the New York–based Human Rights Watch, "Chinese authorities have not discriminated between peaceful and violent dissent. Their fight against 'separatism' and 'religious extremism' has been used to justify widespread and systematic human-rights violations against Uighurs, including many involved in non-violent political, religious and cultural activities."

> ### Reliable Resources
>
> At every meeting of the Shanghai Five—an informal association of China, Kazakhstan, Kyrgyzstan, Tajikistan, and Russia, set up in 1996 at China's initiative—China emphasizes the need to prevent cross-border "activities undermining national sovereignty." One focus of the Shanghai Five is cooperation in order to counter Islamic radicalism in the Xinjiang region. Beijing has received ample assurances from the Shanghai Five that Xinjiang opposition groups will not be allowed to operate.

In the 1990s, the Turk peoples of Xinjiang grew increasingly discontent with Chinese rule. Rioting by pro-independence Muslims broke out in 1997, and China subsequently increased the number of troops in the region.

Then, after September 11, 2001, the Chinese Government charged that Uighur groups had links with the Taliban in Afghanistan and were supported from abroad by other radical Islamist organizations. According to Human Rights Watch, "China has used these claims to justify ruthless repression in Xinjiang against religious activities, personnel and individual believers in what are known as 'campaigns to rectify social order.'"

Today, Xinjiang remains the only province in China where execution of political prisoners is common. According to Amnesty International, more than 200 people were executed between 1997 and 1999. Among conflict watchers, Xinjiang is now one of the most closely scrutinized areas on earth.

China and Russia

After the founding of the People's Republic, Chinese leadership was concerned with ensuring national security, consolidating power, and developing its economy. To those ends, it formed a united front with the Soviet Union.

Mao traveled to Moscow to negotiate the 1950 Sino-Soviet Treaty of Friendship, Alliance, and Mutual Assistance. Under this agreement, China gave the Soviet Union certain rights in return for military support, weapons, and large amounts of economic and technological assistance. China acceded, at least initially, to Soviet leadership of the world Communist movement and took the Soviet Union as the model for development.

But the relationship would quickly be strained. In the late 1950s, disputes over ideology, borders, and economic development caused the rift. During the 1960s, this ideological dispute deepened and spread to include territorial issues, culminating in 1969 in bloody armed clashes along the long Russian-Chinese border. Both sides drew back from the brink of war at the last minute.

This seesaw relationship was down in the 1970s as Beijing began a rapprochement with Washington as a counterweight to the perceived threat from Moscow, but up again in the 1980s, when Soviet leadership changes provided openings for renewed diplomacy.

After the fall of the Iron Curtain, however, things turned icy once again. China was the last large Communist nation on Earth (albeit a communist in capitalist clothing), and the Russian Federation, with its emphasis on democracy, rattled Beijing.

The countries flip-flopped again in 2000, when Russia's lower House of Parliament (the Duma) ratified a groundbreaking treaty with China that aimed to end decades of suspicion and border conflicts between the two nuclear-armed neighbors.

The treaty prohibited the two countries from launching nuclear strikes against each other or even targeting one another with such weapons. It also recognized Beijing's "sovereignty" over Taiwan and pledged Russian support of Chinese military operations in any conflict over the island, which potentially would involve the United States.

China and the United States

China's relations with the other superpower, the United States, have followed a similarly uneven course. Chinese leaders expressed an interest in possible economic assistance from the United States during the 1940s, but by 1950, Chinese-American relations were openly hostile.

The Korean War was a major reason for this because it contributed to the United States policy of *containing* the Chinese threat through a trade embargo and travel restrictions, as well as through military alliances with other Asian nations.

After the Soviet Union's invasion of Czechoslovakia in 1968 and the border clashes with the Soviets in 1969, China decided that its major threat was the Soviet Union rather than the United States, and thus sought a closer relationship with Washington. President Richard M. Nixon thereafter made his dramatic trip to China in 1972.

As the Chinese began to open up their one billion-person market to the West, relations continued to thaw. The United States granted China the trading status of Most Favored Nation, and in 2000, China joined the World Trade Organization.

Diplomatic Dialogue

Containment is a foreign policy strategy that was pursued by the United States after World War II wherein America pursued a plan of long-term, patient, and firm containment of communist expansion.

Yet the lesson of the Soviet Union and China must be kept in mind. Countries who are your friend can easily become your enemy. Countries promote what they believe to be their best interest. China and the United States had good relations at the turn of the millennium because China wanted access to the West's technology and the West wanted access to China's vast market. That could change at any time, for any number of reasons. Today's friend is tomorrow's foe.

Landmine!

As reported by Newsmax.com, according to the Rand Corporation, by 2000, China's military was narrowing its technology gap with the United States. However, Jack Spencer, a defense analyst and fellow at the Heritage Foundation, claims the Chinese military is preparing itself for a future war with America. "Of course China is narrowing the technological gap. They are in the midst of a major military buildup that is driven by the belief that the United States will be its primary future competitor," Spencer told Newsmax.com.

The Old Guard Versus the New Guard

Since the founding of the Communist regime in 1949, Chinese political life has been dominated by the Chinese Communist Party. A dictatorial, brutal, repressive regime, the Party is dominated by (mostly) old-school hardliners who are loath to share power.

That monopoly on power was threatened for the first time ever in 1989 with the fall of Iron Curtain. The wave of democracy that was lapping over the world found a beachhead in Tiananmen Square, the center of Beijing, and thus the center of China.

In 1989, students—seeing how students in other Communist countries were changing their world by large peaceful demonstrations, and who had long wanted to change China, too—decided that the time was right to take on the old guard.

In April and early May 1989, students and intellectuals began to occupy Tiananmen Square. The students understood that world attention would soon be focused on China because of Soviet President Mikhail Gorbachev's upcoming visit to china at the end of May. Because Gorbachev had opened the Soviet Union to democracy, the students believed that occupying the square prior to his arrival could help bring about similar democratic reforms in China.

The movement quickly gained speed. Thousands upon thousands of people began to join the students. On May 13, workers joined, and a hunger strike began. The students were becoming more and more persuasive in their calls for radical reform. Soon, more than a million people filled the square.

The scene inside Tiananmen Square was too much for the Chinese hierarchy. The movement was perceived as a threat to their power. According to secret transcripts smuggled out of Beijing 10 years after the event, the Associated Press quoted Communist Party Chairman Deng Xiaoping saying at a meeting at the Party Central Office, "A tiny minority is exploiting the students; they want to confuse the people and throw the country into chaos. This is a well-planned plot whose real aim is to reject the Chinese Communist Party."

Because power corrupts, and absolute power corrupts absolutely, the Communist Party of China was determined to retain its stronghold on power and use whatever means necessary to crush the rebellion. On May 18, Deng told a high-level party meeting that "After thinking long and hard about this, I've concluded that we should bring in the People's Liberation Army and declare martial law in Beijing."

Deng was encouraged by several members of his inner circle, including Wang Zhen, who said, "The students are nuts if they think this handful of people can overthrow our Party and our government." On May 20, Deng declared martial law in China. The students still didn't dissipate. In fact, they called on the Party leadership to resign.

On June 4, 1989, Deng had seen enough. He ordered Chinese troops to kill Chinese civilians. Troops moved into Tiananmen Square and opened fire on the demonstrators. The brutal action killed hundreds, and thousands were arrested in a nationwide crackdown.

According to the Associated Press, "two days after the violent crackdown, Deng reportedly defended the decision in a Central Politburo Standing Committee meeting. 'If we hadn't been firm with these counterrevolutionary riots, if we hadn't come down hard, who knows what might have happened? … If the plots of the people who were pushing the riots had gotten anywhere, we'd have had civil war.'"

Although the scene inside Tiananmen Square was remarkable, maybe the most remarkable site of the democracy movement was that of a lone man bravely walking in front of, and thereby stopping, a line of tanks.

However, despite his bravery, the man didn't change history, and the issues that sparked those mass protests across China in 1989 still plague the country today: general dissatisfaction with the Party, increased demands for democracy, and the widening gap between the rich and the poor. If political freedom does not catch up with economic freedom, the resulting dichotomy in the country could be disastrous.

What are China's real intentions? No one knows for sure, but it might help to keep the following quote in mind: When threatening Taiwanese voters not to choose Chen just before their 2000 presidential elections, Chinese Prime Minister Zhu Rongji said, "People making such calculations (that China could not take Taiwan) don't know about Chinese history. The Chinese people are ready to shed blood and sacrifice their lives to defend the sovereignty and territorial integrity of the motherland."

The Least You Need to Know

- The Communist revolution created the split with Taiwan.
- The Chinese have brutally repressed Tibet.
- They have done the same thing in Xinjiang.
- China and Russia have had a hot/cold relationship.
- China and the United States have a relationship of mutual convenience.
- The Tiananmen Square massacre might foreshadow what is to come in China.

Cain and Abel: India and Pakistan

In This Chapter

- ◆ Kashmir in conflict
- ◆ Three wars and the birth of Bangladesh
- ◆ Sikh separatists in India
- ◆ The nuclear option

India and Pakistan are home to two of the world's largest populations. India has more than 1 billion people to feed, clothe, and house every day, and Pakistan has 150 million of its own. They have gone to war three times so far, they detest one another, and now both countries have the bomb. Is it any wonder that many analysts believe that if there ever will be a nuclear war, these are the countries who will have it?

To understand the depth of this conflict, you must examine the main conflict in Kashmir, the wars it has spawned, as well as the nuclear capacity of both countries.

India and Pakistan are locked in a potentially dangerous conflict.

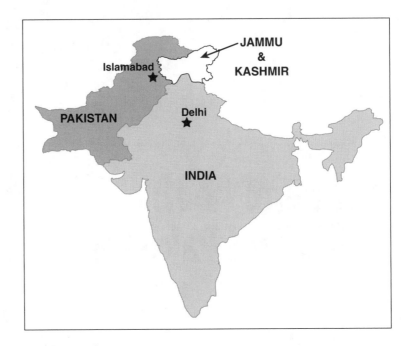

The Indian Subcontinent

The Indus Valley civilization is one of the oldest in the world, going back at least 5,000 years. Aryan tribes invaded about 1500 B.C.E. and merged with earlier inhabitants to create what is now known as Indian culture. Arab invasions began in the eighth century, and Turkish ones started in the twelfth century.

By the late fifteenth century, European traders had begun to rise in influence in the region, and in the nineteenth century Britain had assumed political control of virtually all Indian lands.

Peacekeepers

Mohandas Gandhi is often referred to as "Mahatma" Gandhi, but that is not his name. The people of India gave that moniker to him. It means "great soul."

Mohandas Gandhi invented nonviolent resistance as a way to rid the Indian subcontinent of foreign rule once and for all. It was a long, but ultimately successful campaign, and in 1947, independence was achieved. Thereafter, the subcontinent was divided into the large Hindu state of India and the smaller Muslim state of Pakistan. This dichotomy—two states, two religions, and two people—has led to bloodshed, war, poverty, and strife.

Pakistan Versus India

The people of Pakistan, being overwhelmingly Muslim, always wanted independence, not only from the British, but also from India. Their wish was realized on July 18, 1947, when the British parliament passed the Indian Independence Act, creating two new countries—India and Pakistan. The Act also provided for the complete end of British control over Indian affairs. Pakistan took the opposite route, not surprisingly, choosing to become part of the British Commonwealth of nations.

It was after independence that the full extent of the differences between the two new countries would become apparent.

Roots of War

The first issue that they had to deal with was their long border with one another. It was agreed that a Boundary Commission would be set up to delineate the borders between India and Pakistan. The British government appointed a Boundary Commission to demarcate permanent borders. The boundaries had to be fixed in such a manner that areas which were predominantly Muslim went to Pakistan, whereas the Hindu ones went to India. This was not always readily apparent, nor easy to do.

In an almost frantic hurry, the commission divided districts, villages, farmlands, water, and property into the two new countries. Thousands of people were caught in the middle, and the result was that many hastened across the border to one side or the other, leaving their homes, land, and personal property to seek refuge.

The partition of the subcontinent caused tremendous dislocation of populations. The Legacy Project, a global exchange on the lasting consequences of the tragedies of the twentieth century, reports that the ensuing war and violence cost more than 1 million lives; and forced some 3.5 million Hindus and Sikhs to move from Pakistan into India, while about 5 million Muslims migrated from India to Pakistan. Overall, the demographic shift was the first of many causes that resulted in extreme bitterness between the two countries.

> **Reliable Resources**
>
> There are 750 million Hindus in the world, and most of them live in India.

Kashmir Becomes a Problem

Adding to the tensions was the issue of the three different areas and what to do with them:

- Junagadh
- Hyderabad
- Kashmir

Junagadh was (and is) a Hindu-majority area, but its leader was a Muslim. Although the leader wanted to join to Pakistan, a *plebiscite* was held, and the state chose to join India.

Diplomatic Dialogue

A **plebiscite** is a direct vote in which a population exercises the right of self-determination.

Hyderabad also had a Muslim ruler of a Hindu-majority populace. Rather than join either country, his plan was to gain independence for his state. After more than a year of negotiations, India finally decided to send its army into the region and Hyderabad became part of India in 1948.

The real problem was, and is, Kashmir, whose subjects were roughly 80 percent Muslim. Its Hindu leader, Maharaja Hari Singh, had also wanted Kashmir to remain independent, but the large Muslim population wanted to become part of Pakistan.

In 1948, frustrated and nervous, the Muslims in Kashmir revolted. Singh then fled to New Delhi (in India) and there agreed to place Kashmir under the dominion of India in exchange for military support and the promise of a referendum on independence. Indian troops thereafter flew to Kashmir to engage the rebels, who by then were being supported by Pakistan.

Diplomatic Dialogue

When a fact exists, whether it is legal or not, it is said to be **de facto**. For example, when two countries are in a de facto state of war, they are waging war, whether one country has actually declared war or not.

A cease-fire was arranged in 1949, and the cease-fire line created a *de facto* partition of the region. The central and eastern areas of Kashmir came under Indian control as the Jammu and Kashmir states, whereas the northwestern quarter came under Pakistani control as Azad Kashmir and the Northern Areas.

Although a U.N. peacekeeping force was sent in to enforce the cease-fire, and remains there to this day, the dispute was never resolved. A U.N. resolution, adopted after the war, allows the people of Kashmir to join either India or Pakistan. The United Nations urged both countries to allow the people of Kashmir to choose which country they wanted to join by holding a plebiscite; to this day the plebiscite has not been held.

The Indian position today is that Kashmir belongs to India because of the Instrument of Accession signed by Maharajah Hari Singh, which handed over the "princely state" to India. Pakistan maintains that Kashmir is a heavily Muslim region, and if allowed to determine its own path via a vote in a plebiscite, it would become part of Pakistan.

Whatever the case, the seeds of animosity had been firmly planted, only to intensify over the years.

Act Two

In 1965, Pakistan sent guerrilla forces into the Indian part of Kashmir. Their mission was to stir up a rebellion that would either oust the Indians or at least force the issue back onto the international agenda. The Pakistani forces, however, were unable to round up sufficient support among the Kashmiri population, and by August fighting had spread.

A process of escalation culminated in a full-scale Indian offensive against Pakistan in Kashmir, and between September 6 and 23, the parties engaged in a full-scale war. A U.N.–brokered cease-fire took effect thereafter, and in January 1966, President Ayub Khan of Pakistan and Prime Minister Lal Bahadur Shastri of India met at the invitation of the Soviet government and agreed to the mutual withdrawal of troops to the positions held before the war.

Reliable Resources
Sir Francis Young Husband reportedly described Kashmir in his travel diary as follows: "The huge lake is twice the length and three times the width of the lake of Geneva, completely encircled by snowy mountains as high, and higher than Mount Blank, while mighty glaciers came wending down, and valleys tipped the edge of the water."

In Concert with Bangladesh

While the Kashmir conflict simmered, a new problem was brewing for Pakistan in the late 1960s and early 1970s: the emergence of the East Pakistan independence movement.

After Pakistani parliamentary elections gave the East Pakistani separatist party a majority in the 1970 elections, Pakistan refused to acknowledge these demands for greater autonomy in the east. So, in March 1971, fed up East Pakistani leaders proclaimed the independent state of Bangladesh.

Pakistani forces were called in to suppress the revolt—without much success. In the ensuing civil war, Pakistani troops murdered an estimated one million Bengalis (the largest ethnic group in Bangladesh) in one of the largest genocides of the twentieth century. More than 10 million more Bengalis took refuge in India.

On December 3, 1971, India, which had provided secret aid to the Bangladesh independence movement, began a large offensive against Pakistan in support of the Bangladeshi cause. The U.N. Security Council voted in support of Bangladesh's independence and called for a cease-fire. On December 17, 1971, almost 100,000 Pakistani troops surrendered to Indian forces in Bangladesh. Another war was over. In 1974, Pakistan formally and finally recognized the independence of Bangladesh.

Reliable Resources

The end of the war left Bangladesh in shambles. Soon afterward, Bengali Ravi Shankar, a good friend of ex-Beatle George Harrison, casually asked Harrison to help with a benefit concert for Shankar's home country. Shankar was hoping to raise about $25,000. Harrison took it to the next level, renting out Madison Square Garden and getting Bob Dylan, Eric Clapton, and even Ringo Starr, among others, to come out and play in the Concert for Bangladesh. The first ever rock benefit for a cause had just occurred.

In 1972, India and Pakistan signed the Simla Agreement, which called for a bilateral solution to the Kashmir issue. Although the Simla Agreement reaffirmed the Line of Control between Pakistani and Indian administered Kashmir that was arrived at after the 1947 war and eased tensions, theirs was an uneasy truce.

Sikhing Freedom

Besides Muslims and Hindus, this part of the world also contains many Sikhs. And, apparently like every other ethnic group or religion discussed in this book, the Sikhs too want a land to call their own and are willing to kill people in order to get it. Since 1973, Sikh separatists in the Indian state of Punjab have campaigned to secede from India and form an independent state. Their fight has often been a violent one.

Reliable Resources

The essence of being a Sikh is that one lives one's life according to the teachings of the Sikh Gurus, devoting time to meditating on God and the scriptures, and doing things to benefit other people. Sikhs believe that there is a single, all-powerful God, who created the universe and everything in it. Sikhism emphasizes social and gender equality, and stresses the importance of behaving altruistically.

The insurgency in the state of Punjab originated in the late 1970s when an age-old fear in the Sikh community—that of being absorbed into the Hindu fold—reemerged more strongly than ever before. One of the leaders of this revivalist movement was Sant Jarnail Singh Bhindranwale, a politically ambitious Sikh preacher. Bhindranwale and his followers soon became a source of mayhem and disruption in Punjab.

In 1984, Bhindranwale and his followers took over the Golden Temple complex in Amritsar, Punjab. This temple is Sikhism's most holy of shrines. Indian Prime Minister Indira Gandhi responded by ordering the Indian army to get them out. Negotiations failed, and so Gandhi ordered the army to storm the temple.

A variety of army units, along with substantial numbers of paramilitary forces, surrounded the temple complex. Demands to surrender were met with gunfire. After a day-long siege and firefight, the Indian army successfully regained control of the temple. According to the Indian government, 83 Indian army personnel died and 249 were injured in the battle. Almost 500 Sikhs were also killed and 86 injured.

Needless to say, the massacre at the Golden Temple inflamed the Sikh community. In retaliation, that same year, Indian Prime Minister Indira Gandhi was assassinated by her Sikh bodyguards. In the reprisal's reprisal, mobs massacred Sikhs throughout India.

Things seemed to be finally settling down until one September day in 1995. That was the day that Beant Singh, India's Chief Minister of Punjab, was killed when a powerful plastic explosive near one of his convoy of sedans exploded just as he was stepping into his bullet-proof car. The blast killed Singh and 15 others instantly, injured 14 more, shattered windows in the capital, and was heard two miles away.

> ### Reliable Resources
>
> In 321 B.C.E. Alexander the Great entered Punjab and demanded that all local chieftains submit to his authority. All did, save one. Instead, Porus went to battle against the legendary Alexander. After losing his sons and getting hurt himself, a defiant Porus was brought in front of Alexander the Great. Alexander inquired of Porus, "How should I treat you?" Porus replied, "As one king treats another king." So impressed was Alexander that he returned the defeated kingdom back to Porus.

It's not surprising that Singh was murdered; he was both despised and a symbol of Indian control over Punjab. According to *Time Magazine* (September 11, 1995), "Singh's tactics were often ruthless. There were complaints of human rights abuses: More than 120 court cases involving more than 450 policemen [were then] pending against the Punjab police. Corruption and nepotism were rampant, and the Singh administration had 17 high court indictments against it."

India shows no signs of giving in to the demands of the Sikh separatists. As in Kashmir, India seems resigned to protecting its territories; damn the consequences.

Nuclear Roulette

The real problem today on the Indian subcontinent is not that India and Pakistan have so far failed to resolve their differences over Kashmir, that they have two of the largest populations on earth, or that they hate each other. No, the problem now is that they both have nuclear weapons; the same dispute that might have killed 10,000 people yesterday could well kill more than a million people today.

Briefing Book

On May 18, 1974, India detonated its first nuclear device, saying that it is for atomic research and not weapons. Why it did so is a matter of some debate, but the fact is, it did. India thereafter began an inexorable climb up the nuclear mountain in search of the plutonium at the end of the rainbow.

Why did it go down the nuclear road? Having a nuclear bomb forces other countries to think twice. That is as true for the United States and Russia as it is for India. The deterrence effect of having a nuclear weapon cannot be underestimated. India understood and wanted this.

> ### Reliable Resources
>
> Throughout the Cold War, the United States based its defense policy on a deterrence theory called M.A.D., which stood for "mutually assured destruction." The theory was that the Soviet Union would be crazy to attack the United States because doing so would ensure its own destruction. It worked, too.

Now it is true that India has legitimate security concerns, not just from Pakistan, but from other countries as well. In an interview with the *Deccan Herald News Service*, former Indian Prime Minister I.K. Gujral explained India's security concerns. According to Gujral, the Indian coastline is nearly 7,000 miles long and is in an area that is "heavily nuclearized." Moreover, Gujral says the U.S. military base in Diego Garcia sits in the Indian Ocean , and is also home to nuclear weapons., Gujral also pointed out that warships, submarines, and aircraft carriers with nuclear weapons constantly sail in the Indian Ocean.

Even more disturbing, in India's eyes, is that after the disintegration of the Soviet Union, the United States, being the world's sole super power, has abused its strength against much smaller and more venerable nations, Iraq, Yugoslavia, and Afghanistan to name but three examples.

So it was of little surprise that India's tests of nuclear weapons in 1998, were very popular among Indians. The *Times of India* reported that 91 percent of Indians approved of the tests. Fully 82 percent further believed India should build nuclear weapons.

A typical analysis of why so many in the third world supported India's bold move was written by Nawab Khan in the *Iran Times*. In his piece, titled "Nuclear Tests, Why Not India?" Khan wrote

> The argument that Western powers are democratic and hence their nuclear arsenals are under strict control and can never be misused are not quite convincing. American democracy did not prevent it from dropping the atomic bomb twice on Japan. The lesson to be learnt from the Pokharan nuclear blasts is that there cannot be one law for the haves and another for the have-nots.

Yet not everyone was so enthusiastic. India and Pakistan, after all, had already had three wars. So, if the five nuclear tests conducted by India at Pokharan were not bad enough, that they were followed three weeks later by six nuclear explosions conducted by Pakistan was worse. Both countries now had the bomb.

Landmine! _____

In 1966, the year the United States had the greatest number of nuclear weapons in its stockpile, the number of warheads it had available was 32,193.

You Started It!

According to an article by M. V. Ramana and A. H. Nayyar published in *Scientific American* titled "India, Pakistan and the Bomb," both countries had actually been working on their nuclear programs practically since independence. India's first prime minister, Jawaharlal Nehru, stated in 1948 that India should "develop (atomic energy) for peaceful purposes." Nehru also believed, though, that "if we are compelled as a nation to use it for other purposes, possibly no pious sentiments will stop the nation from using it that way."

Like many countries that developed nuclear capabilities, for Indian leaders, India's nuclear program gave the country political clout and a sense of joining the modern world. Accordingly, for the next 20 years, India built and operated nuclear reactors, mined uranium, and extracted plutonium.

When India finally tested its bomb in 1974, the news was, not surprisingly, greeted with enthusiasm in India and apprehension abroad. Western countries retaliated by cutting off any further nuclear assistance and restricted the export of nuclear technologies and materials to nations, like India and Pakistan, that refused to sign the Nuclear Non-Proliferation Treaty.

Because these two countries are so linked (whether they like it or not), once India entered the nuclear game, Pakistan was sure to follow, and it did. Pakistan operated its first nuclear reactor in 1965, and opened its first commercial reactor in 1970.

Pakistan made up for its lack of trained nuclear scientists by shipping more than 600 scientists and engineers to the West for training. Pakistan was therefore able to get its nuclear research laboratories in place by the mid-1960s.

Success for Pakistan finally came in 1979 when it enriched a small amount of uranium: a process necessary for isolating the "bomb-usable" isotope uranium 235. Since that time, it is estimated that Pakistan has developed enough uranium to arm between 20 and 40 nuclear bombs.

Reliable Resources

After the 1965 India-Pakistan war, many Pakistani politicians wanted to get a jump start on their nuclear program. Pakistani Foreign Minister Zulfikhar Ali Bhutto, put it bluntly when he stated that if India ever developed an atomic bomb, Pakistan would, too, "even if we have to eat grass or leaves."

Pakistan's bid for nuclear parity with India was bolstered in the spring of 1990, as events in Kashmir threatened to erupt into another full-scale war. According to a 1993 *New Yorker* article by Seymour Hersh, U.S. surveillance satellites detected a convoy of suspicious trucks moving toward an air base as the latest Kashmir crisis accelerated.

> ### Reliable Resources
>
> Pakistani Islamic fundamentalist Qazi Hussain Ahmad declared in 1993: "Let us wage jihad for Kashmir. A nuclear-armed Pakistan would deter India from a wider conflict."

This information was relayed to India by the Americans, and a worried India therefore decided to recall the troops it had amassed at the border. Pakistan concluded that its nuclear weapons were a strong deterrent. Indian officials never acknowledged the story; doing so could be construed as a sign of weakness.

Whatever the case, this event led India to double its efforts to make a usable bomb, a plan encouraged by the rise of Hindu nationalism in India. The Bharatiya Janata Party (BJP), an ultra-nationalist party that had long called for India to acquire nuclear weapons came to power in 1998. It ordered nuclear tests immediately, giving Pakistan a reason to do the same.

The First Ever Nuclear War?

The subcontinent now has all the necessary ingredients for a nuclear war: a contentious and ongoing conflict in Kashmir, extremist pressures, possession and development of nuclear bombs, inadequate fail-safe precautions to avoid unauthorized use of these weapons, geographical proximity, and jingoistic leaders.

Evidence of just how bad things can be now that both countries have the bomb was seen in November 2001 when suicide terrorists stormed the Indian parliament building in Delhi. Twelve people were killed, including the five attackers. It is believed that the terrorists were Pakistanis demanding a free Kashmir.

Both countries sent massive amounts of troops to the Kashmir border. India accused Pakistan of coddling terrorists, with an external affairs minister saying "Like the United States in the case of Taliban, we have launched a comprehensive diplomatic offensive to apprise the international community of Pakistan's active role in fomenting terrorism on Indian soil."

Envoys from both countries were recalled, and plans for war were underway. The question this time was far more serious—would they go nuclear? Somehow, cooler heads prevailed, and both countries backed off from war when Pakistan took concrete steps to reign in those responsible.

What Does the Future Hold?

If there is any good news in all this, it is that the actual size of seismic signals from the 1998 tests of both countries has cast doubt on the declared explosive yields of their respective bombs. But if there is any more bad news that can be had, it is that both countries are sure to become better bomb makers and are more apt to be trigger happy to beat their enemy to the nuclear punch.

In January 2001, Indian officials declared that they were ready to deploy the country's new long-range missile, if necessary. A month later, the Pakistani deputy chief of naval staff announced that Pakistan was considering to equip at least one of its submarines with nuclear missiles.

And the meltdown continues.

The Least You Need to Know

◆ Kashmir will likely remain a source of conflict for the foreseeable future.

◆ India and Pakistan have fought three wars, one of which created Bangladesh.

◆ Sikh separatists cause India additional pressures.

◆ India and Pakistan might well be the first countries ever to engage in nuclear war.

Chapter 13

Religious and Ethnic Animosity in Indonesia

In This Chapter

- From authoritarian rule to East Timor's independence
- The isle of Irian Jaya and the Spice Islands
- Sulawesi
- Killing in the name of God in Kalimantan
- Acceh's independence movement
- Terrorists and Indonesia

Indonesia is not only the world's fourth most populous nation and one of the world's most populous Muslim nations, but it is also the world's largest archipelago, containing more than 13,000 islands—of which 3,000 are inhabited. Only one of its islands has captured popular imagination—Bali.

And, with more than 300 tribal and ethnic groups and 250 different languages, the country is beset with interethnic and interreligious hatred. Even the largely predominant Muslim religion is characterized by regional variations.

Indonesia is a vast archipelago.

The End of Colonialism and the Rise of a Dictator

After winning independence from Spain in 1581, the Netherlands became one of the world's major seafaring powers. A Dutch fleet entered Indonesian waters in 1596, and in 1602 the United East India Company was formed. The city of Jakarta became the Indonesian capital of the burgeoning spice trade, and the company would go on to rule Indonesia for two hundred years.

In the nineteenth century, Indonesia saw the replacement of Company rule by Dutch government, as well as the transformation of Java (the main island) into a colonial society that spread throughout the *archipelago*. The modern state of Indonesia is therefore a nineteenth-century creation.

> **Diplomatic Dialogue**
>
> An **archipelago** is any sea or broad sheet of water interspersed with many islands or with a group of islands.

Independence Day

Japan invaded China in 1937, and in 1942, the Battle of the Java Sea resulted in the Japanese defeat of a combined British, Dutch, Australian, and U.S. fleet. On March 9, 1942, the Dutch government surrendered Indonesia to the Japanese.

Although Japanese occupation was a watershed in Indonesian history, Japanese control of Indonesia would not last long. As its war effort became more desperate, Japan announced in 1944 that Indonesia would become independent. This announcement was a vindication for the Indonesian nationalist leader, and soon-to-be first president, Achmed Sukarno, and his communist allies.

Sukarno believed that the new country should have a strong presidency and a constitutional form of government. This was agreed to, although many in the country's large Muslim population had misgivings about forming Indonesia as a secular state. Nevertheless, Sukarno formally declared the nation's independence on August 17, 1945.

The Rise of Suharto

Ruling such a vast, populous, heterogeneous country would prove, and not for the last time, to be a very difficult thing to do. By 1965, Indonesia had become an unstable place. Sukarno was a despotic ruler who instituted martial law in 1957. His ruling party (PKI) aroused the hostility of many Islamic groups, as well as the military. In addition, the United States and China had used Sukarno and Indonesia to wage a bloody proxy war. So, many despised Sukarno's rule.

By 1965, the population had fallen into two camps—those supporting Sukarno and the ruling PKI and others who supported Major General Suharto. On September 30, 1965, an attempted coup d'état occurred. Although unsuccessful, it proved how disliked Sukarno had finally become, and eventually it would lead to his displacement from power.

In the wake of the coup's failure, there was a violent reaction. Many in the country wanted to be rid of the PKI. By December 1965, mobs were engaged in large-scale rioting and killings. Paramilitary groups carried out a war against the PKI. Estimates of the number killed vary widely; 300,000 dead is believed to be an accurate number.

The end result of this conflict was that Indonesia would get itself a new leader, yet another strongman, General Suharto. Suharto's military government was, if nothing else, a stable one. Given the instability of the Sukarno years, that alone was a salve for the Muslim country. After Suharto took power, he solidified his power base and ruled with an iron will. Rebellion had become sporadic and, until recently, unsuccessful.

> **Reliable Resources**
>
> In the 1983 movie *The Year of Living Dangerously*, Mel Gibson plays an Australian reporter assigned to Indonesia during the calamitous summer of 1965. Linda Hunt played the local who helped him, and she won an Academy Award for best supporting actress.

CAUTION

> **Landmine!**
>
> The elimination of the PKI was one of the bloodiest events in postwar Southeast Asia.

Revenge of the Sukarnos

However, with stability came repression. Suharto would repressively govern Indonesia for the next 30 years. He remained in power until 1998 when charges of corruption were leveled against him and his family. Coupled with the ongoing crisis in East Timor (see the following section) and an economic crisis throughout Southeast Asia, the Indonesians had had enough. Massive rioting, strikes, and protests finally forced Suharto out, and soon brought new elections.

When Indonesians went to the polls to vote for a successor to the ousted Suharto, they chose a woman, Megawati Sukarnoputri, who had few visible talents as a politician, except for one—Sukarno was her father.

As the heir to Indonesia's first family, the 54-year-old matriarch was reluctantly pushed into politics by opponents of the dictatorship who hoped to use the Sukarno name to rally support. Although her family had been ousted from power by Suharto, it remained part of Jakarta's elite.

What "Mother Mega" found upon taking office was a country bursting at the seams; what with Suharto's ability to crush opposition now gone. Separatist rebellions in some regions and ethnic and religious violence in others showed that the hodgepodge of thousands of islands that became a nation-state only because of their common colonization by Holland was now threatening to disintegrate.

If Megawati is able to curb the many conflicts and hostilities that now beseige her homeland, she will prove herself to be a master politician in her own right.

East Timor Struggles for Independence

East Timor became a colony of Portugal in the sixteenth century and remained so until 1975. In 1974, Portugal decided that all of its territories should have the right of self-determination, and in 1975 representatives of several East Timorese political groups were invited to attend conventions to that end.

But before a decision could be made, the Portuguese authorities withdrew from the country after violent uprisings in East Timor. Thereafter, in November 1975, the Revolutionary Front for an Independent East Timor (Fretilin), a Marxist group, declared the independence of the Democratic Republic of East Timor.

For Indonesia, this was an alarming opportunity. On one hand, having a communist regime in its neighborhood was thought to be a national security threat. The Indonesian government decided that if Portugal was unable to reestablish effective control over its colony, it would be necessary for Indonesian forces to restore order. On the other hand, the communist movement proved to be an awfully handy reason to invade and annex the small country.

Indonesia sent in an army of 10,000, and in December 1975, the establishment of a provisional government of East Timor was declared. Indonesia declared that the people of East Timor had requested Indonesia "to accept East Timor as an integral part of the Republic of Indonesia." Indonesia thereafter incorporated East Timor as part of Indonesia. The slaughter of East Timorese during the 1975 Indonesian invasion foreshadowed the ruthless manner in which Indonesia would come to govern the former Portuguese colony.

Indonesia thereafter began a long and harsh campaign of subjugation and pacification against the East Timorese. Through the late 1970s and 1980s, accounts of military repression and mass starvation repeatedly emerged from the country. An estimated number of as high as 200,000 of East Timor's inhabitants died as a result of the armed occupation.

> **Landmine!**
>
> According to the Federation of American Scientists, "as many as 60,000 Timorese were killed in the initial assault, out of a total population of about 600,000."

The World Takes Notice

Indonesia's highly questionable annexation of East Timor naturally became the subject of much international debate, and East Timor became the focus of two U.N. Security Councils. Security Council resolution 384 (1975) called upon "all States to respect the territorial integrity of East Timor as well as the inalienable right of its people to self-determination." It further called upon "the Government of Indonesia to withdraw without delay all its forces from the Territory." Indonesia ignored the resolutions.

By the 1990s, discontent with Indonesian rule escalated sharply among the younger generation of East Timorese, particularly those born after the island's forced annexation of 1975. With the disintegration of global communism by this time, it was this emerging militancy of East Timorese youth, far more than the remnants of the Marxist Fretilin group, which posed the greatest threat to Indonesia's rule.

In November 1991, peaceful youths were marching in a pro-Fretilin political demonstration in the East Timorese capital of Dili. Video of the event taken by participants caught Indonesian troops firing upon the marchers. At least 70 protesters were shot or clubbed by the troops. The inflammatory video was smuggled out of East Timor, and for the first time in a long time, the plight of the Timorese became world news, showcasing what was widely seen as mass murder by the Indonesian army.

The growing resentment of Indonesia's rule became more evident in November 1994 during the Asia-Pacific Economic Cooperation meeting. At that meeting, roughly 30 East Timorese climbed over a fence surrounding the U.S. Embassy in Jakarta and occupied the embassy compound for two weeks, demanding the release of a Timorese resistance leader. They asked President Clinton, who was attending the summit, to intercede on behalf of the East Timor people. At the same time, rioting in the region of Dili left four people dead, leading to additional clashes with police.

World sympathy was further aroused by the award of the 1996 Nobel peace prize to exiled East Timorese independence leader Jose Ramos Horta and Dili's Bishop Carlos Ximenes Felipe Belo.

Change Is in the Air

With the demise of the Suharto regime in 1998, and the emergence of Megawati Sukarnoputri, efforts to resolve this conflict came to the fore. United Nations–sponsored talks on East Timor gained new momentum; both sides agreed to discuss an Indonesian plan to offer special status for East Timor, which was more than any previous government was willing to concede.

> **Reliable Resources**
>
> Indonesia's surprise announcement that East Timor could eventually become independent was met with resistance from anti-independence East Timorese forces. Pro-independence East Timorese, who are Roman Catholic, became victims of anti-independence Muslim militias.

In May 1999, Indonesia, Portugal, and United Nations Secretary General Kofi Annan signed an agreement in New York, which would grant the right of self-determination to East Timorese through a plebiscite. The historic agreement called for Indonesia to be responsible for ensuring a peaceful environment in East Timor so that the voting process could take place as scheduled.

The Plebiscite

At the end of August 1999, despite an intense climate of fear, a healthy 98.6 percent of all East Timorese registered voters went to the polls. During the five days that it took the United Nations to count the ballots, Indonesian-backed violence escalated, and thousands of civilians fled to the hills and mountains. In the end, the East Timorese voted overwhelmingly for independence.

The agreement had stated that "all sides must lay down their arms and subsequently disarm," but this was easier said than done. Immediately after the vote, the Indonesian military and its militia brethren began to attack and destroy the East Timorese population and infrastructure. Estimates are that 70 to 80 percent of Dili's businesses were destroyed, and half of all homes were burned to the ground.

After 10 days of turmoil, and under intense international pressure, President Clinton suspended all U.S.–Indonesian military ties on September 11, 1999. On September 15, the Security Council endorsed the deployment of an Australian-led peacekeeping force to East Timor.

The international pressure proved to be too much, and the Indonesian military finally began to withdraw from the country it had occupied for nearly a quarter century. U.N. peacekeeping forces took control.

As all parties realized that the ruined country was not quite ready for full independence, the United Nations created the United Nations Transitional Administration for East Timor. UNTAET was established to administer the region and institute a transitional government during the transition period. To that end, UNTEAT works in close cooperation with the East Timorese.

Peacekeepers

Today we suspended all military sales, and continue to work to try to persuade the Indonesians to support the United Nations' operation to go in and help to end the violence and secure the safety of the people in East Timor.

—President Bill Clinton, September 11, 1999

Finally, on January 30, 2002, United Nations Secretary General Kofi Annan invited the leaders of all 189 U.N. member states, as well as the Pope and Switzerland, to attend a May 20 ceremony marking the full independence of East Timor. Its mission completed, UNTAET folded up shop, and East Timor was finally free.

Papua, A.K.A. Irian Jaya

Irian Jaya is the eastern-most island in the Indonesian archipelago and forms half of the island of New Guinea. The island reportedly was discovered during the 1800s by a Portuguese spice merchant who named the island Papua: the Malay word for curly haired people. Today, the eastern half of the island is Papua New Guinea, a territory that was administered by Australia until it gained independence in 1975.

The western half is called Irian Jaya—Glorious West Guinea—by Indonesia, which took over from Dutch rule in the early 1960s. With the hand over to Indonesia, Irian Jaya was promised eventual self-determination, but, typically, that never occurred.

As a result, the Free Papua Movement (or OPM) emerged in opposition to Indonesian rule and has waged a battle for independence that has lasted for 30 years. In 1996, the OPM attracted international attention when it kidnapped more than 20 people. Two were killed during a rescue operation by Indonesian special forces. The next year, OPM took control of the streets of Jayapura, and thousands of people gathered in the capital, demanding independence.

Reliable Resources

Irian Jaya's 2.4 million people represent only one hundredth of the Indonesian population, but in land area, it is the largest and one of the most resource rich parts of Indonesia. Its people are the poorest of all Indonesians.

The pressure on the Indonesian government to give the people of this mostly Christian territory a greater voice in their own future was mounting. In response, new President Megawati Sukarnoputri decided to grant the province a far greater degree of autonomy than ever before.

The new laws went into effect on January 1, 2002. The main changes, as summarized by BBC regional analyst Nicholas Nugent were ...

- The government allowed the province to change its name to the preferred name of Papua.
- The Papua flag was allowed to fly next to, although lower than, the Indonesian flag.
- The Papuan provincial government was allowed to retain most of the revenue from oil and gas production as well as from mineral and forestry activity. Given the province's enormous natural reserves, this compromise was worth hundreds of millions of dollars.

Peacekeepers

President Megawati Sukarnoputri's father, Indonesia's first president Sukarno, first promised autonomy to the region nearly 40 years ago.

Maybe surprisingly, many Papuans rejected the package. OPM demanded nothing less than a plebiscite on full independence, along the lines of that held in East Timor in 1999. But the government, fearing that the people of Papua would follow the Timorese precedent if given the chance, ruled out an independence referendum for the province.

The likelihood that this long simmering conflict would end peacefully diminished greatly after pro-independence leader They Eluay went missing. The 64-year-old Eluay was later found dead, suffocated in his overturned car. Indonesian police ruled the death a murder.

The Spice Islands, A.K.A. the Moluccas

The outside world has barely noticed how this region has slipped into a spiral of Muslim-Christian murder. As reported in a January 17, 2000, *Time Magazine* article, "Mobs armed with automatic weapons roam the streets of Ambon, the capital city, sometimes dragging the decapitated bodies of their enemies around with them. ... Units of the supposedly neutral security forces have been seen firing on crowds and even at each other. Curfew starts at 10 P.M., but the streets are empty long before then."

Peacekeepers

The name Spice Islands originally comes from the fact that cloves, nutmeg, and mace once grew only there.

An almost even number of Christians and Muslims have lived in peace and make up the Moluccas. Yet now, today, the one thing they share is fear of each other. How could this have happened?

In 2000, rioting erupted after, of all things, a dispute arose between a Christian bus driver and a Muslim passenger. Subsequent incidents led to even more rioting and violence. Full blown civil war came next.

How bad are things now? According to *Time*'s Terry McCarthy ...

♦ Few people now choose to travel by road on Ambon because the two sides have set up roadblocks.

♦ The main business street in Ambon is now sadly called "Sniper's Alley."

♦ Christians and Muslims now patrol their own neighborhoods after sunset.

Some believe that the violence is a result of the power vacuum left by the fall of Suharto in 1998. After that, they say, long simmering tensions between the two religions came to the fore. But in actuality, no one is really sure why these two religious groups have started killing each other. While neither group seems to have anything to gain from the conflict, nobody has any idea how to stop it either.

Landmine! _____

In 2002, in Jakarta, Muslims in the city's central square called for a jihad against Christians in the Moluccas. One man held a sign that read "Tolerance Is Nonsense, Slaughter Christians."

Sulawesi

Central Sulawesi has been described as a remote and backward province. Farming and fishing are the occupations of most people who live there, and the economy is of little significance. As in the Spice Islands, the Christians and Muslims here have lived side by side in peace. But in 1998, all that changed when religious violence erupted in the small town of Poso. And, as with the Spice Islands, a seemingly insignificant event was able to turn neighbors into killers.

It was nothing more than a stupid drunken fight between a Christian and Muslim youths that was the catalyst for the violence and rioting that ensued. After a period of relative calm, violence again broke out in 2001. By the time the insanity subsided this time, Poso was practically destroyed. An estimated 1,000 people were dead, and many more Christians were no longer welcome there.

The actual cause of the animosity and violence is a matter of speculation. Some say that it is a result of similar fighting in the Moluccan Islands to the east. Christians say it is because of a rise in Islamic fundamentalism. No one is really sure. What is clear, however, is that the Christians and Muslims here continue to kill each other.

Kalimantan

Violence has erupted on the island of Borneo as well. Ethnic and religious riots broke out in the Indonesian controlled side of Borneo, called Kalimantan, in late December 1996. In this case, it was a matter of two different tribes battling one another—the ethnic Christian Dayaks versus immigrant Muslim Madurese.

The immigrants arrived as part of a resettlement program that lasted for 40 years, until 2000. The program was unwelcome by many as the government was accused of ignoring the local Dayaks. It seems evident again that the end of the Suharto rule created an opening for this long festering feud to break out in full.

> **CAUTION**
>
> **Landmine!**
>
> According to a CNN.com report on Indonesia, "Before Indonesia's former Dutch colonial rulers outlawed headhunting in the late nineteenth century, the Dayaks were widely believed to be cannibals. In traditional Dayak belief, consuming the flesh of an enemy endows the eater with the victim's strength."

Although several peace agreements were signed following the first clash, none held. Rioting continued to take place as Madurese men went on rampage that included the burning down of a Catholic school. The fighting between the Dayaks and the Madurese then spread to other parts of the Kalimantan province. Murder and rampage begat revenge and retribution on both sides.

Government officials said the body count from one "incident" stood at around 500, nearly all them Madurese, adding however, that the death toll could be as high as 1,000 as uncounted bodies lay rotting in houses and fields. Local Christian church leaders have calculated the number of missing Madurese in the thousands.

Indonesia's military then cracked down on both groups. Although the Army has successfully taken control of many of the most problematic areas, in the interior, beyond the military checkpoints, Dayaks continue to hunt for Madurese.

Hopefully, the recent peace agreements signed by the two tribes signal an end to this violent conflict.

Aceh

On December 27, 1949, the Dutch left Indonesia, including the province of Aceh. The Republic of Indonesia was born. The problem here is that even though Aceh had never formally been incorporated into Dutch colonial possession, upon the creation of Indonesia, Aceh was made part of the new country.

Subsequently, the Indonesian government annexed Aceh. Since annexation, the Acehnese have continued to resent what they consider foreign occupation. The Aceh independence movement was born.

Aceh Merdeka (Free Aceh)

Recognizing the problem, the Indonesian government gave Aceh the status of "special territory" in 1959. This conferred upon it a high degree of autonomy. But even so, the desire for an independent Islamic state did not die.

In 1976, the Aceh Merdeka movement ("Free Aceh") was founded. In the 1970s, Indonesian authorities arrested members of the group and shut down their activities until 1989.

Escalation

The conflict has turned increasingly brutal. According to *Human Rights Watch*, "By mid-2001, so many killings were taking place in Aceh of people suspected of belonging to Aceh Merdeka that it was difficult to keep an accurate tally." It adds, "there is ample evidence that Indonesian forces deliberately and systematically employ executions to deter villagers from supporting (the independence movement)."

Diplomatic Dialogue

According to its own website, the **Human Rights Watch** "is dedicated to protection the human rights of people around the world. We stand with victims and activists to bring offenders to justice, to prevent discrimination, to uphold political freedom and to protect people from inhumane conduct in wartime. We investigate and expose human rights violations and hold abusers accountable. We challenge governments and those holding power to end abusive practices and respect international human rights law. We enlist the public and international community to support the cause of human rights for all."

By the same token, Human Rights Watch adds, "[Rebel] abuses include killings of suspected military informants, as well as of family members of police and military personnel, unlawful detentions, forced expulsions, and other terrorizing of non-Acehnese; destruction of property, including homes, and systematic extortion."

In 2002, peace talks were at a stand still and as the new year dawned, The governor of Aceh province declared that the region had implemented Islamic "Sharia." The strict Muslim code provides rules on alcohol, dress, and personal conduct, but also in theory demands amputation for theft and execution for adultery.

Osama and Indonesia

Because of its vastness, as well as its Islamic ties, there was widespread belief in Washington that al-Qaeda was operating out of Indonesia. And, as the U.S. War on Terror began, Washington found Indonesia to be a hard country to deal with. Washington was frustrated by the unwillingness of the Indonesian security forces to rein in Islamic militants.

This is so, despite the fact that the head of Indonesia's National Intelligence Agency said that al-Qaeda members had been fighting on the island of Sulawesi. Apparently, the militant Islamic organization Laskar Jihad had links with al-Qaeda and was responsible for sending in thousands of armed fighters to Sulawesi to support local Muslims.

Even this is not surprising, considering that Indonesian General Abdullah Hendropriyono admitted in late 2001 that international terrorists, including Osama bin Laden's al-Qaeda network, have training camps on Sulawesi.

If Indonesia didn't have enough conflict already, a war against the United States is the last thing it needs.

The Least You Need to Know

◆ Suharto's authoritarian rule clamped down on conflicts.

◆ East Timor is finally free.

◆ The isle of Irian Jaya wants to be free.

◆ The Spice Islands are wracked by religious-based unrest.

◆ Sulawesi is an extremist Muslim breeding ground.

◆ In Kalimantan, people kill in the name of God.

◆ Aceh is demanding independence.

◆ Islamic terrorists find a home in Indonesia.

Chapter 14

More Asian Atrocities

In This Chapter

- ◆ Why do they even want the Spratly Islands?
- ◆ Who owns the Diaoyutai Islands?
- ◆ Muslim separatists in the Philippines
- ◆ Burma's heroine
- ◆ Sri Lanka's long civil war

Conflict is born of many mothers. Asia, being one of the most densely populated parts of the planet has learned that overpopulation can often create conflict; countries with too many mouths to feed might look with envy and ill will toward their neighbor's resources.

Conflict also arises when one group thinks that its philosophy can care for the people better than that of another group. It might also come about when competing countries lay claim to the same parcel of land. And finally, let's not forget the vices of power and greed as potential causes. When it comes to conflict, Asia has it all!

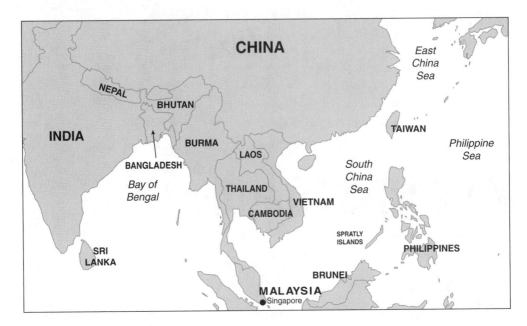

Asia: Little room to expand.

The Spratly Islands

On some tiny islands in the South China Sea, six nations stand ready to do battle. The islands they all want to control are often underwater. For centuries, these "islands" were virtually unknown.

Located in southeastern Asia, the Spratly Islands include about 100 islets, small islands, atolls, shoals, coral reefs, and seamounts. The largest island in the chain has a total area of .46 square kilometers and a maximum elevation of about 15 feet.

Landmine!

February 14, 1999 (BBC): "The disputed territory of the Spratly Islands in the South China Sea offers one of the region's major potential flashpoints for the twenty-first century. If conflict ever did break out there, no less than six nations could quickly find themselves in the midst of a bruising encounter."

The problem here (and it easily could soon be a large one), is that some or all the islands are variously claimed by China, Malaysia, the Philippines, Taiwan, Vietnam, and Brunei. The whole of the Spratly Islands are claimed by China, Taiwan, and Vietnam.

China and Vietnam are the two main actors in the dispute, but make no mistake about it, all parties involved stand ready to fight. Why? Surrounding the islands are some of the world's richest fishing grounds. And underneath the seabed, there are thought to be massive reserves of oil and gas.

Vietnam's claim to the islands, which they call the Truong Sa islands, rests on history. Vietnam maintains that the islands were part of the early Vietnam Empire of Annam. Indeed, in 1815, Annam King Gia Ng did send an expedition to chart the sea-lanes and settle the islands.

Thereafter, in 1884, France occupied Vietnam, becoming Vietnam's colonial rulers. The French then began to conduct patrol trips of the area, and in 1927, it conducted a full scientific survey of the islands.

The first hint of controversy came in 1932 when China contested France's sovereignty over the Spratlys. China explained that the 1887 Sino-French Convention "specifically states that islands … belong to China." Of course France disagreed, and in 1933, France annexed the Spratlys.

By 1941, Japan had become a power, especially in South Asia, and was able to forcibly occupy the Spratlys, claiming them as her own. Japanese troops remained in control of the archipelago until the end of the war. But in the peace treaty ending World War II, Japan renounced "all right, title, and claim to the Spratly Islands." Alas, the treaty never specified to which country the islands were ceded.

Vietnam thereafter maintained that the islands became its again because it was the rightful inheritor of the French possessions, and the French had lost the islands to the Japanese.

Now Things Get Murky

Enter the Philippines. In 1956, the Philippines claimed "ownership, by discovery and occupation, of all the (Spratly) territory."

A 1978 Philippines Decree outlined Manila's claims to the Spratlys (which it calls the Kalayaan Islands). The Philippines maintain that it has occupied a part of the islands for hundreds of years. So, in 1976, the Philippine government set up a garrison on the island of Palawan, and in 1978, it stationed soldiers on seven of the islands. In 1979, the Philippine government explained to the rest of the world that it only wanted those seven islands under its control, and not the rest of the archipelago.

Peacekeepers

The United States refuses to take sides in the Spratly Islands dispute, insisting that the various parties must resolve this matter on their own.

Enter the big dog. Beginning in 1985, Beijing assumed a newfound interest in the Spratlys, which it had always called the Nansha Islands. By 1987, the Chinese Navy began conducting patrols in the waters of the archipelago; at one point the Navy even staged a mock assault on one of the islands. The Chinese then occupied one of the "main" islands in the chain, establishing, within a short period of time, their first permanent base in the region. In 1987, China claimed that the Hainan Island, the closest to Chinese territory, was a Chinese province that would be developed as a special economic zone.

But Vietnam continued to occupy parts of the chain too, and by March 1988, it had troops on 18 islets. This all came to a head when, for the first time, violence broke out over the Spratlys. A gun battle erupted between Chinese and Vietnamese forces after the Chinese landed on one of the islands. When it was over, three Vietnamese ships were sunk and 70 Vietnamese troops died.

To make matters more complicated, Taiwan also claims sovereignty over the Spratlys, based on its assertion that it is the true China. According to both Taiwan and China the islands were discovered by Chinese navigators, have been used by Chinese fishermen for years, and have been under the administration of China since the 1400s. Furthermore, the Taiwanese had sent a naval expedition to the islands and left a battalion on one of the largest islands.

In February, 1995, the Philippines' armed forces discovered Chinese-built concrete markers on the appropriately named Mischief Reef, which are inside waters claimed by the Philippines. The Philippine government ordered its air force to destroy the Chinese-built structures.

Diplomatic Dialogue

The United Nations **Convention on the Law of the Sea** lays down a comprehensive regime of law for the world's oceans and seas by establishing rules governing all uses of the oceans and their resources. The Convention resolves conflicting claims, interpretations, and measuring techniques by setting a 200-mile limit as the boundary of a country's continental shelf.

What About International Law?

Brunei too lays claims to the Spratly Island, based on the *Law of the Sea Convention*. Brunei states that the southern part of the Spratly chain is actually a part of its continental shelf and is, therefore, its territory.

Like Brunei, Malaysia also lays claim to the Spratlys due to the Law of the Sea Convention because, it says, the islands are part of its continental shelf.

So far, the dispute has not been taken to any official forum, although Indonesia has encouraged the disputants to to start talks. No decisions on sovereignty have ever been reached. If in fact oil is discovered there, you can bet that this dispute will turn ugly quickly.

The Diaoyutai Dispute

The Diaoyutai Islands are a group of eight uninhabited islands located 120 miles off the northeast coast of Taiwan. For several centuries, they were administered as part of Taiwan and have always been used by Chinese fishermen.

The problem here is that in 1874, Japan took the nearby Liu Chiu (Okinawa) Islands from China by force, although the Diaoyutai Islands remained under the administration of Taiwan, as a part of China. Taiwan (including Diaoyutai) was later ceded to Japan after the first Sino-Japanese War in 1895, and was returned to China at the end of World War II. What was not given back, however, was Taiwan's claim over the Diaoyutai Islands; the United States decided to keep the Liu Chiu islands, including the Diaoyutais, for bombing practice for its Okinawa-based forces. In 1968, large deposits of oil and natural gas were discovered in the Diaoyutai region.

In 1969, the United States and Japan signed the Okinawa Reversion Treaty, which, among other things, returned Liu Chiu (Okinawa) to Japan. As such, Japan began to claim that it owned the Diaoyutai Islands.

At first, the U.S. government supported the Japanese claim, but because of the emerging American need to improve relations with China, the U.S. government later took a neutral stance over the dispute, claiming that America's involvement could, "in no way prejudice any underlying claims. The United States considers that any conflicting claims are a matter for resolution by the parties concerned" (Congressional Record, November 9, 1971).

Nevertheless, since 1969, Japan has insisted that the islands are part of Japanese territory. To that end, the Japanese have repeatedly sent naval forces to expel Chinese fishermen from the islands and have also tried to build a heliport on Diaoyutai. China maintains that the islands were never the Americans' to give back.

> **Reliable Resources**
>
> Japan's own maps prior to 1945 did not include the Diaoyutai Islands.

The conflict was exacerbated by a 1978 incident wherein a Japanese right-wing political group called Nihon Seinensha illegally erected a lighthouse on Diaoyutai in an attempt to legitimize Japanese territorial claim over the islands. (There are many ways to protest things. Erecting a lighthouse has to go down in the record books as one of the strangest.)

In 1990, the Japanese government decided it would grant Nihon Seinensha permission to renovate the lighthouse it had erected on Diaoyutai in 1978. Taiwan, claiming to be the legitimate Chinese government, sent two boatloads of protestors to the islands to demonstrate its own claim to the Diaoyutais. The Japanese Coast Guard prevented this force from landing on the islands.

In July 1996, Nihon Seinensha made another landing on the Diaoyutais, erecting a new lighthouse. Despite a series of warnings issued from both China and Taiwan, the Japanese government continues to maintain its control over the islands and has repeatedly prevented Chinese fishermen and reporters from entering the Diaoyutai waters.

In 1996, a group of Hong Kong protesters headed by David Chan, the leader of "Global Chinese Defend Diaoyutai Alliance," set sail for the Diaoyutai Islands. Their objective was to destroy the lighthouse and reassert Chinese sovereignty by raising a Chinese flag on the islands. It would be comical if it weren't so serious to all those involved.

Their attempts to reach the islands, however, were thwarted by a fleet of 17 Japanese Coast Guard vessels and a helicopter. After an hour of standoff with the Japanese forces, the group had to concede defeat and abort the mission.

China and Japan have since agreed to put off a solution to this thorny problem for another day. Taiwan says that it is the one that Japan should be talking to.

The Philippines

Like much of the rest of Asia, the Philippines is a country where tensions between Muslims and Christians is a constant. A massive U.S. resettlement program early in the twentieth Century resulted in 80 percent of the largest island of Mindanao becoming Christian, thereby causing deep resentment among local Muslims.

Ferdinand and Ferdinand

The Philippines was first discovered by the West (and by Christians) when Ferdinand Magellan arrived in 1521. Of course he claimed the archipelago for Spain, and equally predictable was the response of local chiefs who disapproved of Magellan's plan and killed him.

But European colonizers were not easily discouraged, and in 1543, Ruy Lopez de Villalobos followed Magellan, named the territory Filipinas after Philip II of Spain, and by 1571 the country was totally under Spanish control.

Spanish control continued until the turn of the twentieth century, when the United States bought the Philippines from the Spanish for $20 million. Japan invaded in 1942 and ruled until the United States reinvaded two years later. The Philippines received full independence from the United States in 1946.

The country struggled economically, and the Christian-Muslim split was evident even then. Filipinos thought they had an answer to their problems when, in 1965, they elected Ferdinand Marcos president. Seven years later, they were proven wrong when Marcos declared martial law and thereafter ruled the country as his own personal *fiefdom*.

For example, it was later proven that Marcos and his royal wife Imelda looted their land of perhaps $5 billion. But typically, Imelda Marcos once cavalierly

> **Reliable Resources**
>
> The Philippines is an archipelago of 56 million people and more than 7,000 islands.

> **Diplomatic Dialogue**
>
> A fiefdom is the estate or domain of a feudal lord. In modern times, the word has come to mean an area over which one dominant person exercises complete control.

remarked, "Here in the Philippines, we live in a paradise. There are no poor people as there are in other countries." At this time, 7 in every 10 Filipinos were living below the poverty level.

Needless to say, throughout his tenure, Marcos's government was attacked by both Communist and Muslim guerrillas. The beginning of the end of the Marcos regime occurred in 1983 with the assassination of prominent opposition figure Benigno Aquino by forces loyal to Marcos.

People Power!

After the assassination, massive anti-government protests erupted throughout the country as people were ready to rid themselves of the despot and his imperial wife. Marcos, who had once been a beloved leader, was, like every dictator mentioned in this book, corrupted by his power and had come to be a despised man. Nevertheless, because he had never lost an "election," Marcos decided to call a snap election and run against the new opposition leader, Aquino's widow, Corazon Aquino.

How out of touch was Ferdinand Marcos by this time? On election day in February 1986, despite the fact that more than 700 foreign journalists were watching the election closely, Marcos had his goons destroy ballots, intimidate voters at gunpoint, and buy votes.

> **Reliable Resources**
>
> Upon filling out her application for the presidency, Cory Aquino stated that her occupation was "Housewife."

Then the amazing began to happen according to *Time Magazine*. Thousands of poll watchers, singing and burning candles, formed a human barricade and carried their ballot boxes through the streets to election stations. Government vote tabulators walked out in protest. The country's Catholic bishops condemned the election, and the U.S. Senate immediately echoed the protest.

After it was over, both parties claimed victory, but Aquino was widely believed to have won. In any case, the fraud tainted whatever little legitimacy Marcos had left. But even so, power is an aphrodisiac, and those with it are loath to give it up. Marcos stood ready to inaugurate himself back into power.

But freedom is an aphrodisiac as well, and people want it. Marcos's top military commanders broke ranks with him, alleging that Aquino was the true winner. They then barricaded themselves inside two military camps. Before long, tens of thousands of Filipinos began what Aquino called a "People Power" revolution. They offered the rebellious military food and protection. With nothing but Filipino flags and flowers, they took up positions to defend the defiant military men.

Landmine! _____

How extravagant were the Marcoses? After their palace was overrun by Filipinos, 1,220 pairs of Imelda's size eight shoes were found left behind.

Marcos's tanks rolled toward the crowds, but they stood no chance against People Power. Nuns knelt in the path of the tanks and stopped them. Grandmothers went up to gun toting military men and hugged them. Little girls offered troops flowers and made them cry. In the face of this simple heroism, Marcos loyalists defected. Ferdinand Marcos and his wife were forced to flee the country to Hawaii.

For her determination and courage in leading a democratic revolution that captured the world's imagination, Corazon Aquino became *Time Magazine's* Woman of the Year for 1986.

Hangover

The Philippine revolution was, needless to say, a watershed event in the country's history. And, although it did restore democracy, little of the root problems that then afflicted the country have ever been solved. The Philippines is still wracked by poverty and religious animosity.

According to BBC News, there are four main groups at odds with the Manila government:

- **The Moro National Liberation Front (MNLF):** This is the first group that fostered a Muslim separatist rebellion.

  A 1996 agreement might have been a breakthrough. The agreement gave some Muslim areas of the Philippines a far greater degree of self-rule by setting aside land specifically for Muslims. Called, ARMM, the area is a semiautonomous area. The founder of MNLF, Nur Misuari, was installed as governor of the area, but his rule ended in violence when he led a failed uprising in November 2001.

- **The Moro Islamic Liberation Front (MILF):** This is a militant group that split from the MNLF in 1977. The government and MILF concluded a cease-fire agreement in 2002, but MILF continues to oppose it.

Peacekeepers _____

The MNLF and MILF are not all that much different. MILF is the more Islamic of the two.

- **Abu Sayyaf:** This is the most radical of the Islamic separatist groups in the Philippines. A series of kidnappings received both a lot of attention for the group and several high payoffs. Abu Sayyaf became a target of the American War on Terrorism after the group was linked with al-Qaeda.

- **The New People's Army (NPA):** It is strange to think that Communist insurgents are still in the world, but they are. They seem to be like Rip Van Winkle, sleeping through the demise of global Communism since the late 1980s. Nevertheless, in the Philippines, the NPA has waged a bloody guerilla war against the government that had lasted more than 30 years, and more than 40,000 people have been killed.

Burma's Close Shave with Democracy

A largely rural, densely forested country, Burma (or Myanmar, as it is also known) is adorned with ample symbols of Buddhism, manifested most vividly by the thousands of pagodas and Buddhas throughout its ancient towns. Yet this peaceful vision of the Buddha couldn't be more discordant with modern Burma.

Burma is ruled by a military junta, which has a history of gross human rights abuses, including the forcible relocation of civilians and the widespread use of child labor. The military controls key Burmese industries, and corruption is a hallmark of the black market economy. The armed forces are also said to traffic in heroin.

> **Reliable Resources**
>
> Burma is the world's largest exporter of teak and is a principal source of jade, pearls, rubies, and sapphires. It also has important offshore oil and gas deposits. Yet it remains one of the poorest countries on earth.

The Savior?

Aung San Suu Kyi is the daughter of the late Burmese nationalist leader, General Aung San. According to the BBC, after attending school in the Burmese capital of Rangoon, Suu Kyi went on to live in India and then moved to Britain for her university education, where she met and married an Englishman.

In March 1988, Suu Kyi went back to Burma alone to attend her ailing mother. At the same time, as they had throughout the world at this time, student protests were also breaking out in Burma, demanding democracy.

On August 8, 1988 (8/8/88), the famous 8-8-88 mass uprising began in Rangoon and spread to the entire country, drawing millions of people to protest against the government. On August 26, Aung San Suu Kyi addressed a half million people in a mass rally in Rangoon, calling for a democratic government.

Inspired by the nonviolent campaigns of Mahatama Gandhi and Martin Luther King, Aung San Suu Kyi began to organize nonviolent rallies throughout Burma, calling for free elections.

> **Reliable Resources**
>
> The movie *Beyond Rangoon* tells the story of these chaotic days in Burma, through the eyes of Patricia Arquette, who plays an American doctor stuck in the country during the crisis.

On September 18, 1988, Suu Kyi was placed under house arrest and held without charges or trial. The next year, despite her continuing detention, her National League for Democracy party won a landslide victory in the general elections by securing 82 percent of the vote.

As can now be expected from what you've read so far in this book, the military junta that ruled Burma refused to recognize the results of the election. In protest to her continued detention, Suu Kyi went on a hunger strike and many of the elected NLD representatives fled the country, maintaining a government in exile. In 1991, while still under house arrest, Aung San Suu Kyi was awarded the Nobel Peace Prize. In the meantime, many western governments have enforced sanctions against Burma until the military government steps down.

Reliable Resources

Nobel Peace prize winners include the following:

1906	President Teddy Roosevelt
1919	President Woodrow Wilson
1964	Martin Luther King
1973	Henry Kissinger
1979	Mother Theresa
1983	Polish leader Lech Walesa
1984	South African Bishop Desmond Tutu
1989	Dalai Lama
1990	Mikhail Gorbachev
1998	U.N. Peacekeeping Forces

Amazingly, although he was nominated in 1937, 1938, 1939, 1947, and 1948, the strongest symbol of peace and nonviolence in the twentieth century, Mahatma Gandhi, never won the Nobel Peace Prize.

Indeed, the military junta continues to wage war against its own people. Violence against various groups have forced over a million refugees to flee Burma.

Finally, in 1995, after six years in jail, Aung San Suu Kyi was released, only to be put under house arrest again in September 2000. Although she was able to live at home, her phone was disconnected and she was unable to travel freely. In fact, when her husband Michael died of cancer in 1999 in Britain, she was unable to leave Burma, fearing the junta would never allow her back into her country.

In October 2000, Suu Kyi entered into talks with the ruling military junta, aimed at ending the country's political deadlock. And in 2002, she was again released. But she will never be truly free until popular will runs her beloved homeland.

Trouble in Paradise

In Sri Lanka, a small island off the coast of India, Hindu Tamils are the majority in the northern part of the country, but are a minority in the country overall (accounting for only 12 percent of the population). Buddhist Sinhalese are the majority.

The Tamils are violently demanding (what else?) independence. The Tamils believe that because they have their own history, traditions, culture, and language, they deserve their own homeland. The problem is that Sri Lanka is a very small place.

The most powerful Tamil group in Sri Lanka, the LTTE, began its armed conflict with the Sri Lankan Government in 1983. Often called the Tamil Tigers, the group utilizes a traditional guerrilla/terrorist strategy to forward its aims—the group's elite Black Tiger squad conducts suicide bombings against various Sri Lankan targets, and all rank-and-file members carry a cyanide capsule so they can kill themselves should they ever get caught before their mission is accomplished.

In 1987, the Sri Lankan government went on a major military offensive against the Tigers, ignoring objections and warnings by the Indian government that it would intervene if it thought the Tamils were being starved. (India has a population of about 55 million Tamils.)

In July 1987, India and Sri Lanka signed an accord in an attempt to settle the dispute by giving greater autonomy to the Tamils and including an Indian Peace Keeping Force that would disarm the rebels. At first, the LTTE was game to the accord.

The accord broke down in 1989 after opposition by some Sinhalese natives who turned violent. In 1990, India withdrew its troops, and civil war was again on. Since then, the LTTE has turned out to be a very active, very violent group:

◆ In 1991, it assassinated Indian Prime Minister Rajiv Gandhi.

◆ In 1993, a suicide bomber attacked and killed Sri Lankan President Ranasinghe Premadasa.

◆ In 1996, they exploded a massive truck bomb at the Sri Lankan Central Bank and another at the Colombo World Trade Center the next year.

◆ In 2000, they murdered C.V. Goonaratna, the Sri Lankan Minister for Industries.

◆ They have also attacked several ships in Sri Lankan waters, including foreign vessels. They also attack trains, buses, and power stations.

Landmine! ———————

The elections held in 2001 were the most violent in recent Sri Lankan history—17 people were killed on polling day alone.

According to the BBC, "The government says its strategy is to defeat the Tigers militarily while simultaneously pursuing a constitutional settlement to Sri Lanka's troubles. The Tigers say they will not stop their struggle until they have secured an independent homeland."

And so it goes.

The Least You Need to Know

- Six nations continue to battle over the tiny Spratly Islands.
- It is unclear who owns the Diaoyutai Islands.
- Muslim separatists in the Philippines have spoiled the People Power revolution.
- Aung San Suu Kyi is Burma's brave heroine.
- Sri Lanka's long civil war has no signs of ending.

Part 4

Europe

Europe has been the center of more violence and conflict in the last 100 years than any other place on earth. World War I, World War II, The Cold War, and the Northern Ireland conflict have raged in Europe.

Although things are calmer today, they might be no less volatile. Russia has problems aplenty with her many neighbors, the Balkans have recently been the scene of a bloody conflict, and simmering animosities linger throughout the land.

Chapter 15

The Balkan Mess

In This Chapter

- The players and their politics
- The rise of Slobodan Milosevic
- The Croatian and Bosnian wars
- The Dayton Accords
- Mass Murder in Kosovo
- Milosevic's downfall

There was a time, just before the beginning of the horrific wars within what would soon become the "former Yugoslavia," when things were much different. The country was on the brink of European Union membership and its people took holidays. Yugoslavia was the freest and most economically advanced of all the communist countries.

You may recall that during the Cold War, much of the world was divided into two camps—the West (or democratic countries) and the East (communist countries). East Block countries were those that were part of the Soviet Union's Warsaw Pact and sphere of influence—countries like East Germany, Poland, Romania, and Czechoslovakia.

Yugoslavia was different as it was the only communist country not under Soviet domination. But upon the disintegration of Yugoslavia, things went downhill fast. Instead of peace and prosperity, the country was plunged into war and poverty. After the Cold War ended, ethnic animosities took precedence, and the region broke out in the worst violence Europe had seen since World War II. Ethnic cleansing, murder, rape, and torture became commonplace.

Today, with the possible exception of Slovenia, all parts of the former Yugoslavia are now far, far behind former East Block countries such as Hungary and Poland; countries that once envied the Yugoslav standard of living. Today, the Balkan countries that make up what was once Yugoslavia lay in ruins. Genocide can do that.

Hence the Term—Balkanization.

Break Out Your Scorecard

To understand the Balkan mess, the first thing you must do is know who the players are. Once you can tell them apart (and it can sometimes be a bit confusing), understanding this conflict becomes much easier.

You Say Slavonia, I Say Slovenia

In 1914, Austria-Hungary invaded Serbia, triggering World War I. After the war, the Balkan countries of Croatia, Slovenia, Vojvodina, Serbia, Montenegro, and Macedonia joined forces to form a new country called "The Kingdom of Serbs, Croats, and Slovenes." Smartly, the name was soon changed to Yugoslavia. As time went by, the main three groups that would make up Yugoslavia were the Serbs, the Croats, and the Bosnians.

In 1945, the Communist Party under Josip Tito came to power. During his presidency, Tito walked a fine line between the two superpowers, and remained unaligned with either the West or the Soviets. Besides being a tightrope artist, Tito was also a tyrant, and when he died in 1980, long simmering resentments between the many nationalities that made up Yugoslavia were able to come to the surface.

Reliable Resources

The unity fostered by Marshall Tito in Yugoslavia took precedence over ethnic differences. Tito was considered by his countrymen to be a benevolent father figure, who inspired songwriters to compose rousing songs. Even today, you can find his portrait in some homes and public buildings. Children throughout the land honored him every year on his birthday. What few knew was that Tito maintained this semblance of unity by shipping dissidents off to work camps or demoting them from positions of power.

After Tito's death, the Yugoslav presidency became a post that rotated between nine elected members of the government. In 1986, a Communist Party *apparatchik* named Slobodan Milosevic got his turn in the seat. The vision he would begin to espouse was that of a "Greater Serbia"; a land untainted by foreign blood or other Balkan blood. It was a vision that would lay to waste an entire region.

Diplomatic Dialogue

Under Communist rule, loyalty to the party was one of the most respected traits. An **apparatchik** was an unquestioningly loyal subordinate or bureaucrat.

Serbia

The Serbs are the bad guys. With a population of almost 10 million, compared to Croatia's 5 million and Bosnia's 4 million, the Serbs were the dominant force in the old Yugoslavia and wanted the same power in the new region. They were in a far better position to create that, too, because, as Yugoslavia disintegrated, the Yugoslav People's Army generally followed orders from the Serbs, and thus, Milosevic. Therefore, almost by default, he became the dominant player in the region.

The problem for Milosevic was that Serbs didn't just live in Serbia—they lived in Bosnia (the so-called Bosnian Serbs), as well as other areas in the region. His desire for a Greater Serbia threatened Croatia and Bosnia because Greater Serbia, if it were ever to be, would be carved partially from those countries.

Needless to say, Slovenia and Croatia were alarmed at Milosevic's grand plan, and as such, declared themselves independent of Yugoslavia in June 1991. This signaled the end of Yugoslavia as the world had known it. (Today, Serbia and Montenegro still call themselves "Yugoslavia.")

Slovenia

Slovenia has a population of less than two million, and few of them are Serbs. So when the country declared independence from the crumbling Yugoslavia on June 25, 1991, Milosevic did not care. Slovenia's independence had no impact on his Greater Serbia plan.

Croatia

Croatia immediately followed suit, declaring its independence on the next day, June 26, 1991. Milosevic was also prepared to let Croatia have its independence, *if* it was willing to give up Slavonia, a region with a heavy Serb population. (Note: Slavonia and Slovenia are different.) Croatian President Franjo Tudjman was, like any president of any country, unwilling to simply give part of his country away to the dictator next door. Conflict became inevitable.

Bosnia

Bosnia was created out of desperation. Despite opposition from other member states in the European Union, Germany had formally recognized the new states of Slovenia and Croatia in December 1991. Other EU countries soon followed. For Bosnia, this was a disaster.

The new political landscape left what remained of Yugoslavia as a Serbian-dominated state—a situation intolerable for Muslims in Bosnia, who had lived amicably with Serbs and Croats in Bosnia for 40 years, but who suddenly became a vulnerable minority in a state ruled by Serb nationalists. Bosnia thus wanted to become independent too, to protect its large Muslim population from the newly ethnocentric Serbs.

A vote on Bosnian independence was held in early 1992, but the Bosnian Serbs decided to boycott the vote as they did not want to be separated from their Serb brothers in Serbia. Yet even so, because Muslims made up about 65 percent of Bosnia's population, the election resulted in an overwhelming vote for independence.

So the stage was now set for a massive war. Milosevic, and his much better-armed Yugoslav army, was ready to attack Croatia and Bosnia in order to both reunite all Serbs and kill any non-Serbs (that is, Muslims).

The Great Dictator

Slobodan Milosevic was born in 1941 near Belgrade. His was not a happy childhood. His father left home just after World War II and committed suicide in 1962. He was brought up by his mother, a strict communist schoolteacher.

At university, Milosevic met Mira Markovic. She so believed in her Slobo that she often boasted that one day he would be as glorious a leader as Comrade Tito himself. Little did she know that Milosevic would turn out to be the opposite of the beloved Tito.

Milosevic then began a long, slow climb up the Communist Party ladder. By 1986, he had become head of the Serbian Communist Party. It was the issue of Kosovo that transformed Milosevic from a dull bureaucrat into a jingoistic politician.

"No one will ever beat you again!"

According to BBC News, "In 1987, Milosevic was a middle ranking and virtually unknown Yugoslavian communist official who was sent to calm local Serbs who had been complaining about abuses by the ethnic Albanian population in Kosovo. When he got there, he was greeted by an angry crowd that was being beaten by the mainly Albanian Kosovo police."

Milosevic gave a fiery speech and, according to the BBC "uttered the words that transformed him from apparatchik [into a hero] telling the frightened Serbs: 'No one will ever beat you again!' The result was amazing. State television began broadcasting the remarks around the clock. Newspapers analyzed the event, and suddenly, Milosevic came to symbolize the resentments Serbs had felt during Tito's reign; they thought that their interests had always come last since Tito was a Croat.

By lifting the lid on the long-standing taboo of ethnic rivalries, Milosevic was able to use the event as a springboard to reinvent himself. Serbian

> **CAUTION**
>
> **Landmine!**
>
> Milosevic's mother also committed suicide, in 1972. He also had an uncle who committed suicide. In all, three very close relatives of the Serbian leader killed themselves.

> **Reliable Resources**
>
> In 1389, Turkish forces defeated the Serbs at Kosovo Polje. As a result, Christian efforts to free the Balkans from Ottoman rule ended, and the Serbs would be part of other countries for another 500 years. Serbs thus view the place of this defeat—Kosovo—as their spiritual home.

nationalism became his calling card, and his newfound popularity allowed him to soon take control of the Serbian state.

As the BBC put it, "In 1989, on the anniversary of the historic battle of Kosovo Polje, Milosevic gathered one million Serbs at the site of the battle to tell them to get ready; changes were coming. He then began to arm and support Serb separatists in Croatia and Bosnia and to prepare his own army for the battles ahead. The Balkans' long nightmare of civil war was beginning."

The Croatian War

Once Milosevic was firmly in control of Serbia, it was clear to all concerned that his aspirations were far greater than merely leading his country into the post–Cold War world. He obviously aimed to take over other Serb-dominated areas by force if necessary. As he said at the time, "We believe that Serbs have the legitimate right to live in one country. If we must fight then by God, we will fight!"

When Croatia declared independence, it set off an immediate war with Serbia. Serbs were no small minority in Croatia at the time, and many believed in Milosevic and his grand plan. Encouraged and armed by Serbia, Serb guerrillas inside Croatia were quickly able to take control of about one-third of Croatia, driving out members of other ethnic groups in the process.

In May 1995, the Croatian army went on a major offensive, bent on gaining back Croatian territory it had lost in 1991. The Croat army entered Krajina Serb enclaves inside Croatia, and either expelled or murdered the Serb residents. Three months later, Croatian troops had retaken the disputed territory and had sent more than 100,000 Serbs fleeing.

The Siege on Sarajevo

Following Croatia's lead, Bosnia declared independence in April 1992, and violence immediately broke out there, too. Milosevic vowed to defend the Serbs living in Bosnia. But he didn't need too much help: Serbs inside Bosnia, the "Bosnian Serbs," already controlled the military. In fact, since 1991, Radovan Karadzic (a former psychiatrist) had been creating a renegade army within Bosnia with the support of Milosevic. In 1992, under Karadzic's leadership, Bosnian Serb nationalists began a systematic policy of "cleansing" large areas of Bosnia of non-Serbs.

Serbia then began to do its part by attacking the main Bosnian city of Sarajevo, shelling the city from hilltop positions above. In an orgy of murder, the Serbs took the ancestral lands of the Muslim population and sent hundreds of thousands of Muslims fleeing. This became the largest refugee movement in Europe since WWII as Muslims fled to other parts of Europe.

> ### Peacekeepers
>
> In 1984, before the insanity, Sarajevo hosted the Winter Olympics. The city, adorned with cafés, restaurants, pubs, shows, theaters, and public art, put on a magnificent party. Three-time defending world champion Scott Hamilton won gold in men's figure skating, and East German Katarina Witt won gold on the ladies' side. The British ice dancing team of Torvill and Dean amazed crowds and judges with nine perfect sixes to take the gold.

The Serbs were indiscriminate in their killing. They shot and bombed hotels, schools, hospitals: Even mourners in graveyards were killed. All the while, governments in the West continued to do little to stop the bloodshed.

In August 1992, television began to display images of Muslims in Bosnia in newly built Serbian concentration camps. Alarmed by this and other evidence of Serbian "ethnic cleansing," the United Nations created a War Crimes Tribunal; the first such tribunal since Nuremberg.

> ### Peacekeepers
>
> In 1945, four nations—the United States, Great Britain, France, and Russia—issued an indictment against 24 men and 6 organizations, charging them with the systematic murder of millions of people and with planning and carrying out World War II. Twenty-one of the indicted men eventually sat in the dock in the Nuremberg courtroom. All were found guilty, as were the Nazi SS, the Gestapo, and all political leaders of the Nazi Party.

Despite the atrocities (or maybe because of them), the war raged on and by 1993, Serbs controlled almost two thirds of Bosnia. The Croats, whose war with Serbia had spilled over to Bosnia, had taken over nearly one third of the country.

Genocide

In May 1993, the United Nations designated six U.N.–protected "safe areas" in Bosnia: all of which were Muslim areas that had been under siege by the Bosnian Serbs. U.N. peacekeeping forces were to provide limited military protection and assist in humanitarian aid efforts to those who could get there.

In the summer of 1995, Serb forces began to attack these safe havens. Ethnic cleansing had come to Srebrenica. Srebrenica was supposed to be the world's first U.N. Safe Area, but safe was the one thing it was not. The worst case of genocide in Europe since World War II would occur there. In July 1995, the Bosnian Serb army staged a violent takeover of the small, spa town and its surrounding region. During a period of five days, the Bosnian Serb soldiers separated Muslim families and systematically murdered more than 7,000 men and boys.

After the fall of the Srebrenica "safe area," the international community finally seemed to realize that if this war didn't end soon, it could spill over into the rest of Europe—thereby possibly creating a much larger conflagration. NATO threatened air strikes against Bosnian Serbs if they attacked any of the remaining safe areas in Bosnia. Ignoring the warning, they launched attacks against the "safe areas" of Zepa, Bihac, and Sarajevo.

On August 30, 1995, Operation Deliberate Force began against Bosnian Serb military targets. Air attacks continued until September 14, dropping more than 1,000 bombs on Serbian targets.

Apparently, military might is the only thing Slobodan Milosevic understands. After three weeks of being brutally shelled by NATO, the Serbian strongman agreed to peace talks, but not before more than 200,000 people had died in the fighting.

The Dayton Accords

In December 1995, President Milosevic of Serbia, President Alija Izetbegovic of Bosnia, and President Franjo Tudjman of Croatia met in Dayton, Ohio under the prodding of the Clinton Administration.

From the outset, the outcome of the negotiations was in doubt. So intransigent were the warring parties that on the last day; as President Clinton put it, "our American negotiators had their bags packed and were ready to head home without an agreement." However, the Balkan leaders finally decided to make peace. They did so because the alternative was too terrible: more war, ethnic cleansing, mass graves, refugees, economic ruin, and international isolation.

The Dayton Peace Accords that they signed did several things:

- ◆ It affirmed Sarajevo as the capital of Bosnia.
- ◆ It carved Bosnia into two autonomous and ethnically based entities separated by a demilitarized zone.
- ◆ It rewarded the Serbs for their aggression by giving them 49 percent of the territory of Bosnia. The Bosnians received the remaining 51 percent of their own country.

Shortly after the accords were signed, a NATO-led peacekeeping force of 60,000 soldiers (called SFOR) arrived in Bosnia. SFOR maintained the cease-fire and forced the parties to pull back their forces and weapons from the demilitarized zone. Nearly all heavy weapons were placed under SFOR supervision, and many were destroyed. More than 100,000 soldiers were demobilized.

SFOR also stopped the widespread killing of civilians and restored security to Sarajevo. Virtually all prisoners of war were released. SFOR moved to take down internal checkpoints, and, while far from perfect, freedom of movement improved. The force was downsized to 20,000 troops by 2002.

One would think that this should be the end of the story. But it's not: not in the Balkans. Although the fighting was over in Bosnia, Milosevic had already set his sights on another minority, the Albanians living in the Kosovo region of Serbia.

Kosovo

Beginning in 1997, Serbians began a systematic mass murder of Albanians in Kosovo. Many victims were murdered or expelled. Serbian forces also expelled the majority of Kosovar Albanians from urban areas. Those who remained behind were used as human shields.

It was also reported that the Serbian forces stole personal belongings and documentation telling the Albanians they would never return to Kosovo. Hundreds of villages and thousands of homes throughout the region were burned to the ground.

Kosovar Albanians also allege that Serbian forces systematically executed ethnic Albanian men—ranging from as young as 14 to 59. Mass graves found later confirmed this.

Serbian forces also allegedly burned bodies in an apparent attempt to destroy forensic evidence of their crimes.

Rape also became a staple of the Serbian form of war:

- Kosovar Albanian women have stated that they were raped repeatedly by Serbian soldiers.
- Serbian forces especially focused on raping young Kosovar Albanian women.
- Numerous Kosovar Albanians have also claimed that they were gang raped by the Serbs.

> **Reliable Resources**
>
> Most Serbian homes and stores were not damaged during the conflict. How? Serbian forces knew that an "S" painted on a door meant that it was Serbian property.

NATO, having intervened in the Balkan atrocity once already, finally decided that it would have to act again. In March 1999, wave after wave of NATO warplanes and missiles struck Serbia, pummeling army barracks, power plants, and air defenses in an effort to force Slobodan Milosevic to cease his genocide of Kosovo Albanians.

The NATO attack came after months of diplomacy failed to end a year of fighting that left more than 400,000 homeless in Kosovo. The campaign took far longer than anyone had anticipated—11 weeks—but in the end, Serbia capitulated. Although Milosevic withdrew his troops from Kosovo, he still didn't admit defeat.

Serbia's infrastructure was destroyed, and its economy was in ruins, but Milosevic tried to turn the devastation to his advantage. In a propaganda campaign waged through the state-controlled media, he styled himself as the rebuilder of the nation.

Thankfully, the End

By the time Milosevic called elections in the fall of 2000, the country was already crippled by sanctions and poverty. Milosevic was finally being seen by his countrymen for what he was—a genocidal murderer.

But his undoing came when he refused to recognize the election victory of an opposition leader. Hundreds of thousands of people took to the streets and went on strike. Important allies of Milosevic then dropped their support, including the Serbian Orthodox Church.

Ten days after the election, protesters stormed the parliament and the state television station, setting both buildings on fire. Policemen joined the protesters, and the country unraveled. It was finally the end for Slobodan Milosevic.

Milosevic was arrested soon thereafter and sent to the International War Crimes Tribunal in The Hague, Netherlands where he was set to be tried. The charges? Crimes against humanity and genocide for actions in Bosnia, Croatia, and Kosovo.

The Least You Need to Know

- The former Yugoslavia was made up of many conflicting nationalities.
- The Bosnian War saw horrendous atrocities.
- The Dayton Accords ended the war between Bosnia, Serbia, and Croatia.
- Kosovo was the last place in the Balkans where ethnic cleansing took place.
- Milosevic is a war criminal.

Chapter 16

The Russian Bear

In This Chapter

- ◆ The Russian revolutions
- ◆ Chechen rebels: friend or foe?
- ◆ Radical Islam in the Caucuses
- ◆ Russia and the West

For much of the last century, Russia (then known as the Soviet Union, or the USSR) was one of the most feared countries on earth. Seemingly indifferent to the desires of the rest of the world, and aided by a huge nuclear capacity, few wanted to tangle with the USSR, including the various republics that made up the huge, diverse country.

However, the break up of the Soviet Union in 1991 unleashed forces that continue to effect life there to this day. Long forgotten feuds were apparently not so forgotten, and conflicts that lay dormant for years once again rose to the surface.

Russia is simply too vast to discount for long.

Russian History 101

The defeat of the Russian Empire in World War I created the opening for a communist revolution in Russia. Vladimir Lenin (1870–1924) led his *Bolsheviks* to power in 1917, creating the first communist state in history. Lenin was able to harness power despite a bloody civil war, famine, and an unknown path toward an untried communism.

Lenin ruled Russia until his death in 1924 and was succeeded, after a three-year power struggle, by Josef Stalin. Stalin proved to be one of the most ruthless, despotic leaders of the entire twentieth century; a feat not easy to achieve. Upon seizing power in the Soviet Union, Stalin quickly took measures to make his reign absolute by expelling and demoting his most hated rivals from the party.

Believing that the West might attack the USSR at any moment, Stalin began to militarize his country and solidify his power. Beginning in 1934, he also began to purge the country of supposed enemies, and his grip on power tightened even more. Internal concentration

Diplomatic Dialogue

The **Bolsheviks** (meaning "majority") split from the original Russian Socialist movement in 1903, and developed into a small, organized, revolutionary, Marxist group. In November 1917, they took over a country torn by civil war. Upon gaining power, the Bolsheviks renamed themselves the Communist Party of the Soviet Union (CPSU).

camps for those who opposed the state became a fixture of life inside the Soviet Union, and both party members and citizens alike were afraid to question Stalin or his policies.

The "cult of personality" that blossomed around Stalin would not only lead some countrymen to revere him (or fear him, as the case may be), but also would ingrain Russians for generations to come with the idea that the good leader is probably an authoritarian leader.

During World War II, the Soviet Union emerged as a formidable world power. The Russian forces resisted the German advance and eventually overwhelmed them, reaching Berlin in April 1945. Thereafter, with his troops already in place, Stalin

> **Reliable Resources**
>
> Who was the most murderous person of the twentieth century? It is hard to say. Hitler can probably claim the top prize—between those killed in the war he started, as well as those killed in concentration camps and other forms of intentional murder he sanctioned, probably 34 million people died because of him. Stalin comes in a close second, having caused the deaths of probably 20 million people.

was able to control, either directly or indirectly, most of Eastern Europe. When the war ended, he immediately began to establish communist rule in these countries.

The Cold War

As a result, the post-war world was suddenly divided between East and West. The East was dominated by communism, the USSR, and puppet states such as Poland, Hungary, Czechoslovakia, and East Germany. The West was lead by democracy, the United States, and European allies such as Great Britain, France, Italy, and West Germany.

Fearing this newfound Soviet strength and its dominance over Eastern Europe, the West decided to enter into a mutual defense commitment in 1949, and the North Atlantic Treaty Organization (NATO) was born. NATO was intended to counter what was now being called the "iron curtain."

Peacekeepers

From Stettin in the Baltic to Trieste in the Adriatic an "iron curtain" has descended across the Continent. Behind that line lie all the capitals of the ancient states of Central and Eastern Europe: Warsaw, Berlin, Prague, Vienna, Budapest, Belgrade, Bucharest, and Sofia; all these famous cities and the populations around them lie in what I must call the Soviet sphere, and all are subject, in one form or another ... to control from Moscow. The safety of the world, ladies and gentlemen, requires a unity in Europe ....

—Winston Churchill, Westminster College, Fulton, Missouri, March 5, 1946

The newly emerging Cold War was named that because, unlike a "hot" war, the two combatants rarely squared off directly against one another. Rather, they operated in a series of proxy battles intended to either strengthen their team or harm the other. The number of actual conflicts that occurred during the Cold War (1946–1991) is numerous, but the major ones are these:

- **The Berlin Airlift**: After World War II, Germany was divided into four zones administered by four nations: the United States, Great Britain, France, and the Soviet Union.

  In June 1948, the Soviet authorities, claiming "technical difficulties," halted all traffic by land and by water in to or out of the Western-controlled section of Berlin. In response, the West chose to airlift in supplies. For the next 11 months, the Berlin Airlift sustained the city's two and a half million residents.

- **The Berlin Wall**: In an effort to stem the tide of people escaping communist East Germany, the East German government, on August 12, 1961, decided to close the Berlin border. The next day, just after midnight, East German troops erected barbed wire barricades and roadblocks.

  Construction of the concrete Berlin Wall began five days later. Eventually, the wall would use guard dogs, machine-gun nests, floodlights, and observation towers to keep people in. From 1961 to 1981, almost one thousand East German citizens were killed by East German troops in attempts to escape, and tens of thousands were imprisoned for planning to do so.

- **The Bay of Pigs**: On March 17, 1960, President Eisenhower asked the CIA to "organize the training of Cuban exiles [for] a possible future date when they might return to their homeland," invade, and take out Castro. President Kennedy inherited the dubious plan, was never committed to it, waffled when it began, and when it was launched, saw it turn into an utter disaster as Cubans killed or captured the American forces in a matter of hours.

Landmine!

After the Cuban Missile Crisis, Khrushchev said of Castro, "He was a young hotheaded man, so he thought we were retreating and capitulating. He did not understand our action was necessary to prevent military confrontation."

After the Bay of Pigs, relations between the United States, Cuba, and the Soviet Union deteriorated rapidly. It is speculated that it was Kennedy's indecisiveness during the Bay of Pigs that encouraged new Soviet leader Nikita Khrushchev to send missiles to Cuba soon thereafter.

- **The Cuban Missile Crisis**: For 13 days in October 1962, the world stood on the brink of nuclear annihilation as the United States attempted to get the USSR to withdraw nuclear warheads it had placed in Cuba.

President Kennedy, after receiving advice that ranged from the continued use of diplomacy to preemptive air strikes to a blockade of Cuba, finally settled on the latter. Soviet ships carrying more missiles were turned away, the missiles that remained were soon removed, and a bigger crisis was averted.

Détente

In 1968, the virulent anticommunist Richard Nixon was elected president of the United States. Whatever else can be (and has been) said about President Nixon, it cannot be said that he did not understand international relations. Among the things he realized was that the Cold War was dangerous business for all concerned. So, just as he had decided to go to China, he also decided to warm relations with the Soviet Union. He called his plan *détente*.

> **Diplomatic Dialogue**
>
> From the French, **détente** is the relaxation of strained relations or tensions.

The results were the SALT I (Strategic Arms Limitations Talks) and Anti Ballistic Missile (ABM) Treaties, opening the decade of the 1970s on a positive note. And, although SALT II followed, the Soviet invasion of Afghanistan in 1979 ended the decade on a very sour note. With the election of Ronald Reagan the next year in the United States, the Cold War was back with a vengeance.

It is yet unknown whether Reagan actually intended to bankrupt the Soviet Union, or if that was simply a byproduct of his plan to massively increase American defense spending. Either way, it worked. The Soviets were unable to match either American resolve or its deep pockets throughout the massive arms buildup the United States undertook in the 1980s. Cracks in the Soviet system finally began to emerge.

In 1985, Mikhail Gorbachev came to power in the Soviet Union. Understanding that his country was unable to continue along on the course it had been following, Gorbachev began to steer a radically new path for his country. In 1986, he ended economic aid to Soviet satellite countries. That same year, Reagan and Gorbachev resolved to remove all intermediate nuclear missiles from Europe.

Gorbachev's plan was twofold. In an attempt to unleash his society, he introduced "glasnost" (openness). And, in an attempt to revive his moribund economy, Gorbachev introduced "perestroika" (restructuring). What he didn't anticipate was that his attempts to modernize communism would inadvertently unleash forces that would change the world.

In 1989, Hungary declared its independence from the *Warsaw Pact*. In November of that year, the Berlin Wall fell. In December, communist governments in Czechoslovakia, Bulgaria, and Rumania fell. In 1990, Germany reunited.

Diplomatic Dialogue

To counter NATO, the Soviet Union created the **Warsaw Pact** in 1955. Participating countries included Albania, Bulgaria, Hungary, East Germany, Poland, Rumania, and the USSR. In July 1991, all members agreed to end the 36 year alliance.

In late 1991, Mikhail Gorbachev resigned as head of the Soviet Communist Party, and on December 25, 1991, he resigned the presidency of the USSR. Unable to cow its many republics into subservience any longer, the Soviet Union itself soon splintered into 15 independent republics.

Postscript

After 74 years, the USSR faded into history, not with a bang, but with a whimper. The Soviet empire was over, and the Cold War had finally ended. Although Russia would inherit the Soviet mantle, it was largely symbolic. Russia was now seen for what it might have been all along: a *Third World* country with a large army and nuclear weapons.

Diplomatic Dialogue

In politics, the so-called First World refers to the highly developed industrialized nations often considered the westernized countries of the world. The Second World refers to the communist nations as a political and economic bloc. The **Third World** is the aggregate of the underdeveloped nations of the world. Some people even refer to a Fourth World, meaning a group of nations, especially in Africa and Asia, characterized by extremely low per capita income and an absence of valuable natural resources.

Even before the end of the USSR, the new Soviet president, Boris Yeltsin, had set about creating an entity to replace it. On December 8, 1991, Russia, Ukraine, and Belarus signed an agreement to form the Commonwealth of Independent States (CIS), also sometimes known as the Russian Federation. After the Soviet Union collapsed, other nations joined the CIS.

I Want to Get Away

The largest factor contributing to conflict in the old Soviet Union today is the desire of many of the former Soviet republics to be free and the insistence from Moscow that they remain part of the Russian Federation.

This tension was first seen in May 1989, before the dissolution of the USSR, when the three Baltic republics of Estonia, Lithuania, and Latvia declared their sovereignty. The three tiny republics continued to push for separation from the USSR for 19 months.

On January 13, 1991, the Soviet Union sent troops and tanks into the breakaway republic of Lithuania. But a mere nine months later, after the collapse of the USSR, the Soviet parliament acknowledged the independence of the three Baltic republics and the troops were withdrawn.

Seeing what the small Baltic countries were able to do, many other republics followed suit and declared their independence. Some became independent states when the USSR was finally dissolved, whereas others remained a part of the Russian Federation; some unhappily so.

Chechnya

Chechens are a Muslim people who live in the Caucasus Mountains. The Chechens have long engaged in struggles against Russian rule both before and after their surrender to Tsarist Russia in the mid-1800s.

After Soviet rule was established, the Chechen Autonomous Region was created in 1922. In 1934, it became part of the Chechen-Ingush Region and was made a Soviet republic in 1936. But, after the Chechens collaborated with the invading Germans during World War II, Stalin expelled many of them to Kazakhstan, charging them with disloyalty.

Of the 500,000 or more people who had lived in Checheno-Ingushetia in 1939, less than half returned after its restoration in 1957. This troubled past partly helps to explain Chechnya's troubled present and why it is not eager to remain part of the Russian Federation.

The 1994 War

Russia, although accepting its new world order, was yet unwilling to lose all of its republics. Chechnya is one republic that Russia decided must remain part of the federation. Nevertheless, under the leadership of Dzhokar Dudayev, Chechnya declared full independence in 1993, leading to civil war in that republic, as well as several Russian-backed attempts to overthrow Dudayev in 1993 and 1994.

Tensions between the Russian and Chechen governments continued to escalate, and by late 1994, the Russians had decided that they needed to crush the Chechen separatist movement. Russian troops were sent to Chechnya in late 1994 to end the rebellion.

> **Reliable Resources**
>
> Chechnya has large oil deposits, as well as an abundance of other minerals, and its mineral waters have made it a spa center. The population is mostly Chechen, although it does have a sizable Russian minority. The Chechens are Sunni Muslims.

But this Russian army was not the old Soviet war machine. With paydays rare and food scarce, Russian troops were already suffering from low morale. That they were disinclined to attack their countrymen in the Chechen capital of Grozny made matters worse.

Earlier in the year, Moscow had begun to fund and support Chechen rebels who were opposed to President Dudayev. These forces eventually joined the Russian troops, and together they launched a clandestine, poorly organized and badly executed attack on Grozny in November 1994.

By December, Russian forces were pummeling Chechnya with massive aerial bombardments. But the aerial attacks did not have the desired effect. Rather than capitulating to the clearly superior air power of Moscow, the Chechens dug in. And, as so often happens in these "precision bombing" campaigns, many bombs missed their mark, killing an untold number of civilians. This, in turn, was reported by Russian journalists. In Moscow, opposition to the war was growing.

Russian President Yeltsin then sent in thousands more troops. But unlike the Russians, the Chechens believed in their cause. Said Chechen Foreign Minister Shamsedin Yusef, as quoted by BBC News, "They cannot kill every Chechen. There are one million of us, and every one of us will fight." What the Chechen guerilla army lacked in organization and training was made up for in tenacity and intensity.

Moscow finally ordered a massive bombardment of the capital of Grozny in a last-ditch effort to root out the rebels. Tanks and soldiers rolled into Grozny in a show of strength.

However, the following days proved to be a military setback for the Russian forces. In a "David vs. Goliath"-like scenario, Chechen guerilla units used hand grenades to destroy the lead tanks in Grozny's narrow streets. The tanks following behind were forced to halt, and thus they became sitting ducks; the guerillas picked off the Russian tanks and soldiers one by one. Thousands of Russian soldiers are believed to have been killed in the first days of the battle for Grozny.

Russia reacted by increasing its firepower. Journalists reported that the Russian artillery was targeting apartments, homes, and civilians, and Grozny was rocked by the magnitude and severity of the attack. Russia was, in effect, attempting to raze the city.

Peacekeepers

One way the Chechens fought the Russians was by mobilizing entire villages to prevent the passage of Russian tanks.

But the Chechens struck back, and by the third day of the assault, had repulsed the attack. And so, only a few days after its offensive, Russian forces began to withdraw from Chechnya.

But the war wasn't over. Russian forces would return, apparently opting for a war of attrition. Eventually, Grozny began to fall to the Russians under the weight of the attack. According to BBC News, German

Chancellor Helmut Kohl described the events as "sheer madness," and "journalists reported appalling human rights abuses being carried out by both sides."

Although Russian military forces took key buildings in the capital, Chechen rebels kept up their guerilla attacks. Russian soldiers were now facing an enemy they rarely saw and a population who despised them. The invaders grew disheartened.

Reliable Resources

How demoralized was the Russian army in Chechnya? One U.S. military survey reported that Russian soldiers had taken to selling their arms to the rebels in exchange for alcohol.

By May 1995, about two thirds of Chechnya and most of the main towns were controlled by Russian forces. Yet, the Chechen rebels continued to inflict heavy damage on the invaders, operating from bases hidden in the mountain region.

Eventually, the Russian forces had to concede defeat in face of a Chechen rebel force that refused to be contained or have itself crushed. Following a peace deal in August 1996, the troops who had entered the territory to keep it part of the Russian Federation withdrew, leaving behind about 10,000 dead and a country in ruin.

Estimates vary on the total number of casualties caused by the war. Russian Interior Minister Kulikov claimed that fewer than 20,000 civilians were killed, whereas then-Secretary of the Russian National Security Council Aleksandr Lebed asserted that 100,000 had been killed and 240,000 injured. International organizations estimate that up to 500,000 people fled Chechnya during the war.

Round Two

The Russians might have won the battle, but they lost the war. What began as a war of independence for many Chechens turned into a jihad for many others in this Muslim enclave. Radical Islam was able to make strong inroads as a reaction to Russian atrocities and imperialism.

Indeed, many Chechen commanders who started as pro-independence, essentially nonreligious figures increasingly turned to radical Islam as the war continued. And they did so, not just because it might have appealed to them, but also for the far more *realpolitik* reason that doing so enabled them to obtain money, troops, and the moral boost needed to sustain their fight.

The rising influence of Islam in this region was demonstrated in 2000 when the first of what would be many Chechen suicide bombers struck a Russian army barracks. Heretofore, suicide

Diplomatic Dialogue

Realpolitik is politics based on practical and material factors rather than on theoretical or ethical objectives.

bombers had been seen only in the Middle East. But ever since the first suicide bombing in Moscow, more attacks have followed. According to senior analyst Tomas Valasek, "Qoqaz.net reports that at least 500 Muslim Chechens volunteered for martyrdom on these suicide missions."

Surprisingly, this rise of radical Islam, and the events of September 11 actually played into Russia's hand. All of a sudden, the Chechens were no longer "freedom fighters" but rather Osama bin Laden-like terrorists. Russia was able to use these attacks as a pretext to "fight terrorism." In 2001, Russian air strikes targeted Chechen communications and infrastructure while ground troops poured into Chechnya again, a clear sign that Russia once again was mobilizing to reassert its military and political authority in the region.

And now, whereas the Chechen army was once seen in the West as rebels with a cause, the American War on Terrorism changed all that, too. It became clear to Russia-watchers that Russian President Putin was able to extract a promise from U.S. President Bush that the West would ignore Russian carnage in Chechnya in exchange for Russia's help in America's latest war.

> **CAUTION** **Landmine!**
>
> Human Rights Watch asserts that "Russian Forces in Chechnya continue to commit atrocities at an alarming rate. Russian abuses documented by HRW since late 1999 include: summary execution of civilians; arbitrary detention and the beating and torture of detainees; and looting." The Chechens didn't fare much better. HRW also says that "Chechen forces have summarily executed servicemen they have captured as well as physically abused civilians."

More Crisis in the Caucasus

Chechnya, although Russia's biggest problem, is by no means its only one.

The Dagestan Rebellion

In 1999, a number of Islamic rebels started a guerilla war in Dagestan, a republic in the Russian federation, demanding independence. As journalist Sara K. Miller relates in her account of the history and conflict in Dagestan, the rebels are a small, internationally funded militia whose numbers include Arabs and Africans, as well as Dagestanis and Chechens.

The rebels declared Dagestan's independence and a holy war against Russia. In response, Dagestan's next-door neighbor, Chechnya, declared a state of emergency. Russia initially relied on air offensive to combat the rebels, but then ground troops were introduced soon thereafter.

And of course, refugees began to pour out of Dagestan. But international aid organizations were unable to help much as the rebels are not averse to kidnapping or killing relief workers. The end result of all of this is that this conflict is far from over.

The Rise of Islamic Fundamentalism

The big fear for Russia is that this outbreak of fighting in Dagestan, coming as it has on the heels of the fighting in Chechnya, might mean that the Caucasus and Central Asia are turning towards radical Islam. It is, in fact, a regional problem.

In Central Asia, the former Soviet states of Kyrgyzstan, Uzbekistan, and Tajikistan are also battling Islamic groups lodged in the mountainous region where the borders of the three republics converge.

Poverty and the collapse of the Soviet government, when combined with the opening of the borders, have enabled radical Arab missionaries to spread their message in this area. These clerics, part of the fundamental *Wahabi* tradition, are opposed to the more traditional Islam that has long been practiced in the region.

The growth of radical Islam in this area is a cause for deep concern. One reason is that this form of Islam provides a reason to fight, and fighting, as we have seen, produces refugees. Refugees, in turn, are people unable to pursue their professions, and are often forced into poverty. And poverty repeats the cycle—giving people a reason to fight, to wit: If communism didn't work, and capitalism didn't work, maybe Islam is the answer! That many people are disillusioned with the corruption and poverty plaguing the former Soviet republics makes puritanical Islam even more inviting.

> **Diplomatic Dialogue**
>
> **Wahabi** s the most fundamental form of Islam. It was practiced by both the Taliban in Afghanistan and Osama bin Laden.

Russia and the West

Throughout most of the twentieth century, Russia and the West stood ready to do battle with one another. Although they became allies during World War II, because they faced a common enemy, for the most part, Russia was the West's enemy.

The breakup of the Soviet Union in 1991 began to change that perception. Russian Presidents, first Mikhail Gorbachev, and later Boris Yeltsin and Alexander Putin, began to make peace overtures to the West, needing, as they did, Western capital. Old Warsaw Pact countries began to join NATO. Russian and American nuclear arms were greatly reduced. Things seemed to be getting better.

But it might not stay that way. Russia is a huge country with vast resources. Nationalism runs high there. To expect it to remain a second-tier country for long is unrealistic. Russia will likely rise again, and it might well become the West's biggest problem.

Evidence of this occurred as recently as 1993 when Vladimir Zhirinovsky received the largest number of votes for parliament on a neofascist platform. Zhirinovsky, whose autobiography has the same title as Adolf Hitler's (*My Struggles*), pledged to

- Put radioactive waste along the border with Lithuania.
- Reclaim the breakaway central Asian republics.
- Make Russia a superpower again.

Although his support has since diminished, what he stood for survives among many Russians, indicating that the Russian bear may be only hibernating.

The Least You Need to Know

- Russia was in conflict with the West for most of the twentieth century.
- Chechen rebels are now being portrayed as terrorists.
- Radical Islam is making large inroads in the Caucuses and Central Asia.
- Russia and the West might duel yet again.

Chapter 17

Northern Ireland Imbroglio

In This Chapter

- ◆ A history of Ireland
- ◆ Irish troubles
- ◆ The Good Friday Peace Agreement

The current state of the world can be depressing. From one country to the next and one region to the next, people somehow seem to find new and better ways to kill one another. And in this orgy of violence, it might seem that there is no light.

But there is. If anything good can come from all this conflict and hate or from all this war and death, it is that peace is possible. No, it's not easy, and yes, it is rare. But it is possible. The bitter antagonists in Northern Ireland are heroic evidence of that. They are the light.

How the Irish saved their civilization.

The Roots of the Problem

The first British involvement in Ireland began in 1169, when Anglo-Norman troops arrived in County Wexford. During the next 500 years, English rulers attempted to colonize Ireland; moves that precipitated numerous rebellions by the Irish over the years.

By the sixteenth century, the English, a mostly Protestant bunch, were able to expand their power over the weaker Ireland. As such, religious persecution of Catholic Irish grew. This was especially true after the accession of Elizabeth I, a Protestant, to the English throne in 1558. By 1691, with the victory of Protestant English King William III over the Irish forces, Protestant supremacy began to dominate life in much of the British Isles as the British grip and occupation of the predominantly Catholic Ireland tightened.

Reliable Resources

The traditional Irish alphabet uses only 18 letters: the five vowels, as well as the consonants *b, c, d, f, g, h, l, m, n, p, r, s,* and *t.*

Catholics in Ireland suffered greatly under British occupation. In fact, there were laws enacted that …

♦ Prevented Catholics from bearing arms.

♦ Denied them the right to hold public office.

♦ Restricted their ability to get an education.

When combined with the Act of Union, passed in 1800, which legally joined England and Ireland as one, Catholic rights became an oxymoron. The island was now officially governed by London.

Home Rule

Understandably, many Irish wanted to govern themselves, and the campaign for "Home Rule" was begun in the 1870s. Home Rulers wanted a separate Irish government. Yet not all Irish were Home Rulers. In the northern part of Ireland, which was predominantly Protestant, the people wanted to remain part of the British Empire. Wanting to remain in union with England, they were called, quite naturally, "Unionists."

On the other side were the "Nationalists"; those who wanted to have their own nation— a free Irish state. In 1916, these Irish Nationalists stormed the General Post Office and other key buildings in Dublin and proclaimed the formation of an Irish *Republic*. But the uprising failed. The subsequent execution of most of the leaders led to the emergence of Sinn Fein, the Nationalist party that would dominate Irish politics for years to come.

In the 1918 general election, Sinn Fein was demanding full freedom for Ireland and no union with Great Britain. On this platform, it beat the Unionists, who supported continued governance from London. Emboldened by this mandate, Sinn Fein boycotted the British parliament the next year, instead declaring the formation of its own Irish Parliament.

At the same time, Sinn Fein's military wing, the Irish Republican Army (IRA), began a violent struggle for independence from Great Britain. Led by Michael Collins, they began a terror campaign throughout Ireland.

> **Diplomatic Dialogue**
>
> According to Merriam Webster, a **republic** is "a government in which supreme power resides in a body of citizens entitled to vote and is exercised by elected officers and representatives responsible to them and governing according to law."

The Partition of Ireland

The campaign worked: The British government relented and, in 1920, passed the Government of Ireland Act. The Act partitioned Ireland into two areas—southern Ireland and Northern Ireland—with the intention that both would be given limited powers of self-government but would remain part of the United Kingdom.

This partitioning would have a lasting impact on Ireland. By creating two separate parliaments—one in the north and the other in the south, —the British effectively pitted Ireland against itself. And it was done deliberately: The British knew that Northern Ireland had plenty of Protestants who still supported a union with Great Britain.

So in 1921, Sinn Fein and British officials signed the Anglo-Irish treaty, which created an Irish Free State over the 26 southern counties. Although the south was finally free of English rule, the partition left Irish Catholics in the six northern counties cut off from their countrymen, subject to British rule, and dominated by a Protestant majority.

The partition was unacceptable to the Irish Nationalists, who were demanding nothing less than a united, independent Ireland. How opposed was the IRA to partition? They even killed Michael Collins, a signer of the treaty.

The Troubles

In the 1960s, the Catholic population, inspired by the civil rights movement in the United States, began to agitate for change. In 1966, Nationalist councilor Austin Currie squatted in a house in the village of Caledon, setting in motion a tragic chain of events, which became known throughout the world as the Northern Ireland Troubles.

Currie's actions instigated a widespread campaign for civil rights in the province. Although it was intended to be a peaceful campaign, the pro-British unionists viewed it as a covert attempt to destabilize the status quo. There was a violent reaction.

Reliable Resources

Currie squatted in protest to the fact that an unmarried Protestant woman could get housing while many Catholic families remained on the public housing waiting list. Discrimination in housing and an unfair voting system were two of the main grievances of the Catholic community.

Violence Erupts

The feelings of frustration, acrimony, and humiliation that had been pent-up over these many years finally found an outlet. Attacks by the IRA against the Nationalists began in earnest, and the Nationalists fought back. Now it was clear: Catholic was against Protestant, North was against South, England was against Ireland, and Unionists were against Nationalists.

Groups bombed each other's government installations, and, as community tension grew, arson attacks and incidents of intimidation reached a frightening level. In Belfast, entire streets of homes were torched as mobs went on wild rampages. In Londonderry, the police were almost overwhelmed by rioters. The crisis led to the greatest population movement in Western Europe since the end of World War II as thousands of families fled the violence in Northern Ireland.

Landmine!

One of the army's first actions was to build a makeshift barbed wire dividing line between Protestant and Catholic areas. In the years that followed, more permanent barriers were built, many of which are standing today—"concrete" evidence of the deep divisions within Northern Ireland.

Britain responded by sending troops to restore order, suspending the Northern Ireland government, and assuming control of the territory. But, as hostilities continued, the British, caught between rival Protestant and Catholic communities, themselves became the targets of violence.

Although Catholics initially welcomed the army, the relationship deteriorated swiftly when soldiers began to search Catholic homes looking for nationalists. The Troubles worsened.

Sunday, Bloody Sunday

On January 30, 1972, British troops opened fire on a group of Irish demonstrators, killing 13 of them. A fourteenth victim later died of his wounds. The incident became known as Bloody Sunday and became one of the defining moments of the Troubles.

Reliable Resources

Well it was Sunday, bloody Sunday
When they shot the people there
The cries of thirteen martyrs
Filled the Free Derry air
Is there anyone amongst you
Dare to blame it on the kids?
Not a soldier boy was bleeding
When they nailed the coffin lids!

—John Lennon/Yoko Ono, February 1972; *Some Time in New York City*, Apple Records

But Sunday wasn't the only bloody day. Violence came every day of the week now in Northern Ireland. According to official statistics, the death toll in Northern Ireland from 1969 to 1997 was 3,228.

But statistics alone cannot begin to tell the tale of woe suffered by the peoples of Northern Ireland who lived with, among other things:

◆ The bombing of pubs

◆ Car bombings

◆ Firebombings

◆ Assassinations

◆ Extortion

◆ Train bombs

◆ Subway bombs

◆ Kidnappings

Landmine!

On March 1, 1981, an IRA prisoner, Bobby Sands, began a hunger strike to protest his status as a common, rather than, a political prisoner. His eventual passing by starvation, and the death of nine fellow IRA inmates, sparked more outrage and riots, and brought increased sympathy for the IRA's drive for a united Ireland. While on his deathbed, hunger striker Bobby Sands was elected to the British Parliament.

Both Nationalist and Unionist politicians were targeted, and the IRA twice came close to killing the entire British Cabinet—in a bomb explosion at the Conservative Party conference and in a mortar bomb attack on the Prime Minister's home at 10 Downing Street.

At the height of the British presence, in 1972, a massive British police and army presence was deployed in Northern Ireland. Some 21,000 soldiers were stationed there, yet the Troubles would continue for the next decade.

The Good Friday Peace Accords

The search for peace in Northern Ireland has gone on longer than the Troubles themselves. Efforts have ranged from pleas to the terrorists to lay down their arms to complex interparty and intergovernmental discussions.

The problem with any proposal is that a division in Northern Ireland exists that some thought too wide to bridge. Many Catholics wanted to become one with the rest of Ireland, whereas the majority of the Protestants wanted to remain in union with Great Britain. How could a solution connect this seemingly insurmountable divide?

Certainly people were trying. In 1972, three young children were killed when a terrorist getaway vehicle crashed into them after the driver had been shot by soldiers. The "Peace People" organization was formed as a result. The group drew thousands of people who were demanding an end to violence. In 1977, the group's leaders, Mairead Corrigan and Betty Williams, were awarded the Nobel Peace Prize.

Peacekeepers

In 1972, the first direct attempt to broker peace took place. Sinn Fein leader Gerry Adams, then in jail, was released and flown with other senior republicans to London to take part in secret talks with the British Northern Ireland Secretary of State, William Whitelaw. Although the result was but a short IRA cease-fire, a new day had dawned.

Throughout the late 1970s and early 1980s, attempts to end the violence continued, with little to show for it except more death. Finally, according to the *Washington Post*, in 1985, there was a breakthrough. The United Kingdom and the Republic of Ireland (ROI, or the southern part of Ireland) signed an agreement which "gave the ROI an oversight role on behalf of Catholics in Northern Ireland." The deal was a breakthrough as it established for the first time ever "the Irish government as a legitimate player in Northern Ireland politics."

With the door open, British leader John Hume and Sinn Fein president Gerry Adams held secret talks in 1988 aimed at finding a political solution to the problems. The talks continued, off and on, for several years until at last, in 1993, they announced the "Downing Street Declaration."

The deal stated that Sinn Fein could be a partner in any talks on the future of Northern Ireland *if* it renounced violence. Importantly, the declaration also stated that the British and Irish governments would support the democratic wish of the majority of people in Northern Ireland, whether it be a continued union with Britain or a united Ireland.

And then, on August 31, 1994, the amazing occurred: The IRA called a cease-fire. This enabled the talks to get serious. Six months later, in February 1995, the Irish and British governments announced their "Frameworks for the Future"—a document that outlined in general terms what any overall settlement might look like.

However, nothing comes easy in this most intractable of conflicts. Over the next 24 months, there were disagreement over disarmament and the lack of an IRA cease-fire. A new wave of bombings threatened to derail the peace process.

The IRA had become increasingly frustrated at what it considered to be a general lack of progress in the talks. Convinced that the British government would never deliver, the IRA ended its 18-month truce and blew up Canary Wharf in London.

But British Prime Minister John Major was clearly committed to this process by now, and vowed it would continue with or without Sinn Fein. When actual settlement negotiations began, in the absence of an IRA cease-fire, Sinn Fein was locked out.

Meet George Mitchell

In 1996, an international body was formed to help end the deadlock. Chaired by former U.S. Senator George Mitchell, the group endeavored to come up with a comprehensive plan to solve the many issues that threatened peace. The first thing Mitchell did was to offer a compromise to end the stalemate, suggesting that Britain drop its insistence that the IRA begin disarming *before* entering negotiations.

Reliable Resources

George Mitchell comes from humble beginnings. His father was a janitor, and his mother worked in a textile mill. Even so, in 1980, Mitchell had worked his way into a position to be appointed to the U.S. Senate to complete the unexpired term of Senator Edmund S. Muskie. Mitchell was elected to a full term in the Senate in 1982, and in 1989 he became the Senate Majority Leader (until he retired from the Senate in 1995).

Then, in May 1997, Tony Blair became Britain's Prime Minister. In one of his most important acts, Blair offered Sinn Fein entry into the talks *if* it would agree to a cease-fire. Sinn Fein agreed, and in the summer of 1997, Nationalists joined Unionists at Stormont Castle in Belfast, Northern Ireland to decide the future of region.

Pathway to Peace

The parties knew that any agreement would have to do two things: First, if there was to be no overall political union between north and south (and that seemed increasingly unlikely as a majority in the north wanted to remain with Britain), the agreement would nevertheless have to reassure the Catholics that the ROI would still play an important role in the life of Northern Ireland. The agreement also needed to reassure Northern unionists that Protestant Northern Ireland would not be dominated by the ROI.

This was one of the thorniest of issues—how to create an all-Ireland body that still respected Protestant ties to England. It was a balancing act to be sure. Unionists accepted the need for some sort of north-south structure, but they resisted any sort of powerful all-Ireland institution that might give the ROI too strong a say in Northern Ireland affairs while also weakening links with Britain.

Nationalists on the other hand, viewed an all-Ireland structure as critical to a deal. If the ROI was going to dilute its claim to Northern Ireland, they believed that a strong all-Ireland council needed to be set up to ensure stability.

In all, besides the British and Irish governments, nine other parties were included in the talks at Stormont, including, for the first time in 75 years, the IRA and the Unionists.

An Agreement Is in Sight

As could be expected, the talks were contentious and were repeatedly marked by one side or the other walking out, threatening to quit, and actually quitting, as well as by break-downs in negotiations, violence threatening future negotiations, and stalemates.

A frustrated, but equally committed George Mitchell then set a deadline: Either an agreement would be reached, or there would be no peace and negotiations would end. Within a week, Mitchell proposed a draft settlement.

Negotiations then reached a fever pitch. Both Prime Minister Tony Blair and Irish leader Bertie Ahern flew in for crisis meetings with the political parties. But even so, the mood was optimistic. As the days dwindled down to hours, that optimism increased in spite of the difficulties which had to be overcome.

According to the *Washington Post*, "By midnight on April 10, 1998, after 21 months of negotiations, the politicians had in their hands an agreement that no one thought they would ever see. The historic Good Friday Agreement created a new form of self-rule for Northern Ireland. The Accords would give the minority Catholics in Northern Ireland a far greater voice in their affairs and end direct British rule over the area—all while meeting Protestant demands that the province remain a part of Britain."

Peacekeepers

Unionist leader David Trimble and Catholic leader John Hume were awarded the Nobel Peace Prize in 1998.

The Agreement

Specifically, the ground-breaking 69-page deal struck at the Stormont sets out a new constitutional framework and proposals for an assembly and other complex issues. The main details are

◆ **Constitutional changes**: The Agreement explicitly recognizes the principle of majority rule as a method to determine any change in Northern Ireland's status. It also states that Articles 2 and 3 of the Irish Constitution were to be changed (articles that called for reunification). The new formula ended the Irish territorial claim to Northern Ireland but recognized formally its Nationalist identity.

◆ **Institutions**: A new 108 member Assembly, elected by proportional representation, would come into effect. The new body would have full legislative and executive authority on issues. Safeguards would be put in place to ensure that all sections of the community could participate and their rights would be protected by a Bill of Rights.

◆ **North-South reinforcement**: A civic forum was to be established, composed of representatives of business, trade union, and voluntary sectors. A new North-South ministerial council, which was to be made up by the first minister and deputy of the Assembly and Irish ministers, would be created. Meeting twice a year, it would deal with matters of common interest.

Peacekeepers

April 10, 1998 (Associated Press): "Critically, the new Belfast assembly will be expected to cooperate formally with the Irish Republic in a north-south council of lawmakers. This measure is considered essential to win support from the north's Catholics, who generally favor the unification of Ireland. But the Protestant bloc appeared to have won a substantial concession because the Belfast assembly will have the right to approve decisions taken by its members in the cross-border council."

Thus, there would be a new Northern Ireland Assembly, a North-South Council, and a British-Irish Council.

No, the agreement wasn't all or nothing. Neither side won, nor did either side lose. As the Belfast Telegraph political analyst Barry White puts it, "Haven't you learned over the past 30 years, that if the population is divided 60-40 in its loyalty to Britain and Ireland, that means that its institutions must incorporate a bit of both? Most of us would wish that things were different, and that we could be all British or all Irish, but we can't. It is something we have to accept, like it or not."

White continues:

> To my mind, the Agreement sets up a governmental framework in Northern Ireland that could develop in one of two directions. It could consolidate Northern Ireland's position in the UK, mainly by getting the Republic to drop its territorial and psychological claim, or it could swing us in the direction of a united Ireland, if these cross-border bodies get us thinking that links with the Republic could be more advantageous than links with Britain.

> In other words, the Agreement gives us the freedom to expand our horizons and drop our obsession with exclusiveness, either British or Irish. We can be either or both, without having to make any excuses or to regard ourselves as second class.

> We happen to live in (an area) where the majority want to be part of the U.K., but we could change, or the majority could change. What's wrong with that?

Yes indeed, what's wrong with that? And the best part is that no one has to die if someone changes his or her mind now.

The plan was put to a vote. In 1998, following nearly 30 years of bloody conflict, the people of Northern Ireland voted overwhelmingly in favor of the Good Friday Peace Agreement. Peace had finally come to Northern Ireland.

The Least You Need to Know

◆ Irish history is replete with sadness.

◆ The Troubles caused the worst bloodshed in modern European history.

◆ The Good Friday Peace Agreement is a historic document.

Smoldering European Conflicts

In This Chapter

- ◆ Basque Separatists in Spain
- ◆ Armenia and Azerbaijan
- ◆ Cyprus divided

The twentieth century was a century marred by violence from Europe. Both World War I and World War II began, and largely took place, there. The Cold War was also mostly a European phenomenon. Even the late century conflict in the Balkans was a European affair. Europe and war tend to go hand in hand.

In the modern world then, Europe is always a concern. The fear today is that even the smallest of conflicts, conflicts that would barely be a concern elsewhere in the world, must be handled properly and contained swiftly because they are in Europe. No one wants the Continent to again be the spark that lights the world.

Europe ruined the last century for the rest of us.

Basque—in the Shadow of Terrorism

Like many people throughout this book, the Basques are a people without a country. The modern *nation state* is not necessarily designed around specific ethnicities. As such, people like the Kurds have seen their traditional homeland divided into different nations, and so too have the Basques. The Basques, who live primarily in Spain, have a language, culture, and history different from the rest of the Spaniards, but they have no land to call their own.

The Basques have been occupying their tiny corner of Europe since well before Roman times. The historical Basque region includes the four Spanish provinces of Vizcaya, Guipúzcoa, Alava, and Navarra, as well as the

> **Diplomatic Dialogue**
>
> A **nation state** is a political unit consisting of an autonomous state inhabited predominantly by a people sharing a common culture, history, or language.

three former French provinces of Labourd, Basse-Navarre, and Soule (now officially incorporated into the French department of Pyrénées-Atlantique).

No one knows where they came from. The Basque language, known as Euskera, has no links with any other known language and was spoken long before all the Indo-European languages in the rest of Europe. Today, about 80,000 people still speak it in France, and about 600,000 in Spain.

Fiercely proud of their history, language, and culture, the Basques have long wanted a country to call their own. This struggle is nothing new. The Basques have repelled many invaders who have trespassed upon their land, including the following:

◆ Romans

◆ Vikings

◆ Visigoths

◆ Muslims

The Modern Conflict Begins

In the 1930s, *fascism* and fascist leaders were on the rise throughout Europe. Hitler had taken over Germany, Mussolini ruled Italy, and in Spain, a new fascist leader was emerging. General Francisco Franco's fascist troops invaded Spain in July 1936 determined to overthrow the young and unstable Spanish Republic. After three years of intense civil war, Franco's fascist troops were triumphant, and Spain became a fascist country.

During the civil war, the Basques were among the fiercest opponents to Franco's Nationalist troops, and Franco never forgot it. During his 40-year reign, Franco never failed to punish the region for its wartime opposition. Declaring two Basque regions "traitor provinces," he banned the speaking of Euskera in public, and made sure that little economic investment happened in the region.

However, like his predecessors, Franco found it difficult to suppress the Basques. In 1958, the only armed group that would emerge in Spain during

Diplomatic Dialogue

Fascism was a system of government marked by centralization of authority under a dictator, stringent socioeconomic controls, suppression of the opposition through terror and censorship, and usually, a policy of belligerent nationalism and racism.

Franco's rule was born in the Basque region. The Euskadi Ta Askatasuna, or ETA (Basque Homeland and Freedom), was committed to the creation of a Basque state, using violence when necessary.

The ETA's first terrorist action occurred in 1961 with the unsuccessful attempt to derail a train carrying Spanish Civil War veterans who were going to the Basque city of Donostia to celebrate the twenty-fifth anniversary of Franco's victory.

CAUTION

Landmine! _____

Ernest Hemingway was moved to write the following words after witnessing the Spanish Civil War: "They wrote in the old days that it is sweet and fitting to die for one's country. But in modern war, there is nothing sweet or fitting in your dying. You will die like a dog for no good reason."

—"Notes for the Next War: A Serious Topical Letter," in *Esquire* (New York, Sept. 1935; repr. in By-Line Ernest Hemingway, ed. by William White, 1967)

What followed were a series of events, some violent, some not, but all of which were intended to help forge a Basque state out of Spain. And Spain fought back:

- The Basque cities of Bizkaia and Gipuzkoa went on strike in 1962; a strike that would soon spread to the rest of the state.

- In 1968, Basque separatist riots erupted and ETA demonstrators battled with the Spanish police.

- In 1970, ETA rebels came before a Spanish military tribunal. They were charged with illegally organizing and murder. Not a few of the 16 defendants showed signs of having been tortured.

- 1973 saw the group undertake its boldest action when Spanish Prime Minister Carrero Blanco was killed in a car bombing.

Franco Is Still Dead

After Franco's death in 1975 and the return of democracy to Spain, the new government changed course and tried to work with the Basques, granting the region limited autonomy. In 1980, the first Basque parliament was elected.

For the militant ETA, however, this was not good enough. The war was still on. Utilizing car bombs, arson, and terror, the group continued to fight for its cause, killing more than 800 people, many of them Spanish police officers and soldiers. Obviously, the Spanish government was not content to let this rampage go unanswered. And so, for four years, from 1983 to 1987, a secret government-sponsored team killed or wounded roughly 57 members of the ETA.

The ETA's terrorist ways eventually became unacceptable to the Basques, too. By the mid-1990s, although 40 percent of the Basque population wanted an independent state, only 11 percent thought that terrorism was an appropriate means to that end.

Peacekeepers

In 1975, the death of Francisco Franco during *Saturday Night Live*'s first season was a cause for one of the show's very first catchphrases. For several weeks, one of Chevy Chase's stories during *Weekend Update* would be "This just in: Francisco Franco is still dead."

Reliable Resources

According to a BBC news report, "The ETA reportedly produced a handbook for new recruits that spelled out the secrets of avoiding capture and being a 'good activist.' According to the handbook, which was obtained by the press, 'The secret of the success of a good activist lies in him having a normal family, social and working life, with no one realizing or suspecting his underground activities.' The handbook adds, 'Practice with explosives, grenades, bombs etc. will always be conducted underground or underwater so that the detonation and effects will be muffled as far as possible.' It concludes by stating that the group will show 'particular vigilance' in hunting down and executing moles in the organization."

Peace?

In 1998, the ETA called for a cease-fire and said that, although it would continue to press for a Basque homeland, it was willing to do so in peace talks with the government. Many observers thought that the Good Friday Peace Accords in Northern Ireland influenced this decision.

The talks began and continued for many months, but no solution was reached. In the year after ETA's announcement, the peace held, but efforts by the Spanish government and Basque Nationalist parties to find a long-term political solution to the problem were fraught with discord. After a 14-month truce and no settlement, ETA backed out of the talks and the cease-fire was over.

The ETA has since gone back to killing people.

Armenia Versus Azerbaijan

Between 1915 and 1917, Russia occupied most of Armenia. But the Bolshevik victory in Russia ended Russia's involvement in World War I, and Russian troops also left Armenia. Similarly, immediately after the chaotic Bolshevik Revolution, Armenia's neighbor Azerbaijan declared its independence from the Soviet Union. Neither country wanted anything to do with the big Russian bear.

However, the bear wanted them. Azerbaijan was reconquered by the Red Army in 1920, and annexed into the USSR in 1922. Armenia, seeing its neighbor Azerbaijan fold so quickly, decided not to fight. In November 1920, the Armenian government made a political agreement with the communists to enter into a coalition government.

Then, for reasons that are still difficult to decipher, the Soviet Union created the Nagorno-Karabakh Autonomous Region within Azerbaijan in 1924. It did so, even though 94 percent of the region's population was Armenian, and the land sits on the border between the two countries. Just as easily, Nagorno-Karabakh, with its largely Armenian population could have been made part of Armenia. But it wasn't.

Nevertheless, even though the region is Armenian, it became part of Azerbaijan. If one thing is clear, it is that governments are loathe to give up their land, even when keeping that land makes no sense.

Seventy years later, after the collapse of the Soviet Union, both countries finally got their chance to be independent. Azerbaijan declared its independence from the collapsing Soviet Union on August 30, 1991. The next month, more than 99 percent of voters in Armenia also voted to free themselves from the Soviet Union. Both countries were finally free from the Russians.

Peacekeepers

According to a March 8, 2002, BBC News report, "Armenia has seen great changes since the breakup of the Soviet Union in 1991. Once dubbed the Soviet "silicon valley," Armenia's economy collapsed when the Soviet market disappeared. It has also suffered from a trade blockade imposed by neighboring Turkey and Azerbaijan after the dispute over Nagorno-Karabakh erupted."

However, they were not free from each other. Since 1988, Azerbaijan and Armenia have been feuding and fighting over Nagorno-Karabakh. Not surprisingly, the majority of the population of Armenian Christians wanted to secede from the predominantly Muslim Azerbaijan and join with Armenia. Azerbaijan would not hear of it.

In 1988, Armenian legislators in the Nagorno-Karabakh region voted to unify with Armenia. Azerbaijanis responded by killing more than 100 Armenians, and war erupted. Refugees then began to pour out of both Armenia and Azerbaijan as the minority populations in both places came under attack.

Soviet President Mikhail Gorbachev then attempted to solve the problem by granting greater autonomy to Nagorno-Karabakh itself while also granting Azerbaijan authorities greater powers. But this balancing act satisfied neither Armenians nor Azerbaijanis. The fighting intensified. In September 1989, Azerbaijan began an economic blockade of Armenia supply lines through its territory.

In 1991, another referendum was held by Armenians in Nagorno-Karabakh, who decided that they wanted to be associated with neither of

> **Landmine!** _____
>
> In 1992, after taking over the Nagorno-Karabakh region, Armenian rebels expelled all Azerbaijanis. In 1993, they captured the province of Kelbacar, looting and burning the capitals and most of the villages of these regions as they expelled the inhabitants from that area as well.

these countries, opting instead to create an independent state. Nevertheless, Armenia decided to go on the offensive. It sent in large numbers of troops and tanks to the disputed region and soon took control of it, as well as large parts of Azerbaijan. All-out war was the result.

In 1994, after more than 30,000 people had died and 1 million Azerbaijanis had been displaced by the violence, a truce was called. At the time, forces of both Armenia and the "Republic of Nargono-Karabakh" (a government unrecognized by anyone on the outside) occupied the disputed lands, as well as parts of Azerbaijan.

In 2001, even though nothing had changed in the conflict, the United States lifted a ban on aid to Azerbaijan that it had placed during the Nagorno-Karabakh conflict. Why was the ban finally lifted? Because Azerbaijan provided airspace and intelligence following the September 11 attacks on the United States.

Coincidentally, earlier that year, the United States sponsored talks between the parties in Florida and Paris. Nothing came of those talks. Armenia still controls the region, and the economies of both countries are severely damaged after years of war and changing economic trends.

Cyprus on the Verge of a Nervous Breakdown

To understand why Europe could be engulfed in a war over this tiny island, you need to appreciate that the vast majority of Cypriots are of Greek descent, whereas a significant minority are Turkish. If you add that the country was run by Britain for almost 100 years, you begin to see why it is a recipe for conflict.

Under the British, the Greek Cypriot population began to call for union with Greece and an end to British rule. To that end, in 1955, a Greek Cypriot separatist organization (EOKA), began a campaign of (you know it by heart now) terrorism. Tension and terror mounted, especially after British authorities deported the spokesman for the Greek Cypriots.

*Cyprus is too small
for continued division.*

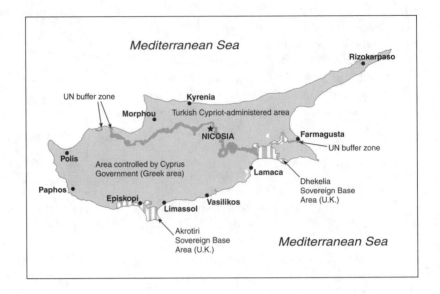

Of course, no conflict would be complete if there wasn't another side that wanted something totally different. The Turkish minority had their own ideas, namely, that the island should be partitioned. Under this plan, North Cyprus would house the Turks and South Cyprus would be Greek.

Negotiations in 1955 among Britain, Greece, and Turkey started, broke down, and went nowhere. In 1959 though, a settlement was finally reached after four arduous years of talks. The agreement provided for Cypriot independence from Britain, along with constitutional guarantees by the Greek Cypriot majority that were supposed to protect the Turkish Cypriot minority.

Reliable Sources

More than three quarters of the population in Cyprus are Greeks who belong to the Greek Orthodox Church. About 20 percent are Turkish Muslims.

But the best laid plans of mice and men often go awry. Cypriot Turks felt like second-class citizens in their own country and large-scale fighting between the Greeks and Turks erupted several times in the 1960s. The clashes got so bad that a U.N. peacekeeping force was sent in.

1974

The major event in this struggle occurred in 1974, when the president of Cyprus, Archbishop Mak-arios, was deposed in a coup orchestrated by Greek Cypriot army officers seeking to achieve union with Greece, and who were supported by Greece's then military government. Rioting and violence erupted throughout the island as a result, and five days later, Turkey sent in the troops. Claiming it was only there to protect the Turkish Cypriots, Turkey soon controlled about one third of Cyprus.

Of course, the Greek Cypriots saw this as an illegal occupation of their country. Nevertheless, the massive show of force by Turkey effectively partitioned the island. Turkish Cypriots occupied the northern third, whereas the Greek Cypriot community held the southern sector. 200,000 Greek Cypriots were displaced in the action. Under the U.N. cease-fire that followed, Turkey was permitted to retain its military forces in the areas it had captured.

In 1975, the island was legally partitioned into Greek and Turkish territories separated by a buffer zone mined and patrolled by U.N. peacekeepers. In 1983, the Turkish-held area declared itself the "Turkish Federated State of Cyprus," and eight years later, it declared its independence as the "Turkish Republic of Northern Cyprus." Unfortunately, the only country in the world that formally recognized it was Turkey.

Throughout the years that followed, successive attempts to resolve the literal and figurative division of Cyprus were met by successive failures. By the late 1990s, it was estimated that over half of the population of Turkish Cyprus consisted of settlers from Turkey. Turkey continued to keep 35,000 troops in the north.

In 2001, with still no resolution in sight, the U.N. Security Council renewed the United Nation's 36-year mission in Cyprus. Some 2,400 peacekeepers continued to patrol the buffer zone between Greek and Turkish Cypriots. Turkey has also warned that it is not averse to simply annexing the Turkish Cypriot part of the island.

> **⚠ CAUTION**
>
> **Landmine!**
>
> According to the BBC, "In 1964, the United Nations sent in peacekeeping troops to support British soldiers manning the so-called "Green Line," which had been set up to divide the warring Greek and Turkish Cypriot sectors in the Cyprus capital of Nicosia."

> **Peacekeepers**
>
> The Turkish north of the island is much poorer than the Greek south, and is politically isolated. It has been subject to U.N. sanctions and economic turmoil.

2001, a Cypriot Odyssey

But encouraging signs also emerged in 2001: Turkish Cypriot leader Rauf Denktas crossed to the south for the first time since the Turkish invasion of 1974 to dine with Greek Cypriot leader Glafkos Clerides. It was an unheard of, landmark event.

The dinner foreshadowed what could be real progress in the deadlock for the first time in 25 years. The impetus was, maybe not surprisingly, money. Both Cyprus and Turkey wanted to join the emerging European Union (EU). The Greek part of Cyprus (which is still called Cyprus) was expected to join the EU at the end of 2002.

Turkey, which also aspires to EU membership, seemed to realize that its chances would be much improved if the Cyprus issue could be resolved. Certainly, if Cyprus joins the EU as a divided island, with Turkey an occupying power, Turkey's prospects of EU membership would be damaged.

Another impetus moving the prospects for peace forward is that Turkish Cypriot leader, Rauf Denktash, who is due to retire in 2003 when he's 83, seemed eager to settle the dispute before he was out of office.

However, peace is never easy, and the problems these two sides face are numerous, including …

- The need for a power-sharing formula.
- Compensation for those who lost land in the division of the island.
- Recognition of injustices done toward each other before partition.
- Fear among the minority Turks that they will again be dominated by the Majority Greeks upon reunification.

Nevertheless, the December dinner created the sort of dramatic breakthrough that can make for great headway. Afterward, the Turkish Foreign Minister, Ismail Cem, remarked that the long-running dispute over the divided island of Cyprus might soon be resolved. Said Cem, "A mutually acceptable resolution should be achieved before the end of 2002. We have a new platform which has created improved conditions for mutual understanding."

The Least You Need to Know

- Basque Separatists in Spain are still at it.
- Armenia and Azerbaijan are still at it.
- Greeks and Turks in Cyprus might finally be over it.

Part 5

South America and Latin America

In South America, civil war is the name of the game. Columbia's civil war lasted more than 30 years. In Peru, although the Shining Path has been vanquished, the problems that lead to its emergence largely have not. Haiti has been wracked by corruption, Cuba has been ruled by a despot, and other countries in the region have their own problems as well.

Chapter 19

Colombia in Conflict

In This Chapter

- ◆ Colombia's history of conflict
- ◆ FARC emerges
- ◆ Drug money
- ◆ Peace talks

Colombia is a country of mixed blessings. One of the largest and most populous countries in South America, Colombia is also a major producer of gold, silver, emeralds, platinum, coal, and oil.

On the other hand, it also has a highly structured class-based society in which the rich families of Spanish descent have gotten demonstrably richer, whereas the indigenous peasants have clearly gotten poorer. This dichotomy has proven to be productive ground for leftist insurgents and guerillas who are funded largely with drug money. Moreover, at the other end of the political spectrum are right-wing paramilitary groups backed by the army and the police. All told, Colombia is a place with more conflict than any one country should have to endure.

Colombia: Maybe "just say no" might work.

A Conflicted History

In the sixteenth century, Spain began to colonize South America, and the settlement of Santa Fé de Bogotá, (subsequently known as Bogotá) became part of the Spanish colony of Peru.

In 1819, the great South American general Simón Bolíívar defeated the Spanish, and the Republic of Gran Colombia was formed from the countries that would later become Colombia, Ecuador, Panama, and Venezuela. After only 10 years in existence, Gran Colombia dissolved when Venezuela and Ecuador split off, eventually followed by Panama, leaving the present-day Colombia.

Reliable Resources

Simón Bolívar was born on July 24, 1783, in Caracas, Venezuela, and he inherited a fortune as a child after his parents died. He traveled extensively throughout Europe as a young man, and later went on to become one of South America's greatest generals. His heroics won independence for Bolivia, Panama, Colombia, Ecuador, Peru, and Venezuela. Bolívar is known as El Libérator (The Liberator) and the "George Washington of South America."

Colombian society has always been split in two—between liberals and conservatives, between the rich and poor, and between indigenous natives and Spanish immigrants. Later, more divisions would emerge—between the government and the rebels, between the drug trade and the police, and between the haves and the many have-nots. At times, these various divisions in the country would practically tear it apart.

The first evidence of that occurred between 1899 and 1903, during the so-called "War of the Thousand Days." It is believed that more than 120,000 people died in this civil war that pitted the right-wing monied class against the leftist poor.

Civil war again erupted 1948. This time, it is estimated that 250,000 to 300,000 were killed during the war. Although many contemporary news accounts label the ongoing Colombian conflict as beginning in the mid-1960s, the roots of Colombia's largest guerrilla group, the Revolutionary Armed Forces of Colombia (FARC), dates back to the peasant armed self-defense movements formed during this civil war: A period known as "La Violencia."

Resolution came in 1958 when the Conservative party and the Liberal party agreed to form a single party—the National Front. In a move that would portend ill for all Colombia, all other political parties were banned. The agreement concentrated control of the state apparatus and bureaucracies in the hands of elites, and prevented the expression of alternative political projects.

The result was that Colombia became a breeding ground for rebels fighting against the powers that be. Their fight would last into the next millennium.

Guerrilla War

Colombia is in the middle of a deadly, decades-long civil war. The conflict pits the Colombian government against both a well-armed, dangerous, violent guerrilla organizations and similarly dangerous, brutal, as well as growing paramilitary forces.

The Guerillas

A 40-year insurgent campaign to overthrow the Colombian Government escalated during the 1990s because of increased funds from the drug trade. Although the violence is deadly and widespread, the movement lacks the overall armed strength and popular support necessary to overthrow the government. However, its support is not insignificant. Accordingly, the insurgency is a major issue in Colombia.

Landmine!

In 2001, Human Rights Watch decried abuses by Colombian guerillas that included killings of civilians, hostage taking, the use of child soldiers, grossly unfair trials, the "cruel and inhumane" treatment of captured combatants, the forced displacement of civilians, and the use of prohibited weapons, including gas cylinder bombs.

As indicated, the roots of the guerrilla movement go back to the civil war of the 1950s, but the emergence of actual insurgent guerilla groups occurred in the mid-1960s, when it was far too evident that Colombia had become a country marked by intense class divisions. The few in the stratified upper classes controlled the country's wealth, power, and resources. There was no middle class. So, the masses of people below increasingly lived in hunger and squalor—a recipe, as we have seen repeatedly, for rebellion.

In 1965, the first of these groups, the Leftist National Liberation Army (ELN) was formed, and the Maoist People's Liberation Army (EPL) soon followed in its footsteps. But, it was the last group that would become the main player in Colombia's long guerrilla war—the Revolutionary Armed Forces of Colombia, FARC.

Over the past 40 years, FARC has grown into a powerful, well-financed military organization. Although much of this growth has been funded by illicit drug money, there is support for FARC among the peasants because of the lack of government response to the hardships faced by peasant farmers. FARC generally lacks any significant support among Colombia's middle class.

FARC's Beginnings

During the first years of FARC, the guerrillas concentrated on expanding their narrow base. The founders of FARC followed the political lead of the Colombian Communist Party and even by the late 1970s, FARC was a marginal guerrilla force.

Peacekeepers

Bogotá is one of South America's fastest-growing areas. After 1940, large numbers of rural Colombians migrated to Bogotá in search of greater economic opportunities, and the population rapidly grew. It currently stands at more than six million.

However, FARC grew and became bolder in the late 1970s as the army failed to subdue them. This was evidenced best in 1980, when FARC took and occupied the Dominican embassy in Bogotá for 61 days, holding many foreign diplomats as hostages. By the end of the siege, 100 were dead, including the president of the Colombian Supreme Court and 10 other justices.

Nourished by the ever-increasing lack of political and economic opportunity for the working class, FARC had now become "the people's army."

FARC Gets Serious

In the 1980s and 1990s the guerillas became more violent as a means to achieve their ends. Kidnapping and extortion became far more commonplace, and in fact became a significant source of revenue as FARC targeted politicians and rich executives.

Despite its violence against the system (or maybe because of it), FARC continued to gain support in some regions of the country. Armed with the ability to control some territory, maintain a presence in others, as well as its ability to exploit rural unemployment, the group has been able to establish legitimacy and support in various regions of the country.

The growth of the insurgency was in do doubt also in part because of the Colombian government's inability, or unwillingness, to deal with the myriad of problems in the countryside. Combined with its tacit, if not express, approval of the growing, ruthless rightwing paramilitary groups, the government is largely seen as being equally responsible for the tremendous loss of human lives, possessions, security, and the integrity of the country.

So, although the guerrillas' military growth is at least partially because of their increased ability to generate revenues through drugs, extortion, and kidnapping, it is equally true that they have grown because of their ability to take advantage of cracks in a highly decayed political system that neglects socio-economic needs of the poor.

The Paramilitaries

In response to the leftists insurgents, rightwing paramilitary groups, supported by the government and the ruling classes, also emerged in the 1980s. They wage war not only against the guerrillas, but also anyone suspected of being a guerrilla sympathizer, such as union members, peasant organizers, human rights workers, and religious activists.

Some paramilitary groups now even extended the parameters of the war against the guerrillas to include drug addicts, alcoholics, prostitutes, petty criminals, and the homeless. These paramilitary groups have been accused of gross human rights violations, including rape, murder, and dismemberment.

CAUTION   Landmine!

In 2001, some 300 armed men belonging to the paramilitary Peasant Self-Defense Force of Córdoba and Urabá spent two days violating residents in every way imaginable. Witnesses told investigators that they tied one six-year-old girl to a pole and suffocated her with a plastic bag. Another woman was reportedly gang-raped. Authorities later confirmed 36 dead. Thirty other villagers were missing. "To them, it was like a big party," a survivor told *The New York Times*. "They drank and danced and cheered as they butchered us like hogs."

According to Human Rights Watch, the Colombian military and police actually work with, support, profit from, and tolerate these paramilitary groups, treating them as a force allied to and compatible with their own. The relationship is so intertwined that

- The army and the paramilitaries communicate with one another via radios, cellular telephones, and beepers.
- They share intelligence, including the names of suspected guerrilla collaborators.
- They share fighters, including paramilitary commanders.
- They share vehicles, including army trucks used to transport paramilitary fighters.
- They coordinate offenses together.

As a result, according to Human Rights Watch, 35,000 people have been killed in the fighting during the past two decades, and "most of them have been poor civilians accused by the Colombian Army or right-wing paramilitaries of collaborating with left-wing guerrillas." Moreover, Colombia has the highest murder rate, per capita, in the world.

Drugs and Money

What complicates matters in Colombia, what makes it different from other places where conflict thrives, are the vast sums of money that come from the drug trade. Drug money influences everything, and has the potential to corrupt anything is in its path. As such, rebels have more money than their counterparts in other countries, the government has more money to fight them, and the stakes are correspondingly much higher.

> ### Reliable Resources
>
> February 5, 1996 (*Time*): "In the 18 months since he became President, Ernesto Samper Pizano has dodged bullet after political bullet, each carrying accusations that his 1994 election campaign received millions of dollars in contributions from the Cali cocaine cartel. He has responded that if drug funds were accepted, it was without his knowledge. But last week the President's evasions were firmly contradicted: a former close associate charged that Samper was indeed aware of the cartel connection."

The War on Drugs

During the late 1970s and early 1980s, the growing contraband export of marijuana and cocaine became a major source of income for the Colombian economy. Not only did the government begin to get proceeds from illicit drug sales, but so did the leftist insurgents and the paramilitaries. Everyone in the country began to drink from the drug teat.

Enter the United States, deciding that Colombia needed to wean itself from its mother's milk. In 1980, after the election of Ronald Reagan, the United States began its War on Drugs. In an attempt to stamp out growing drug use at home and increased production abroad, the Americans began to fund this "war" to the tune of hundreds of millions of dollars. One of the first to receive this largesse was the Colombian government.

In 1984, the Colombian government, aided by the Americans, launched a crackdown on drug trafficking, but it was largely unsuccessful. Drug trafficking continued, and the leftist guerrillas remained. The anti-drug crackdown lost momentum as the drug traffickers and rebels joined forces in some regions.

Part of the problem for Colombia is that the American money goes to support one of the most repressive governments in the hemisphere. The regime then uses this money to crack down on anyone affiliated with the drug trade, including popular leftist guerillas and the poor peasants themselves, who often grow cocoa because it is the only crop that brings in real money. Although the crackdowns might eradicate a bit of the cocaine production, it simultaneously helps to foster more left-wing sentiments and rebellion.

The Medellin Drug Cartel

By the mid-1970s, it had become apparent to American law enforcement that a well-organized effort was exporting illegal drugs into the United States from abroad. Trafficking networks inside the United States, organized from Colombia, were discovered. These networks sold drugs, created and ran stash houses, laundered money, developed distribution networks, and killed their enemies.

The first to dominate this illicit market trade were organized criminal groups headquartered in Medellin, Colombia. The Medellin drug cartel ruled the early drug trade in Colombia.

This network began when Carlos Lehder conceived of the idea of smuggling cocaine into the United States the same way marijuana was smuggled. Specifically, Lehder decided that, rather than hiding small amounts of cocaine in luggage or on airline passengers, large quantities of coke could be put on small, private aircraft and flown into the United States.

To this end, Lehder bought a sizable portion of a Bahamian island about 225 miles southeast of Miami. On this small island, he built an extended airstrip as a refueling stop for the light planes that would be transporting his cocaine to his secret airstrips in the United States.

> **Reliable Resources**
>
> 1998, the U.S. Congress allocated $290 million in anti-drug aid to Colombia to be spent over the next three years. The huge majority of this aid was geared toward purchasing helicopters and weaponry for military and police use in coca eradication projects. Only $45 million of the aid was earmarked for crop substitution programs.

Peacekeepers

Although Lehder was sentenced to 135 years in federal prison, he soon cooperated in the U.S. investigation of Panama dictator Manuel Noriega and received a reduced sentence in return.

Willing to use whatever means necessary to achieve his ends, Lehder was the first in what would be a long line of violent criminals from Medellin. In 1984, he was involved in the assassination of Colombia's Justice Minister, Rodrigo Lara Bonilla. Outraged by the terrorist tactics employed by the Medellin organization, the Colombian Government turned Lehder over to the U.S. Drug Enforcement Agency and extradited him to the United States in February 1987.

Besides Lehder, the infamous Pablo Escobar also ran the Medellin cocaine cartel. Under Escobar, Medellin became the most dangerous city on Earth. Using bribery, intimidation, and murder to get his way, Escobar created an equally ruthless organization. Informants were bombed, planes were blown up, and bounties were put on the lives of police officers. As many as 2,000 police officers and civilians were murdered each year during the 1990s in Medellin.

In 1992, he escaped from prison and for the next 17 months was the target of the largest manhunt in Colombian history. Finally, in December 1993, Escobar was killed in a firefight with the police at a private residence in downtown Medellin.

The Cali Mafias

With the elimination of most of the major figures in the Medellin groups, drug-trafficking groups in Cali, Colombia, came to the fore. Unlike their predecessors, the members of the Cali cartel avoided obvious acts of violence, instead trying to pass themselves off as legitimate businessmen.

Reliable Resources

According to Bartleby, "Most of the world's coca is grown in Peru, Bolivia, and Colombia. For the farmers, it is a well-paying crop. They harvest and dry the leaves, which are then processed into coca paste. Cocaine base is extracted from the paste in laboratories. Further processing continues, where the white powder, cocaine hydrochloride, is produced for export. Once in the United States, the cocaine is diluted with ingredients such as lactose, and it is sold or further processed into crack."

During the early 1990s, members of the Cali drug cartel generated billions of dollars in drug revenues per year operating sophisticated drug trafficking enterprises.

In the 1986 elections, Virgilio Barco Vargas became president of Columbia. Barco vowed to combat the drug cartels. In August of 1989, the government arrested more than 10,000 people and confiscated the property of suspected drug traffickers. However, despite numerous successes in intercepting cocaine shipments and the chemicals used to refine the drug, the drug trade remained strong; demand creating supply and all that.

Eventually however, the combined efforts of the *DEA* and the Colombia authorities paid off when, in June 1995, the Cali mafia began to disintegrate. That summer, five leaders of the Cali mafia were arrested, and by September 1996, the remaining kingpins had been captured.

> **Diplomatic Dialogue**
>
> The **DEA,** or Drug Enforcement Agency, is a unit of the U. S. government that is charged with enforcing drug laws and eradicating illegal drugs. Since 1973, the DEA has grown significantly, especially during the last several years. The DEA has more than 4,000 agents, and its budget is roughly $1.5 billion.

The Drug Trade Today

Since then, the drug trade has become more decentralized. Power is now passing to new traffickers. By working with their associates in Mexico, the Columbia drug traffickers remain responsible for most of the world's cocaine production and wholesale distribution.

Peace Efforts

In June 1994, Ernesto Samper Pizano was elected president of Colombia. Like Barco before him, Samper too wanted to try and create peace for his country by dealing with the guerillas. FARC and ELN were invited to the peace table, and they accepted that offer. The talks were aimed at the disarmament of, and legislative representation for, the guerrillas.

Breakdown

Despite that hopeful beginning, Colombia entered a political crisis in 1995 after Samper was accused of accepting almost $6 million in campaign contributions from drug traffickers in exchange for leniency. In the meantime, the talks broke down.

Samper's government encountered many difficulties controlling the armed factions within Colombia, and the nation's military was unable to contain the violence.

> **Landmine!**
>
> According to the *Denver Post,* "Colombia is the world's largest processor of cocaine. It supplies about 90 percent of the cocaine in the United States and the great majority of cocaine to other international drug markets. Its latest export is heroin, having increased its production by 25 percent in the past few years."

> **Reliable Resources**
>
> Andrés Pastrana is the son of a former Colombian president. He has a law degree and was a fellow at the Center for International Affairs at Harvard.

Thus, in 1997, leftist guerrillas launched a campaign of violence and intimidation aimed at preventing voters from participating in municipal and regional elections, and paramilitary squads launched a counter campaign of violence, raiding a number of villages and executing individuals suspected of supporting guerrilla activities.

However, prospects of a peaceful settlement to the protracted violence improved in 1998 when, in June, Colombian voters elected Andrés Pastrana as Colombia's new president. Following the election, FARC, ELN, and the United Self-Defense Units of Colombia, a leading right-wing paramilitary organization, all announced their willingness to engage in peace talks with the new government.

Peace Talks

Talks between the Pastrana government and FARC officially opened in January 1999. In October of that year, they signed the "San Francisco Agreement," committing themselves to negotiate a cease-fire. A safe haven for the guerillas, which had been given to them as part of the peace negotiations in 1998, was extended until 2002.

However, peace proved elusive. Both sides walked out and came back to the table several times. The talks struggled on. Cease-fires were followed by ultimatums, which were followed by retractions and declarations. President Pastrana then told the rebels that they had to come up with a viable peace offer or vacate the safe haven (an area twice the size of New Jersey).

FARC's plan was deemed unacceptable, and the long, bloody war—a war marked by civilian death, disappearance, and destruction—was on again.

The Least You Need to Know

- FARC has waged a decades-long struggle.
- Drugs provide money for all sides.
- The War on Drugs hurts the neediest in Colombia.
- Peace talks have led nowhere.

Chapter 20

Hatred in Haiti

In This Chapter

- A brief history of Haiti
- The reign of the Duvaliers
- The coming of Jean-Bertrand Aristide
- The song that never ends

Haiti is a country that has been shattered by conflict, violence, and dictatorship, leaving it among the poorest country in the Americas.

As a result, Haiti is a country deeply divided. It has a huge wealth gap between the black majority and the mulatto minority (one percent of whom own nearly half the country's wealth). Haiti has the hemisphere's lowest per capita income as well as the highest mortality rate. Furthermore, the country's infrastructure is dilapidated, and drug trafficking has corrupted much of the government.

Haiti deserves better.

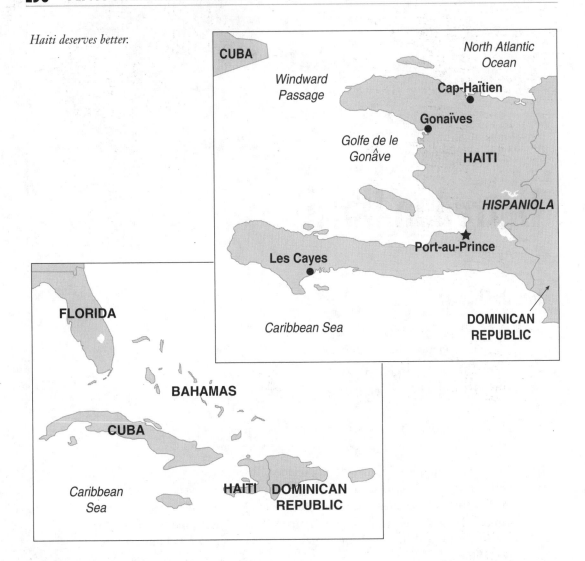

Haiti's History

Haiti is a lush, beautiful, mountainous country with a warm, tropical climate. Its location, history, and culture (epitomized by its traditional music, drumming, and dancing), once made Haiti a desired tourist destination. But the political repression and violence that took root in the last half of the twentieth century killed any desire for people to visit the country.

Land Ho!

Six months after setting sail from Portugal, on Christmas Eve, 1492, Christopher Columbus and the *Santa Maria* ran into a coral reef off the coast of Haiti and sank.

Columbus, helped by local Indians, removed the supplies, dismantled the ships timbers, and proceeded to name the island Hispaniola, or "Little Spain."

In 1496, the Spanish established the first European settlement in the western hemisphere at Santo Domingo (now capital of the Dominican Republic). Europeans would thereafter dominate the Caribbean for the next 300 years.

Spain's dominance in the Caribbean began to wane when Sir Francis Drake of England attacked the Spanish Armada in Hispaniola in 1586. Although Drake failed to secure the island, his raid was part of a pattern of encroachment that gradually diluted Spanish dominance. By the late 1600s, Spain was ready to relinquish control of its colony to the emerging French presence.

The Slave Trade

Many present-day Haitians are slave descendents. The first ever slaves were stolen from Africa and sent to the Americas in the sixteenth century. The slave trade slowly grew, but by the middle of the 1600s, African slave labor had become an economic lynchpin for both the colonists and the colonies. In the Caribbean, these slaves were used mostly for sugar production.

In 1791, Haitian slaves began a revolt against their inhumane lives. An uprising in the French West Indian colony of Santo Domingo helped to create what was probably Haiti's first guerrilla leader as a former black slave named Toussaint Louverture led the resistance movement. In 1801, Louverture attacked the French in Hispaniola, defeated them, conquered the island, abolished slavery, and proclaimed himself governor-general of an autonomous government.

On January 1, 1804, the region declared itself a free and independent country. The name of the new Republic, "Haiti," comes from the Creole word, "Ayiti" which is the name given to the land by the indigenous people who live there. It means "mountainous country."

Big Brother

Conflict in Haiti today comes from three places. First, there is the disparity between elite French mulatto aristocracy and poor black majority. Second, there is the subjugation of the population by the oft-oppressive military. Finally, because of its proximity to the United States, Haiti has often come under the large thumb of the Americans.

Accordingly, and not for the last time, the United States invaded Haiti in 1915 in order to protect America's economic interests that the Americans thought had become threatened by increasing black-mulatto friction. The United States stayed in Haiti until 1934, but maintained economic control over the country until almost 1950.

The Duvalier Era: 1957–1986

After a string of military juntas ruled the country, elections were arranged for 1957. The black candidate was a medical doctor who had served as a rural administrator before entering politics. François Duvalier seemed to most to be an honest leader without either a strong ideological motivation or program. They were wrong.

> ### Reliable Resources
>
> Voodoo is the major religion of Haiti. It is taken seriously by young and old, rich and poor alike. In voodoo, there are three important categories of other spiritual beings: lwa (spirits), the twins (forces of contradiction: good and evil, happy and sad, and so on), and the dead (souls of one's own family members). Voodoo doctors heal with herbs and faith healing (with the help of lwa and other spirits).

Duvalier's only opponent was the scion of a prominent family. As a result, Duvalier scored a significant victory at the polls. His followers took two thirds of the legislature's lower house and all the seats in the Haitian Senate.

Papa Doc

In 1961, Duvalier, or "Papa Doc" as he was known, replaced the bicameral legislature with a unicameral one. Despite a 1957 prohibition against presidential re-election, Duvalier ran for office again that year and won with an official tally of 1,320,748 votes to zero!

Apparently, winning by so wide a margin was not enough for Papa Doc. In 1964 he declared himself "president for life." His regime, which would become the longest in Haiti's history, was a brutal reign of terror and incompetence:

- ◆ Political opponents were summarily executed.

- ◆ The population was kept in a state of fear by Duvalier's notorious paramilitary organization, the Tonton Macoutes.

- ◆ The economy of Haiti deteriorated steadily.

- ◆ The illiteracy rate remained at about 90 percent.

> **CAUTION**
>
> **Landmine!** _____
>
> Duvalier had a personal police force called the Tonton Macoutes. Responsible only to Duvalier, they were given license to torture, kill, and extort.

Yet, although his rule was marked by political repression, Duvalier was often a popular leader. One reason for this was that his medical experiences in the countryside helped him understand the everyday concerns of the people, including their inclination toward paternalistic authority. In fact, it is that attitude that caused his patients to refer to him as "Papa Doc": A nickname he loved. What Duvalier especially understood was the central role voodoo played in the lives of the black majority population.

Duvalier was rumored to be a houngan, a voodoo sorcerer. In fact, he recruited such sorcerers and incorporated them into the Tonton Macoutes. His public acceptance of voodoo and its practitioners, as well as his reputed practice of magic and sorcery, helped to enhance his popularity and legitimized his otherwise repugnant reign.

Duvalier's rule was marked by terror—an estimated 30,000 Haitians were killed for political reasons during his tenure. Duvalier's unrivaled authority led to the megalomaniacal conviction that he was, in his words, the "personification of the Haitian fatherland." Fittingly, at the time of his death in 1971, François Duvalier designated his son, Jean-Claude Duvalier, as Haiti's new supreme leader.

Baby Doc

And so it was that Jean-Claude Duvalier, at age 19, was proclaimed "president for life." But Baby Doc, as he came to be known, cared little for politics, leaving the day-to-day machinations to his father's old cronies, a group known as "the dinosaurs."

What seemed to interest Baby Doc far more than politics was money. Much of his wealth, which

> **Peacekeepers** _____
>
> Although the moniker "president for life" might seem a bit egocentric, in Haiti, no one thought much of it. Each of the previous seven rulers before the Duvaliers also dubbed themselves "president for life."

amounted to hundreds of millions of dollars, came from the Haitian Tobacco Administration. Baby Doc used this agency as his own, private tobacco monopoly. Later, he expanded it to include proceeds from other government enterprises, creating, in effect, a government-sponsored slush fund. Already minimal, public services deteriorated as Jean-Claude and his gang misappropriated millions of dollars from the national treasury.

In 1980, Jean-Claude married a mulatto woman, causing great consternation in the country. One reason his father ruled for as long as he did was because of his support of the black lower and middle classes and his opposition to the established mulatto elite, endearing Papa Doc to the Haitian black majority. But by marrying a mulatto, Jean-Claude appeared to be abandoning this bond. The fact that the wedding cost a reported $3 million didn't help either.

A growing, seeping discontent with Baby Doc came to the fore in 1983 when Pope John Paul II visited Haiti. The Pontiff declared that "Something must change here," and called for …

- More equitable distribution of income.
- A more egalitarian social structure.
- More concern for the well-being of the masses.
- More popular participation in public life.

The Pope's words galvanized the public and contributed to increased mobilization among the masses. Indeed, Baby Doc's kleptocracy was so enormous that, even in this poorest of nations, his drain on the national treasury was felt throughout the country. The economy was in shambles, public health was in crisis, and Baby Doc fiddled.

> **Landmine!**
>
> Why do other countries hate the United States? Consider this example: African Swine Fever (ASF) is a highly contagious and fatal disease. ASF plagued pigs in the Dominican Republic in mid-1978. The United States, fearing that the disease would spread to North America, pressured the Duvalier government to slaughter all of Haiti's black pigs and to replace them with ones supplied by the United States. The Haitian government complied, but in doing so, failed to understand that black Haitian pigs were not only a form of "savings account" for peasants because they could easily be sold for cash, but they were also exceptionally well-suited to rural Haitian environment. The replacement pigs were not.

The first real revolt began in the city of Gonaïves in 1985, when street demonstrators made raids on food-distribution warehouses. By 1986, protests had spread to six other cities. Duvalier then cut food prices by 10 percent, shut down radio stations, and ordered a crackdown by police and army units. However, these moves failed to end the popular uprising. Jean-Claude's wife and advisers, wanting to keep their profitable grip on power, urged him to put down the rebellion at all costs. He did.

But in 1986, with even more mass protests erupting throughout the country, the army decided that it was finally time for the Duvaliers to go. Military conspirators demanded their departure. Left with no bases of support, Jean-Claude and Michele Duvalier departed from Haiti on February 7, 1986, for France. They left behind a country economically ravaged, bereft of functional political institutions, and devoid of self-rule.

In 1988, Leslie Manigat became president, but was soon ousted in a coup led by Brigadier-General Prosper Avril, who installed a civilian government under military control. Elections were called again in 1990.

Election Time

Jean-Bertrand Aristide was born in poverty and raised in a religious atmosphere. At 16, he entered the seminary in Port-au-Prince. He did advanced studies abroad in the Dominican Republic, Great Britain, Canada, Rome, and Jerusalem, and in 1982 he was ordained in the Roman Catholic Church as a member of the Salesian Fathers.

In 1985, Father Aristide was back in Haiti and rose to national prominence through the broadcasts of his sermons on the Catholic station, Radio Soleil. Outraged by what had become of his homeland, Aristide became an outspoken critic of the Duvalier regime. At one startling, defiant mass, Aristide called for change in the country and bluntly criticized the dictatorship of Jean-Claude Duvalier. This mass by Aristide is often cited as one of the sparks that set off the popular uprising and demonstrations that led to the ouster of Duvalier a year later.

After Duvalier's departure in 1986, Aristide led a march in memory of the thousands of Haitians who had lost their lives there under Duvalier. The Haitian military then opened fire on the crowd; Aristide bravely continued his live broadcast during the massacre, reaffirming his reputation as a courageous opponent of the corrupt regime.

Peacekeepers

The San Juan Bosco Organization, directed by Salesian Father Laurent Bohnen in Port au Prince, Haiti, was created in 1954. Father Bohnen began with a one-classroom school. He later added a cafeteria for the students to whom he gave beans, rice, and a sandwich every day. His is now considered "the largest cafeteria in the world," having served more than 70 million meals in 40 years.

These sorts of actions earned Aristide the lasting enmity of the army, police, and Tontons Macoutes. In 1988, his church, St. John Bosco, was destroyed by arson.

Jean-Bertrand Aristide, however, clearly was a man who was not easily distracted. In 1990, Haiti prepared for new presidential elections. When Aristide announced his candidacy that fall, it electrified the country. After a six-week campaign Aristde won, garnering an astounding 67 percent of the vote. He took office in February 1991.

His government began the difficult tasks of cleaning out a corrupt civil service, enforcing tax laws, fighting drug trafficking, and delivering much-needed services. For the first time in a long time, Haiti lived in relative security, with military violence and criminal activity declining. Human rights organizations reported a drop in violations, and the flow of refugees ended. The international community applauded the reforms and pledged funds to the new government.

The Predictable Coup

All of this ended on September 30, 1991, when the Haitian military violently overthrew the Aristide government after only seven months in office. Aristide was forced into exile, first to Venezuela, and then to America.

From October 1991 to June 1992, Joseph Nerette led an unconstitutional regime, and the Haitian military unleashed a horrific campaign of violence, killing more than 5,000 Haitians over three years and forcing tens of thousands to flee their homeland by boat.

By this time, Haiti's problems had made it onto the international radar screen, and over-throwing a legitimate, popularly elected president was not something the international community takes lightly. In June 1993, the United Nations imposed an oil and arms embargo on Haiti. This eventually had the effect of forcing the Haitian military to the negotiating table.

In 1993, a U.N.–brokered agreement established a process for the restoration of both Aristide and constitutional government in Haiti.

But once again, the Haitian military had other ideas. In order to retain power, the military undertook a campaign of repression and assassination, torture and rape.

As a result, tens of thousands of Haitians began to flee the country. Many attempted to sail into American territorial waters and enter the United States. These so-called "boat people" became both a political and social crisis.

The United Nations and the United States had seen enough. On July 31, 1994, the United Nations adopted a resolution that authorized member states to use "all necessary means" to restore constitutional rule to Haiti, as well as the return of Jean Bertrand Aristide.

Operation Restore Democracy

The United States thereafter took the lead in carrying out the U.N. mandate. "Operation Restore Democracy" would foster democracy and reduce the flow of illegal immigrants.

> **Peacekeepers**
>
> According to the United States State Department, "Between 1945 and 1988, there were 13 U.N. peacekeeping operations, limited mostly to the Middle East and aimed at discouraging the renewal of conflict after a cease-fire between hostile states. Most other proposals for U.N. peacekeeping action ran into Soviet veto power, severely limiting the number of potential U.N. peacekeeping operations." However, after the fall of communism, there were some 26 new and separate peace operations authorized and commanded by the United Nations between 1988 and 1995.

An invasion involving almost 4,000 U.S. army paratroopers was readied. With U.S. troops prepared to immediately enter Haiti, President Clinton dispatched a negotiating team led by former President Jimmy Carter (and including a civilian Colin Powell, retired from the Pentagon) to tell the Haitian leadership that it was time for them to go. In the face of this massive, imminent U.S. invasion, the negotiations proved successful, and the military in Haiti relinquished control of the government. U.S. forces landed unopposed.

Operation Restore Democracy then set about paving the way for the return of civilian rule to Haiti. Its mission was to …

- ◆ Restore democracy.
- ◆ Return Aristide to power.
- ◆ Ensure security.
- ◆ Assist with the rehabilitation of civil administration.
- ◆ Train a police force and judiciary.
- ◆ Help prepare for new elections.

The mission succeeded. Democratically elected government was restored, and emigration was greatly reduced. On March 31, 1995, peacekeeping responsibilities were transferred to the United Nations.

The Return of Aristide

On October 15, 1994, President Aristide victoriously returned to Haiti, where he completed his presidential term. One of his first acts was to dismantle the worst parts of the Haitian military. His government also created Haiti's first civilian police force.

With the support of the United Nations, legislative elections were held in 1996. Because he was constitutionally barred from running in successive elections, Aristide watched as Haiti witnessed its first peaceful transition from one democratically elected president to the next.

In 2000, Aristide could legally run again, and he did. Although there were some charges of voter fraud, Aristide won another resounding victory.

Postscript: Tuesday, 18 December, 2001 (BBC), "Armed commandos stormed Haiti's National Palace on Monday, taking over radio communications and killing at least five people before the building was recaptured by police.

The attackers, reported to be former members of the Haitian military, were pushed back in an intense exchange of gunfire by security guards at the palace, which is President Jean-Bertrand Aristide's official residence.

Pro-Aristide protesters erected barricades of burning tires to block off main roads and set fire to the headquarters of the Democratic Convergence opposition alliance in retaliation.

At least five people died, including two policemen. "We have defeated the coup, but it is not over yet," Aristide said after returning to the palace.

The Least You Need to Know

- Haiti is mired in poverty and corruption.
- The Duvaliers ruined the country.
- Aristide tried to restore democracy.
- The military is loath to give up power.

Chapter 21

More Latin and South American Standoffs

In This Chapter

◆ Crises in Cuba

◆ Peruvian guerrillas

◆ Coups in Ecuador and Paraguay

During most of the Cold War, Central and South America were pawns in the superpower struggles. The Soviet Union poured guns and money into America's backyard in an effort to destabilize the region and the United States responded by doing the same for mostly right-wing dictatorships. The result was a virtual standoff.

A by-product of those efforts was that the region had far too many weapons readily available for any would-be rebel. Insurgencies abounded.

South America struggles with insurgencies.

Castro's Cuba

The most obvious example of Cold War conflict in the Americas is Cuba. What was once a thriving resort destination became the focal point of international intrigue, and practically the cause of global thermonuclear war.

Rebel Yell

Cuba has always been a place where revolution has thrived. In 1933, an uprising known as the "Revolt of the Sergeants," led by Fulgencio Batista, took over the country. The new revolutionary government, although it lasted but 100 days, engineered lasting and radical changes in Cuba:

◆ It created the 8-hour workday.

◆ It established a Department of Labor.

♦ It opened the university to the poor.

♦ It granted peasants the right to the land they farmed.

♦ It gave women the right to vote.

♦ It reduced the electric rates by 40 percent.

One of President Franklin Roosevelt's advisors, Sumner Wells, called these changes "communistic" and "irresponsible," and the U.S. government refused to recognize the new government. But one person who liked the new Cuban government was mobster Meyer Lansky, who met with Fulgencio Batista and forged a friendship and business relationship that would last three decades.

> **Reliable Resources**
>
> In 1946, famed mobster Lucky Luciano called a summit in Havana. Attendees at the Hotel Nacional meeting included the who's who of mobsters—Meyer Lansky, Frank Costello, Tommy Lucchese, Vito Genovese, Joe Bonanno, Santo Trafficante Jr., and Moe Dalitz. Among the topics discussed was the assassination of fellow gangster Bugsy Siegel. Coincidentally, Frank Sinatra made his singing debut in Havana that year.

In 1938, Batista legalized the Cuban Communist Party, and the country adopted a new constitution in 1940. The document protected individual and social rights, supported full employment and a minimum wage, extended social security, called for equal pay for equal work, and outlawed the huge plantations known as *latifundias*.

Fidel Castro

In 1953, rebel leader Fidel Castro led a revolt in which 100 men and women attacked the Moncada army barracks near Santiago de Cuba. The attack was a failure: Castro was arrested and sentenced to 15 years in prison. Two years later, the government called for a general amnesty, and Castro was released. However, revolution was now in Cuba's blood, and Castro was its new leader.

Four years later, on January 1, 1959, Castro's revolutionary forces took control of Havana. Che Guevara and Camilo Cienfuegos led the rebels into the capital, and Fidel Castro arrived about a week later. One of the first acts of the new Cuban government was to reinstate the Constitution of 1940, which had been suspended by General Batista in 1952.

Originally, Castro was not a communist, but circumstances forced him into the Soviet camp.

> **Reliable Resources**
>
> On December 10, 1959, the Hotel Riviera opened in Havana. It cost $14 million, and most of the money was supplied by the Cuban government to its American owner Meyer Lansky. The floorshow in the Copa Room was headlined by Ginger Rogers. On opening night, Lansky complained that Rogers "can wiggle her ass, but she can't sing a goddamn note."

Diplomatic Dialogue

A **trade embargo** is a prohibition by a government on certain or all trade with a foreign nation. By preventing both imports and exports with that country, an embargo can sometimes be an effective way to punish one's enemies.

After the revolution, Cubans with money were afraid of being able to keep their holdings and defected mostly to the United States. This in turn caused a drain on an already poor economy. Castro went to the United States for economic aide. He was turned down. So, in order to keep what assets remained in the country, Castro decided to nationalize some of Cuba's businesses, and in the process some U.S. businesses were taken over. The United States suddenly became anti-Castro.

Castro then did the logical thing—he met with Soviet foreign minister Anasta Mikoyan and secured a $100 million loan. The Soviets, happy to have a beachhead practically in the United States, became Castro's benefactor. And that is how it came to be that Castro's regime became a communist one. The United States followed this by imposing a *trade embargo* on Cuba, and the stage was set for conflict.

Cuba and the United States

From 1960 on, the United States and Cuba engaged in a prolonged, drawn-out, multi-faceted conflict. Amer-ica was threatened by the communist presence a mere 90 miles from its border, and Cuba was afraid of its huge neighbor to the north. The result was a relationship that careened from invasion to embargo to near irrelevance.

The first confrontation, as mentioned in Chapter 16, was the Bay of Pigs. The disastrous failed invasion set the stage for many problems between the United States, Cuba, and the Soviet Union. Certainly the Cuban Missile Crisis can be traced to the failed Bay of Pigs invasion and the subsequent increased Soviet military support for Castro. Similarly, around the globe, U.S. prestige was hit hard, and the glow quickly came off the Kennedy administration. Kennedy's first foray into foreign affairs was an unmitigated disaster.

Peacekeepers

The CIA tried to get rid of Castro for years. It tried to kill him using poisoned pens, fatal bacteria, and deadly capsules. It also tried to embarrass him by putting a powder in his shoe that was supposed to make his beard fall out. It's surprising that they didn't slip him an exploding cigar!

Of course, the next confrontation was the nuclear missile crisis. On October 16, 1962, John F. Kennedy called a secret meeting of his closest advisors at the White House. Late the night before, the CIA had produced detailed photos identifying Soviet nuclear missile installations being constructed on Cuba.

After 13 tense days, the crisis was resolved, but not before an already bad relationship had grown much worse. After the missile crisis, Cuba became a constant problem and threat to America. Never big enough to fret over too much, but always strategic enough to be concerned about, Cuba remained a problem for every U.S. president thereafter.

Throughout the 1970s, the relationship played itself out both near and far. Locally, Cuba provided support for rebel movements throughout Latin America. And outside the Western hemisphere, it participated in a number of extracurricular activities.

For example, in 1978, at the request of the Ethiopian government, thousands of Cuban troops—supported and led by Soviet and East German officers—helped repel a Somali invasion of Ethiopia. In response, U.S. Secretary of State Cyrus Vance stated that he could not foresee the normalization of relations with Cuba because of the presence of Cuban troops in Africa.

Tensions increased in the 1980s under conservative, anticommunist President Ronald Reagan. Reagan instituted the most hostile policy against Cuba since the Bay of Pigs. Despite conciliatory signals from Cuba, the new U.S. administration …

- Announced a tightening of the embargo.
- Began four weeks of exercises in the Caribbean, with the stated intent of "sending a message to Cuba."
- Reinstituted a travel ban.
- Prohibited U.S. citizens from spending money in Cuba.
- Allowed a 1977 fishing accord to lapse.

> **Landmine!**
>
> In 1985, Radio Martí, backed by Reagan Republicans and Cuban hard-liners, began to broadcast news, information, and anti-Castro propaganda from the United States to Cuba. In 1990, TV Martí, an anti-Castro, U.S.–taxpayer funded station was also launched. The signal was jammed by the Cuban government.

The Fall of Communism

The fall of communism throughout most of the globe in the late 1980s had a profound impact on Cuba. Without its Soviet sponsor, Cuba's economy faltered markedly, and its ability to intervene elsewhere declined correspondingly. In 1991, all Soviet troops left Cuba and Castro was finally on his own. Emigration from the island, already a problem, jumped dramatically as people tried to escape any way they could.

In 1992, the U.S. Congress passed the Cuban Democracy Act, which prohibited trading with Cuba by foreign-based subsidiaries of U.S. companies, traveling to Cuba by U.S. citizens, and remitting to family in Cuba.

At this time, 70 percent of Cuba's trade with U.S. subsidiary companies was in food and medicine. Many claimed the Cuban Democracy Act was thus in violation of international law and United Nations resolutions that food and medicine cannot be used as weapons in international conflicts.

In 1994 at least 35 men, women, and children died at sea when their boat, en route to Florida, sank seven miles out of Havana. Castro then declared an open migration policy. The United States, which had always welcomed Cuban refugees, was not prepared for what came next. 30,000 Cubans set sail from Cuba bound for the United States. Some made it, many did not, and others were picked up by the U.S. Coast Guard and taken to the U.S. naval base in Guantanamo Bay. A migration agreement was thereafter reached between the United States and Cuba, which allowed for a minimum of 20,000 immigrants per year.

> ### Reliable Resources
>
> Guantanamo Bay, originally a vacation resort, was leased to the U.S. Navy in 1898. The terms of the lease are contained in three documents—two agreements and a treaty. The lease calls for Washington to pay rent. Set a century ago at 2,000 gold coins a year, it is now worth just over $4,000. The lease can only be voided by a mutual agreement or abandonment of the land by the United States.

Yet even so, mass migration attempts continued to flummox both countries. In late 1999, the most celebrated of these immigrants, Elián Gonzalez, was rescued at sea after the boat he was on capsized, killing his mother and 10 others. On June 28, little Elián was returned home to Cuba.

Somehow, someway, Castro survived it all. He survived more than four decades of U.S. embargos and conflicts. He survived Khrushchev, Brezhnev, Gorbachev, and Yeltsin. He survived the fall of the Berlin Wall. However, whether his revolution will survive the many expatriates who loathed Castro is another matter altogether.

Indeed, there are many wealthy Cuban expatriates living in south Florida today who would love the opportunity to remake Cuba once Castro dies; men and women with both political clout and financial wherewithal. The possibility of a war over Cuba once Castro dies is very real.

Peru's Problems

Communism is a philosophy that attracts people who want to help the poor. Its altruistic belief of "from each according to his abilities to each according to his needs" seems to be a panacea in a troubled world.

Yet even though communism never worked and it brought economic ruin to almost every place it was tried, it somehow remained a potent political philosophy. This has been as true in Peru as anywhere else.

A Not-so-Shining Path

Founded in 1970 by Abimael Guzmán Reynoso, Peru's Shining Path was supposed to be an orthodox Marxist-Leninist offshoot of the Peruvian Communist party. But in 1980, the group turned to terrorism and became nothing more than another bloodthirsty, power-hungry group. By the 1990s, Shining Path was considered by many to be the most dangerous and violent terrorist organization in the world.

> **Diplomatic Dialogue**
>
> **Communism** is political system in which property is held in common. Based on the works of Karl Marx, and interpreted by Vladimir Lenin, communism's aim is to overthrow capitalism by revolutionary means and to establish a classless society. Communism must be distinguished from socialism, which seeks similar ends but by evolution rather than revolution.

The group derives its name from Mariategui, an avowed Marxist, who once stated that Marxism was a "shining path to the future." The goal of this organization was the destruction of the existing Peruvian government in favor of an Indian-run socialist system. Shining Path waged a bloody battle for the ensuing 13 years.

Shining Path was able to garner some popular support, mostly among students, teachers, the unemployed, and peasants in more rural areas where the government's reach was weaker.

Funding for the group came primarily from robberies and other crimes, although a significant revenue source was the "tax" that Shining Path extorted from businesses and individuals. Recruits came from well-established indoctrination programs that frequently targeted young teenagers who are more easily molded into the fanatical terrorists.

Between 1989 and 1992, Shining Path's terror campaign shook the foundation of the government in the capital of Lima. But the Peruvian state did what states do—it struck back.

Martial Law

In 1992, Peruvian President Alberto Fujimori used the ongoing crisis with the rebels to suspended congress and the courts and declared emergency rule to combat corruption and Shining Path terrorism. This act endowed his administration with the power to operate much more aggressively against the guerrillas.

Peacekeepers

According to CNN, "Among Peruvians, Fujimori was initially popular for defeating the powerful guerrillas, who controlled much of Peru's countryside and shantytowns, and ending annual inflation that topped 7,000 percent when he took office in 1990."

Fujimori cracked down hard on Shining Path. His Special Intelligence Group, a small elite police unit, uncovered a trail of clues that would eventually lead them to the head of Shining path, Abimael Guzmán Reynoso. Between the emergency rule and the work of the special police units, Guzmán was eventually located, arrested, and sentenced to life in prison.

In addition, aside from giving the president protracted dictatorial powers, the net result of Fujimori's emergency rule was the capture of more than 2,500 additional Shining Path terrorists. In 1993, more than 1,000 Peruvian terrorists were convicted on various charges, including Shining Path Regional Chief "Comrade Albino," who was, in 1995, convicted of ordering the murders of more than 100 people and sentenced to life in prison.

Even with the arrests, it is unlikely that Shining Path will disappear completely from Peru's political stage. However, given its vastly reduced size, any conflict it creates should be much less severe.

If Peruvians have anything to fear these days, it might be their own government.

Human Rights Abuses

In 2001, after 10 years in office, Fujimori ran for election for a third time. This time, the outcome was much less certain. His National Intelligence Service was blamed for harassing opposition candidates, the press, the courts, and the electoral bodies in an effort to secure Fujimori's reelection. It worked. Fujimori was officially reelected, but his new government was deemed illegitimate from the start.

At his inauguration, the Lima police fired tear gas on thousands of protestors. Then the opposition party staged a walkout, as it believed that Fujimori's was an unconstitutional government.

Reliable Resources

Ancient Peru was the seat of several prominent Andean civilizations—most notably that of the Incas, whose empire was captured by the Spanish conquistadores in 1533.

Furthermore, according to Human Rights Watch, Fujimori subjected his actual or potential critics to legal harassment and character assassination. Through his influence over the courts and the taxation office, Fujimori had secured the support of several television channels and radio stations previously critical of him. Bogus criminal accusations were launched against independent media.

In 2000, beset by ridicule and upheaval, Alberto Fujimori resigned as president of Peru. Although violence and insurrection are horrible things, the Peruvian story exemplifies that power can also prove to be a very dangerous drug.

Coup of a Kind

If Africa is the king of coups and attempted coups, South America must follow close behind. These countries seem to attract rebellion, insurgency, and government takeovers.

Ecuador

Ecuador's capital of Quito was once a center of the Inca Empire. It also has some of the best-preserved early colonial architecture on the continent.

Ecuador was long an agrarian country, until oil was discovered there in the 1960s. This resulted in rapid growth and brought about progress in health, education, and housing. The bad news is that this oil wealth also fuelled inflation, boosted consumer imports, which in turn increased foreign debt.

Peacekeepers

Because Ecuador exports products such as oil, bananas, and shrimp, changes in world market prices can have a substantial impact on the country. Although Ecuador joined the World Trade Organization in 1996, it has failed to comply with many of its rules.

Even worse, as is the case throughout much of South America, the traditionally dominant Spanish-descended elite gained far more than the indigenous peoples during the boom years. Sixty percent of the Ecuadorian population lives in poverty, and most of those are native Indians.

All this has lead to a lot of instability in the political arena:

- In 1987, the president was kidnapped and beaten up by the army.
- In 1995, the vice president sought political asylum in Costa Rica so as to escape charges of corruption.
- In 1997, the President was deposed on the grounds of mental incapacity.

In 2000, a coup occurred when the head of the armed forces in Ecuador announced the formation of a three-man council to take over the country. The military chief said that the council would be made up of himself, an indigenous Indian leader, and a former Supreme Court judge. According to the leader of the coup, he did what he did "to work against corruption."

Paraguay

Unlike much of South America, Paraguay has a racially homogeneous population; 95 percent of Paraguayans are people of mixed Spanish and Native American descent. Paraguay is also unique in that it experienced the region's longest dictatorship, under Alfredo Stroessner, who ruled the country for 35 years until 1989.

What makes Paraguay like much of the rest of South America, however, is the large wealth gap, with an estimated 60 percent of urban and 80 percent of rural dwellers living below the poverty line.

Such need has created much political instability:

- In 1989, although Stroessner was deposed in a coup, his military-backed Colorado Party won a majority in the first free multiparty elections.
- In 1998, even though allegations of fraud abounded, Colorado Party candidate Raul Cubas was elected president.
- In 1999, President Raul Cubas ordered tanks to the streets of the Paraguayan capital of Asuncion after protesters demanded his removal from office.
- In 1999, President Cubas did in fact resign in the wake of the assassination of Vice President Luis Maria Argana.

> **Reliable Resources**
>
> Tuesday, 17 October, 2000, (BBC): "The president of Paraguay, Luis Gonzalez Macchi, has dismissed rumors that a military coup would attempt to force him from office."

In 2000, rebels attempted to overthrow the government altogether in a coup attempt. They attacked parliament with tanks and took over several radio stations, calling for the overthrow of the government.

The coup attempt was quickly put down, and 75 people were detained or arrested in connection with it. Most of those arrested were members of the state security forces. They were said to be supporters of the country's former army commander, General Lino Oviedo, who was blamed for the uprising. A state of emergency was put in place throughout Paraguay.

There have been 45 coups or attempted coups in Paraguay in the past 100 years.

The Least You Need to Know

- Cuba was the focus of some of the most important conflicts in the twentieth century.
- Peru has successfully battled communist guerillas.
- Ecuador and Paraguay are politically unstable places where attempted coup d'états occur frequently.

Part 6

North America

Although it might seem at first glance that North America is probably the most peaceful place on the planet, that would be a false impression. To begin with, Mexico is in flux: With a large drug trade, the loss of power by the ruling PRI, and an active rebellion in the southern state of Chiapas, Mexico has many problems to contend with. By the same token, Canada has been dealing with its own separatist movement in Quebec.

But by far the largest place of conflict is the United States. September 11 merely reinforced the fact that the United States is a nation that has not been unwilling to engage in war and conflict, angering many countries in the process. Combined with its history of poor race relations, the United States is a place simmering with conflict.

22

Life in These United States

In This Chapter

- ◆ The making of a superpower
- ◆ The Cold War
- ◆ Proxy wars
- ◆ The War on Terrorism
- ◆ The ugly residue of slavery

In the past half century, the country that has engaged in the most wars, incidents, conflicts, missions, and violent events has been the United States. Sometimes it was the victim; sometimes the aggressor. But usually, it was in the thick of things.

Part of this has to do with the Cold War and the eventual success of the West. Ending up as the only superpower made the United States both a bully and a target. Part of it also has to do with race relations in the giant country—conflict breeds from within as well as from without.

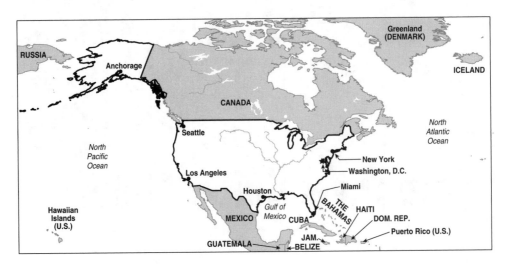

The United States was long protected by two great oceans.

A Star Is Born

Prior to World War I (or as it was known at the time, The Great War), the United States was an emerging industrial society more concerned with its own problems (recovering from slavery and the Civil War) than international relations. World War I changed all that.

There They Go Again

World War I began in 1914 when Archduke Francis Ferdinand of Austria-Hungary was assassinated by a Serbian Nationalist. The causes of the war were, needless to say, far more complicated than that. The main reason for the war was brewing economic, nationalistic, imperialistic, territorial, and economic rivalries among Germany, France, Great Britain, Russia, and Austria-Hungary.

Landmine!

Americans were also convinced to enter the war because, they were repeatedly told, it would be "the war to end all wars."

The war pitted a powerful alliance fronted by Italy, Germany, Austria-Hungary, and Romania against the Allies—France, Great Britain, and Russia. The neutrality of the United States was first imperiled after the Germans sank the *Lusitania* in 1915. The next year, Germany announced that it would begin unrestricted submarine warfare in an effort to break British control of the seas. In protest, the United States broke off relations with Germany, and on April 6, 1917, it entered the war.

America's entry into the war proved to be decisive, both for the war and for America. On the war front, American participation meant that the Allies now had new, enormous, industrial and manpower resources at their disposal. President Woodrow Wilson was able to convince a skeptical American public that war was in its best interest by insisting that the war "would make the world safe for democracy."

Although American entry neither made the world safe for democracy nor ended all wars, it did tip the scale in this war in favor of the Allies. An armistice in their favor was signed on November 11, 1918.

Practically every country, save one, was severely depleted by the war. For the European participants, World War I proved to be a bloody, expensive, exhausting campaign. It ruined economies, and the number of dead and injured was unbelievable: about 10 million died, and 20 million were wounded.

> **Reliable Resources**
>
> The use of chemical weapons is nothing new. In the Middle Ages, a flammable composition known as "Greek fire" (sulfur, naphtha, and quicklime) was used in war. Germans used chlorine and mustard gases against the Allies in World War I.

For United States, however, the war was different:

- One of America's blessings is that it is geographically isolated from much of the rest of the world. When wars break out, it is difficult for them to spread to North America. World War I, having been fought in Europe, devastated Europe, not America.

- Because the United States entered so late, it lost far fewer men.

- The economic push predicated by the war forced the United States to industrialize much more rapidly than it probably would have.

- Finally, because the United States made the difference, it left the war as, if not the king of the hill, one of the kings of the hill.

This newfound American might was soon challenged by the Great Depression (1929–41). Although the policies of President Franklin Delano Roosevelt's New Deal administration did much to mitigate the worst effects of the depression (and to restore a sense of confidence to the American people), a complete economic recovery was not achieved until the government began to spend heavily for defense in the early 1940s.

World War II

History does indeed have a way of repeating itself, and it did in the late 1930s. Once again, France, Great Britain, and Russia found themselves at war with Germany. Once

Diplomatic Dialogue

In politics, **hegemony** is the overwhelming influence and authority of one country over another country or countries.

again, they risked losing if the United States failed to enter, and the American public was skeptical of getting involved in European entanglements.

One person who was not skeptical was President Roosevelt. Roosevelt understood that democracy was truly threatened by the powerful rise of Hitler and his fascist Nazi regime. The German juggernaut had quickly overrun Poland, France, and much of the rest of Europe. Its ally Japan had done the same in Asia. All that stood between German *hegemony* and freedom was a battered, but brave Britain, and a poor, but large Russia. FDR was unwilling to let America stay on the sidelines while the world careened toward darkness.

So, in the late 1930s and early 1940s, Roosevelt quietly prepared America for the war he knew was coming. He was aided greatly in his efforts when, on December 7, 1941, Japan attacked Pearl Harbor. The United States entered the war the next day.

Reliable Resources

Yesterday, December 7, 1941—a date which will live in infamy—the United States of America was suddenly and deliberately attacked by naval and air forces of the Empire of Japan … I believe I interpret the will of the Congress and of the people when I assert that we will not only defend ourselves to the uttermost but will make very certain that this form of treachery shall never endanger us again. I ask that the Congress declare that since the unprovoked and dastardly attack by Japan on Sunday, December 7, a state of war has existed between the United States and the Japanese Empire.

—Franklin Delano Roosevelt, December 8, 1941

When the war ended about three and a half years later, there were but two kings of the hill left standing. In the east, the Soviet Union, though bruised and battered, emerged as the dominant force from Eastern Europe to Asia. And in the West, the United States once again left a war mightier than it had been before it entered.

So conflict and the United States go hand in hand: If it were not for war, the United States would not have become a superpower.

Fighting the Good Fight

The Cold War created even more opportunity for the United States to build its empire, as well as promote democracy and capitalism. Although the Korean War was a virtual standoff (see Chapter 10), neither helping nor hurting American dominance, Vietnam was another matter altogether.

Quagmire

On July 8, 1959, two U.S. military advisors, Major Dale Buis and Sergeant Chester Ovnand, were killed in South Vietnam. They were among the first American soldiers killed in the Vietnam War. Before it was over 14 years later, another 58,000 Americans would die there.

The United States entered into Vietnam slowly, and with much trepidation. However, as the war escalated, the United States often believed that it had no choice but to continue to fight there, incorrectly assuming that losing South Vietnam to communist North Vietnam would endanger democracy throughout Asia.

The first salvo, insofar as the Americans were concerned, occurred in 1961 when Soviet Premier Nikita Khrushchev pledged support for "wars of national liberation" throughout the world. His statement greatly encouraged communists in North Vietnam to escalate their armed struggle to unify Vietnam.

That same month, John Fitzgerald Kennedy was inaugurated as the 35th U.S. president. Kennedy, who was a genuine World War II hero, was keenly aware that the Soviets posed a direct threat to American interests. In his inaugural address, JFK declared that, "We shall pay any price, bear any burden, meet any hardship, support any friend, oppose any foe, to ensure the survival and the success of liberty." In private, outgoing President Eisenhower told Kennedy, "I think you're going to have to send troops to Vietnam."

The Kennedy administration's initial policy was to wage a limited war to attempt to force a political settlement. So that year, he secretly sent 400 American Green Beret "special advisors" to South Vietnam to train South Vietnamese soldiers.

The Kennedy administration failed to understand several things about Vietnam, namely …

- ◆ The will of the North Vietnamese to "win at any cost" (as Ho Chi Minh put it).
- ◆ That the U.S. military was unprepared to fight a guerilla war half a world away.
- ◆ That the American public would not support a war in which it did not feel its national interests were at stake, and that was the feeling about Vietnam.

These were lessons that would be learned much too late.

Guns or Butter

In 1963, Kennedy was assassinated in Dallas, and Lyndon Johnson inherited the war. Johnson was nothing if not a testosterone-driven egomaniac and was not about to lose. By the end of that year, 16,300 American military advisors would be shipped off to Southeast

Asia. By the end of 1964, the number of American troops in South Vietnam was 23,000. (There were an estimated 170,000 North Vietnamese fighters.)

Landmine!

On August 7, 1964, the U.S. Congress passed the "Gulf of Tonkin Resolution." This was not an actual declaration of war. The resolution allowed the president "to take all necessary steps, including the use of armed force" to prevent further attacks against U.S. forces in Southeast Asia. The Gulf of Tonkin resolution passed unanimously in the House and 98–2 in the Senate, and thereby gave almost unlimited powers to President Johnson to wage an undeclared war in Vietnam. (Two Alaskan senators voted against the resolution, with one of them, Ernest Gruening, saying "all Vietnam is not worth the life of a single American boy.")

The war escalated sharply after Johnson's 1964 win. By 1965, 1,000 tons of bombs were being dropped by the United States on the Vietcong, and an astounding 125,000 Americans went to war. Not coincidentally, that same year, 15,000 students marched on Washington in opposition to the war.

By the end of 1966, troop levels had reached 400,000, and Johnson requested an additional half billion dollars to wage war. But the United States, like any other country, did not have unlimited funds. When a country decides to buy guns, it usually must forgo butter. As Reverend Martin Luther King said at the time, "the pursuit of this widened war has narrowed the promised dimensions of domestic welfare programs, making the poor white and Negro bear the heaviest burdens both at the front and at home."

By 1968, opposition at home to the war in Vietnam had hit a crescendo. LBJ couldn't run from the fact that he had led the United States into quicksand from which it could not easily escape. Yet he still shocked the world when he announced on March 31, 1968, "I shall not seek, and I will not accept, the nomination of my party for another term as your president."

Landmine!

On March 1, 1968, Clark Clifford became the new U.S. Secretary of Defense. The very first thing he did was to conduct an intensive study of the entire situation in Vietnam. Clifford concluded that there was neither a concept nor any overall plan anywhere in Washington for achieving victory in Vietnam.

Although President Johnson was not Vietnam's first casualty, he certainly was one of its most tragic. By the time Richard Nixon was elected president in November 1968, troop levels had reached 500,000 and 1,000 young Americans were being killed every month.

It would take another four years for the United States to finally end its bitter folly in Vietnam, and not before it had also invaded neighboring Laos and Cambodia.

Yet somehow with a straight face, Nixon was able to announce, on January 23, 1973, that an agreement had been reached ending the war; an agreement which would "bring peace with honor."

In response to the overbroad authority granted to LBJ in the Gulf of Tonkin resolution, on November 7, 1973, Congress passed the War Powers Act, requiring the president to obtain the support of Congress within 90 days of sending American troops abroad.

The Fifty-Third Hostage

The taint of Vietnam damaged both America's psyche and its image around the globe. A country once thought to be impregnable had been brought to its knees by a band of guerrilla warriors. Maybe America wasn't so tough after all.

Certainly this belief came home to roost in Iran. There, in 1979, the Islamic Fundamentalist revolution overthrew the Shah, and on November 4, militant Iranian students proved that the United States might in fact be a *paper tiger* when they overtook the United States embassy in Teheran.

Diplomatic Dialogue

A **paper tiger** is a country that is seemingly dangerous and powerful but is in fact timid and weak. The phrase was first used by Mao Tse Tung to describe the United States: "U.S. imperialism seems quite powerful, but in reality it isn't. It is very weak politically because it is divorced from the masses of the people and is disliked by everybody and by the American people too. In appearance it is very powerful, but in reality it is nothing to be afraid of: It is a paper tiger."

The Iranian Hostage Crisis occurred after the exiled Shah's admission to the United States for medical treatment. As a result, a crowd of about 500 seized the American embassy. Of the approximately 90 people inside the embassy at the time, 52 remained in captivity until the end of the crisis.

President Jimmy Carter, although a decent and honorable man, also seemed, if not incompetent, at least incapable of solving the crisis. He first attempted to free the hostages using a variety of nonviolent means: applying economic pressure by halting oil imports from Iran, as well as freezing Iranian assets in the United States. He also began several diplomatic initiatives to free the hostages, all of which proved fruitless.

In the end, Carter's own presidency was taken hostage by the Iranian "students" (many of whom were not students at all). He had become, in effect, the fifty-third hostage.

The Tiger Meows

With nothing else working, Carter reluctantly, but finally concluded that he had to try the military option. The problem was that the hostages likely weren't all being held in the same spot. Where they were held was the middle of Teheran, making a rescue mission all the more difficult.

Reliable Resources

When we opened that door, we were taken over immediately. The Iranians swarmed in. One guy looked at me and said, "Walk out the door." So I walked out the door. Two guys grabbed me, one on either side, put my hands behind my back, and tied my hands. They had a long nylon rope that they used to tie us up. After my hands were tied, this guy tried to cut the rope with a knife. The rope slipped and he gouged me, stabbed me in the back. I said, "Ouch!" And he said, "Oh, I'm sorry. I'm sorry. I didn't mean to hurt you!"

—Bill Belk, embassy communications officer

Nevertheless, on April 16, 1980, President Carter met with his foreign policy staff in the White House Situation Room. Also present was Colonel Charles Beckwith, a veteran who had created the elite Delta Force. The Joint Chiefs of Staff had recommended Beckwith to lead a rescue mission.

The plan was this: Beckwith's 132-man team would arrive in Egypt, the staging area for "Operation Eagle Claw." The team would then fly to an island off the coast of Oman. From there, they would fly to Desert One, a staging area in the Iranian dessert, 200 miles from Teheran, where they were to rendezvous with eight helicopters dispatched from the USS *Nimitz*.

The helicopters would refuel at Desert One before proceeding with the Delta Force team to mountains about 65 miles southeast of Teheran. The following night, the rescue team was to enter Teheran in four trucks. The rescuers would then infiltrate the embassy and free the hostages. The helicopters would then fly in, pick them all up, and deliver them safely to an airfield outside Teheran.

What happened instead was this: Beckwith and his men reached Desert One as planned, but a short time later, a bus carrying Iranian civilians happened into the area, and were taken into custody. Then a fuel truck and a pickup appeared in this area that was supposed to be quite remote. The fuel truck was destroyed, but the driver of the pickup escaped.

The helicopters were due at 11:30 P.M., but were late. One of them had lost rotor blade pressure and was forced to land. The remaining helicopters flew into a dust storm, as another lost its gyroscope and turned back. The remaining six reached Desert One two hours late. Once there, it was discovered that another one of the choppers had lost its hydraulic pump and could not take off.

Peacekeepers

Secretary of State Cyrus Vance, who opposed the rescue mission from the beginning, resigned after it was over.

That left five copters: one less than the minimum needed to carry out the plan. Beckwith was forced to scrub the mission. Bad turned to worse when, as the helicopters and transport planes began to depart, one of the choppers collided with one of the planes. The helicopter exploded into flames and eight men died.

444

Back in the United States, the continued failure to resolve the crisis contributed to Ronald Reagan's defeat of Jimmy Carter in the presidential elections of 1980. After the election, with the assistance of Algerian intermediaries, successful negotiations began. On January 20, 1981, just hours before Reagan's inauguration, a final deal was struck. The United States released almost $8 billion in Iranian assets, and Jimmy Carter brought every one of the hostages back home alive after 444 days in Iranian detention just as Reagan was being sworn in.

War by Proxy

As president, Ronald Reagan was far more bellicose than Jimmy Carter. He ramped up the Cold War to heights it hadn't seen in 20 years. And by extension, he led the United States into a series of proxy wars, especially in the Caribbean, where he felt America's security was being threatened by Soviet assistance to various Marxist guerilla groups. The United States was back on familiar ground—in war mode again.

Sandinista!

In 1979, a Marxist revolution led by the Sandinistas ousted the Somoza dictatorship in Nicaragua. In one of his first acts, Reagan authorized the CIA to overthrow the Sandinistas. William Casey, the CIA Director, arranged with Argentine military officials to begin training an opposition group known as the Contras, using U.S. weapons and money.

Reagan tried to drum up support for the Contras within the United States by referring to them as "the moral equivalent of our Founding Fathers." The CIA received $50 million for training programs.

But it turned out that the Contras were typical South American thugs. The group resorted to hit-and-run tactics aimed primarily at women and children. Horatio Arce, Chief of Contra Intelligence, stated, "We attack a lot of schools and health centers. We tried to make it so that the Nicaraguan government cannot provide social services for the peasants." As word of these sorts of tactics spread, American support of the Contras receded.

In 1984, for the first time in Nicaragua's history, free elections took place. The Sandinistas received 69.2 percent of the vote. As a result, in the United States, Congress passed the Boland Amendment, barring U.S. actions to overthrow the Sandinistas.

Stuck but not dismayed, the Reagan administration utilized Oliver North to sell arms to Iran and use the profits to fund the Contras. The resulting "Iran Contra scandal" almost brought down the Reagan White House. Ironically, the Sandinistas were eventually driven from office, but not by guns—they were voted out some time later by the Nicaraguan electorate.

Grenada

On October 13, 1983, the Grenadian Army and former Deputy Prime Minister Bernard Coard led a bloody coup d'état in Grenada. Because Coard was a Marxist and because nearly 1,000 American medical students were then in Grenada, Washington was deeply troubled by the events.

On October 25, 1983, the United States attacked and invaded Grenada. The initial assault consisted of some 1,200 troops. Heavy fighting continued for several days, but as the invasion force grew to more than 7,000, the Grenadian communists either surrendered or fled. Although scattered fighting continued for a few more days, the island quickly fell under American control. By the first of the year, U.S. troops went home and a pro-American government took power.

Panama

In 1968, General Omar Torrijos led a coup in Panama that allowed blacks and the poor to obtain a share of power in the traditionally European-dominated Panama. Torrijos was killed in a plane crash in 1981, and by 1983, Manuel Noriega had become the ruler. Noriega was a Torrijos ally, as well as a friend of U.S. intelligence.

The United States was content to let Noriega run Panama, and its vital canal, as long as he abided by Washington's ways. And he did, for the most part. That he was a known drug trafficker mattered little; in fact, the U.S. government had known that Noriega was involved in drug trafficking since at least 1972, when the Nixon administration considered assassinating him. Yet he stayed on the CIA payroll.

When Noriega began to sow his oats and act more independent than the United States wanted, especially insofar as the Contras went, he became expendable. In December 1989, the United States invaded Panama, capturing Noriega, and bringing him back to the United States on drug charges. The U.S. invasion also had the effect of restoring power to the rich white elite that had been displaced by the Torrijos coup, just in time to ensure a friendly government for the administrative changeover of the Panama Canal on January 1, 1990.

> **Reliable Resources**
>
> In 1903, Panama and the United States signed the original Panama Canal Treaty, which allowed the United States to build and operate a canal connecting the Pacific Ocean with the Caribbean Sea through the Isthmus of Panama. On September 7, 1977, a new Panama Canal Treaty was signed by President Torrijos of Panama and President Carter of the United States that transferred full control of the canal to Panama on December 31, 1999. The United States, by far, uses the canal more than any other country in the world.

The Once and Future King?

Conflict from abroad hit the shores of America for the first time on September 11, 2001. Although, as can be seen herein, the country should have been used to war and conflict, it was not. September 11 was a body blow precisely because all the conflict the United States had engaged in for almost 100 years had happened abroad. It was antiseptic conflict.

September 11 was different. Occurring as it did, not only in America, but also in its most powerful and important cities (Washington D.C. and New York), the terrorist attacks made the United States feel vulnerable like nothing else ever had before, save for Pearl Harbor.

Yet the attacks should not really have been a surprise. Not only had the United States been imposing its will upon lesser countries since at least 1945, but also al-Qaeda had declared war on the United States two years earlier. It was hubris that shielded the attacks.

The resulting War on Terrorism certainly poses risks and potential rewards for the United States. On one hand, it is an opportunity to make the world safer, and despite acting in its own self-interest (as all countries do), there is no small streak of puritanical idealism that runs in Yankee blood. It might surprise the rest of the world that the United States thinks that by attacking terrorists in other sovereign nations, it is making the world a better place for everyone.

The risks are numerous. The first is that the United States might end up being an even larger target. People in countries that might have otherwise ignored America might decide it deserves to be put in its place. Alternatively, others might conclude that the success of the September 11 attacks proved that the United States might be a paper tiger after all. Either way, being the international policeman is dangerous when so many people don't like the police.

The last risk is the most serious. International relations really is not that much different from "king of the hill." The British were once the king, and for a short while, it was the Germans. Both got knocked off the hill. The Soviets were half king for a while, until they got knocked down.

Today, the United States stands alone as king of the international hill. Given that the object of the game is to knock the other guy off and ascend yourself, you can rest assured that someone, somewhere, is making plans to knock America off its pedestal. That is how the game is played.

A Shameful History

Conflict for the United States not only comes from without, but it also has a large race-relations problem stemming from slavery.

Slavery in the United States

During the course of the slave trade, which began in the United States in the seventeenth century, millions of Africans were stolen from their homes and families in Africa and forcibly shipped to America.

Although the European, American, and African slave traders and the politicians, business-men, and slave owners who supported them, did not intend to put into motion a chain of events that would create a brutal and costly civil war, they did.

In all, more than 600,000 people died as a result of the Civil War and its efforts to end the "peculiar institution" of slavery. In the two days it took for the Battle of Gettysburg, for example, more than 50,000 soldiers died. Before the war was over, probably the great-est president the United States had ever had, Abraham Lincoln, was assassinated.

Reliable Resources

Lincoln's pre-presidential life:

1832—Lost job.

1833—Failed in business.

1834—Elected to Illinois state legislature.

1835—Sweetheart died.

1836—Had nervous breakdown.

1846—Elected to Congress.

1848—Lost renomination.

1854—Defeated for U.S. Senate.

1856—Defeated for nomination for vice president.

1858—Defeated for U.S. Senate again.

1860—Elected president.

Of course, the end of the war did not end discrimination toward blacks. Throughout the south, *Jim Crow* laws were enacted to keep the blacks at bay. And even though the United States attempted to make amends of sorts by constitutionally outlawing discrimination based on race, creed, or color in the Thirteenth, Fourteenth, and Fifteenth Amendments, changing racist attitudes proved to be very difficult.

Diplomatic Dialogue

Jim Crow laws barred African Americans from access to voting and employment, as well as to public places such as restaurants, hotels, and other facilities.

We Hold These Truths to Be Self-Evident

In the 1950s and 60s, African Americans began to demand the rights guaranteed them in the Constitution. Both peacefully, through the leadership of Dr. Martin Luther King, and violently, through leaders like Malcolm X, millions of black Americans confronted the white structures that subjugated them.

Many words were said, and far too much blood was shed before laws and—more importantly—attitudes changed. Although the country certainly has made a lot of progress in the area of race relations, an ugly vein of racism remains in the mountain that is America.

According to the Southern Poverty Law Center, in the year 2000, there were 602 active "hate groups" in the United States, categorized as Ku Klux Klan, Neo-Nazi, Racist

Skinhead, Christian Identity, Black Separatist, and Neo-Confederate. These groups, with names like Aryan Nations, Underground Skinhead Action, and the American Nazi Party, are committed to conflict and resistance.

Despite such groups, credit must be given where credit is due. In America, great strides toward equality have been sought and undertaken. No, this conflict is not over, but it is healing. Martin Luther King seemed to be speaking the dreams of many when he said, on August 28, 1963:

> I have a dream that one day this nation will rise up and live out the true meaning of its creed: 'We hold these truths to be self-evident: that all men are created equal.' I have a dream that one day on the red hills of Georgia, the sons of former slaves and the sons of former slave owners will be able to sit down together at a table of brotherhood. I have a dream that my four children will one day live in a nation where they will not be judged by the color of their skin but by the content of their character.

The Least You Need to Know

- Wars made the United States a superpower.
- The war in Vietnam was a mistake from its inception.
- Throughout the 1980s, the United States engaged in several proxy wars.
- The War on Terrorism is a double-edged sword.
- The residue of slavery is an ugly one, although progress can be seen.

Problems for America's Neighbors

In This Chapter

◆ Mexico

◆ The Zapatistas

◆ Canada

Although North America might seem to be a place of relative peace and quiet, it is not. Not only is the most warring nation on Earth, the United States, there, but also its neighbors have their own internal conflicts and problems that are magnified by their proximity to their superpower neighbor.

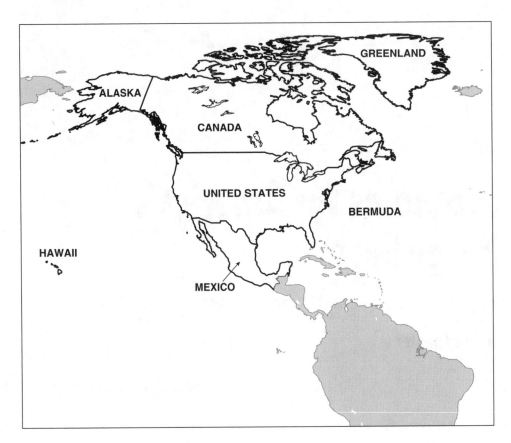

North America is not as peaceful as it seems.

Viva Mexico!

In the early part of the twentieth century, the legendary peasant leaders Pancho Villa and Emiliano Zapata successfully fought for reform in Mexico. Because of this, the 1917 Mexican Constitution contained several provisions concerning worker rights and land reform; ideas that would dominate Mexican politics for years to come.

Reliable Resources
Mexico's reputation for festive fun is well founded. Most months contain a major national holiday or fiesta, and practically every other day is a local saint's day or town celebration. Carnaval is held in late February or early March. Mexico's most characteristic fiesta is the Día de los Muertos (The Day of the Dead), held on November 2.

But not until the presidency of Lazaro Cardenas in 1934 would the revolutionary ideas of Zapata and Villa become part of the government's agenda. The most dramatic proof of this occurred in 1938 when Cardenas nationalized British and U.S. oil firms.

Cardenas was a radical in other ways as well. Most importantly, he created a political revolution that would last for 70 years. Cardenas cobbled together a coalition of the three broad sectors of Mexican society: the peasants, the unions, and the public employees. He renamed his party the Institutional Revolutionary Party (PRI) in 1946, and it remained the ruling party of Mexico for the rest of the millennium.

> **CAUTION** **Landmine!**
>
> Despite its vast oil wealth, Mexico remains a very poor country. Rural areas are generally neglected, and huge shantytowns surround the major cities. Many young, poor Mexicans risk crossing the border to the United States in search of a job.

Problematically for the country, Mexican presidents after Cardenas began to use the PRI's power for control rather than popular participation. As a result, Mexico became a stable, if undemocratic, nation in which power and corruption became a basic element of politics.

The most dramatic evidence of this occurred during the 1960s, which were a time of social unrest in Mexico as they were in many other places around the world. In 1968, Mexican students began to clamor. The two main sources of discontent were the slow progress made in fulfilling the promises of the Mexican Revolution (1910–1920) of eliminating poverty and inequality and the limited levels of democracy. The students were determined to take advantage of the international attention devoted to Mexico during the Mexico City Olympic Games to express their frustration and criticize the government, as well as to demand democratic reforms and social justice.

On October 2, 15,000 students marched through the streets of Mexico City and into the central square—known as Plaza de Taltelolco. But this peaceful student demonstration turned bloody in what came to be remembered forever as the Taltelolco Massacre. Without any warning, the army began to fire against the unarmed student protestors. The massacre was indiscriminate, killing people who were at the plaza for reasons unrelated to the protest. It is estimated that more than 300 people were killed, hundreds were injured, and several thousand were arrested.

This event typifies conflict in Mexico. It is neither condoned nor allowed. The right-wing PRI often uses brute force to keep the masses of poor peasants in line.

Growing Militarization in Mexico

Needless to say, strong-arming factions of the military are nothing new to Latin America. But they have grown especially worrisome in Mexico, especially in light of its poverty and urgent social needs. Thus, for example, in spite of an economic crisis in 1995, the

Mexican government paid an estimated $2.2 billion to the United States that year for military purchases, a 40 percent increase over 1993 expenditures.

Why the increase? There are three reasons.

Cocaine, It's Running All Around My Brain

The first reason for the dramatic growth of the army and right-wing paramilitary groups in Mexico has to do with the drug trade. Marijuana, heroin, and cocaine trafficking have reached ever higher levels in Mexico over the last 20 years. Under pressure from the United States, the Mexican government is making a very serious effort to control the problem, and a significant problem it is:

♦ Roughly 70 percent of South American cocaine and 80 percent of its marijuana comes from Mexico into the United States.

♦ Mexican drug cartels bring in approximately $50 billion a year from drug sales in the United States.

♦ It is estimated by some in Mexico that between 70–80 percent of the police force has been influenced by drug money.

Landmine!

The Mexican army currently deploys more than 20,000 soldiers in counter narcotics operations, including eradication and interdiction efforts. The majority of civilian complaints of army abuses have involved troops participating in counter narcotics operations.

Landmine!

The drug czar was fired after 10 weeks for alleged involvement with the drug cartels.

To overcome the problem of corrupt and abusive police forces, U.S. military advisors began to push for military involvement in Mexican anti-narcotic activities. In a 1995 anti-narcotic plan, President Zedillo mandated a military role in drug interdiction. Subsequently the Mexican army began to take control of numerous provincial police forces and, in 1997, an army general was appointed to serve as Mexico's drug czar.

There have been some successes in the drug war. Several major figures in the cartels were captured and prosecuted. According to an observer of the U.S.-Mexican drug scene, "In 1996, Mexican officials reported two consecutive record years in eradicating nearly 20,000 acres of marijuana and poppy crop: much of this owing to military search-and-destroy missions in the mountainous areas where these crops are grown."

> **Landmine!** _____
>
> Why do other countries hate the United States? Consider the "Drug War." American complicity in drug trafficking is unquestionable. Whereas an estimated 70 percent of all cocaine and 40 percent of all heroin on American streets has traveled through Mexico, in Mexico's view, it is equally true that 100 percent of all these sub-stances travel through the United States. To blame Mexico for drug imports when the United States can claim even less success is seen as utter hypocrisy.

Good Cop, Bad Cop

The second reason for Mexico's increased militarization relates to the aforementioned corruption in Mexican law enforcement. It is said by some that local law enforcement has the choice to either cooperate with the traffickers or face death.

In response to this dilemma, the government began to use the army to deal with the drug runners. But the problem with this solution is that the military is equally corruptible: General Jesús Gutiérrez Rebollo, head of the National Institute to Combat Drugs, was fired from his post in 1996 for taking bribes from the godfather of Mexico's largest drug cartel.

Stand Up for Your Rights

The final reason for Mexico's growing militarization is an increasing disaffection with the federal government. Dissatisfaction in poor, rural areas of southern Mexico especially may indicate the potential for armed rebellion.

Paradise Lost

In the state of Chiapas, high atop a distant mountain sits an idyllic little town inhabited by friendly Indians wearing colorful garb. A sort of Shangri-La, San Cristobal de Las Casas is the sort of place travelers yearn to discover. Its cafés surround the central square, art galleries line its cobble stoned streets, and jazz wafts through the air; or at least it used to. (I was there in 1988 and it was an amazing place.)

The Zapatista National Liberation Army staged an uprising in idyllic San Cristobal de Las Casas on, not coincidentally, January 1, 1994, the day the North American Free Trade Agreement (NAFTA) took effect. A guerrilla group, which was previously unknown to the public, the Zapatistas—under the leadership of articulate pipe-smoking poet "Subcommandante Marcos" (later revealed to be a former university lecturer)—announced a long

Peacekeepers

NAFTA began on January 1, 1994. It removed most barriers to trade and investment among the United States, Canada, and Mexico. Under the NAFTA, all nontariff barriers to agricultural trade between the United States and Mexico were eliminated. In addition, many tariffs were eliminated immediately, with others being phased out over periods of 5 to 15 years.

list of demands. Among them were demands for reforms in health care, land distribution, an opposition to NAFTA, and better education for the indigenous Mayan population.

The 12-day fight between the Zapatistas and the government left an estimated 145 dead and hundreds arrested. Incidents of torture and forced confessions were reported during and after arrests.

The rebellion took the country by surprise. In Mexico, dominated as it had been by the ruling PRI and as militarized as it had become, armed rebellion had not been a common occurrence. This was especially true during the Cold War when social, economic, and cultural problems in Mexico—especially as perceived by the left—were neglected. Said one Zapatista rebel, "if you brought up those problems in the 80s, you were immediately labeled pro-communist, or a puppet of the Soviet Union." Given Mexico's proximity to the United States, such a label was heresy.

When the Cold War ended in the 1990s, Mexico's many social problems began to come to the fore. And unlike other armed rebellions in Latin America, this one was media savvy. The Zapatistas used the news media, books, and the Internet to lobby for local autonomy and economic development for a people they felt had long been neglected by the federal government.

After the rebellion had been quashed, the government signed a cease-fire agreement with the Zapatistas. But even so, the next year, the Mexican army launched a military offensive against them. The Mexican government hadn't bought all those arms for nothing. But the attack failed to defeat the Zapatistas, and Mexico faced strong international criticism.

Yet the government wanted to contain the rebels, so rather than attack them outright, it sponsored paramilitary groups who terrorized on its behalf. These paramilitaries focused especially on the civilian population in an attempt to undermine support for the Zapatista rebellion. Even so, the Zapatistas, and what they stood for, would not go away.

Reliable Resources

In Mexico, troop size has grown 15 percent since 1994, and the military budget continues to rise at a rate of about 16 percent per annum.

The Zapatista rebellion, in fact, signaled the beginning of a dangerous time for Mexico. Later that year, 1994, presidential candidate Luis Donaldo Colosio was murdered. As a result, the election was won by PRI candidate Ernesto Zedillo. The stock market plunged later that year, and the peso lost a third of its value. The next year, former President Carlos Salinas was forced into exile after his brother Raul Salinas was connected with Colosio's murder.

Clearly change was in the air. In 1997, for the first time since its inception in 1929, the PRI lost parliamentary elections. In December, 45 Indians were killed by paramilitary gunmen in a Chiapas village. The incident caused an international outcry, and President Zedillo began an investigation. The governor of Chiapas then resigned, and peace talks with the rebels started up again, although they would break down at the end of the year.

Pandora's Box

Even though the two sides eventually reached an agreement of sorts on greater autonomy for the indigenous Mayans of Chiapas, the insurgency in the southern part of Mexico escalated. A different group, the leftist Popular Revolutionary Army (EPR), also attacked government troops.

These guerrillas stated that their purpose was "to overthrow the anti-popular, anti-democratic, demagogic, and illegitimate government which panders to national and foreign capital interests." The group targeted police stations, government offices, and military installations.

The Zapatistas and the EPR are apparently not alone. It is estimated that as many as eight different armed rebel groups might be operating throughout Mexico.

Landmine!

On January 9, 1998, the Mexican army entered into Chiapas. Sixteen women and nine children were beaten by soldiers. The children, who were carried by their mothers, were injured as the soldiers threw stones at them, hit them with clubs, and tried to snatch them from their mothers. Women and children who had fallen were forced to get up with blows from the butts of rifles and shovels. A seven-month-old baby lost consciousness from blows she received. Two women received deep cuts to their heads.

—Testimony from community members, as reported by Global Exchange

Presidente Fox

The most dramatic change in Mexico in 50 years occurred in July 2000 when opposition party candidate Vincente Fox was elected president, the first opposition candidate ever to do so. His Alliance for Change party beat the institutional PRI by just over 1 percent. The election of

Peacekeepers

According to CNN, "In the tourist markets of San Cristobal de Las Casas today, Zapatista souvenirs are everywhere. You can find Zapatista dolls, key chains, and even T-shirts emblazoned with Zapatista slogans."

Fox was a mandate for change. One of Fox's first acts was to address issues raised by the Zapatistas.

At Fox's urging, the Mexican parliament passed a bill increasing the rights of indigenous people. But Subcommandante Marcos rejected the bill, saying it would leave the Indian population worse off than before. Marcos declared that "the uprising in Chiapas will continue."

Oh Canada!

Other than say, New Zealand, Canada might seem to be about the most peaceful place on earth. But that is a misconception. Would it surprise you to learn that the country came within a hair of disintegrating in 1995?

To understand how this could have happened, you need to travel back in time 500 years, to the earliest explorations of North America by the Europeans.

New France

In 1524, an Italian navigator named Giovanni da Verrazzano was sponsored by King François I of France to explore the New World. Verrazzano explored the American east coast between Florida and Newfoundland, and he named these new lands "Nova Franca." In 1529, his brother Girolamo created a map of the area, and he called the area "Nova Gallia." Over time, the name "Nouvelle-France" (New France) became the norm to identify French possessions of Northeastern America.

French influence really began in earnest when, in 1608, Samuel de Champlain established the first permanent French settlement in North America in Quebec City. Unlike much of the rest of Canada, or North America for that matter, Quebec became a French-speaking Catholic region. More importantly, over the next 150 years, it became a major battleground in the fight between England and France for control of the New World.

The Québécois

The roots of the modern conflict can be directly traced back to 1759. That year, General James Wolfe's British forces routed the French at the Battle of the Plains of Abraham and Quebec City fell to the British. At the Treaty of Paris four years later, France surrendered its North American colony. The residents of Quebec City, the Québécois, numbering about 70,000 then, suddenly became British subjects.

Although the British were not overbearing, with the British army came English-speaking settlers. Threatened by this foreign occupation and their foreign tongue, the Québécois came to believe their very existence was threatened. This continued throughout the nineteenth century because the British minority dominated the French majority in Quebec.

Peacekeepers

The Treaty of Paris was signed in February 1763 and ended the "Seven Years War." The treaty decreed to England all of Canada and all the great interior east of the Mississippi, except for the port of New Orleans.

Resentful of their diminished status and disturbed by the increasing number of English-speaking immigrants, a number of Québécois took up arms against the British in 1837. The rebellion failed, and there were no further nineteenth century rebellions in Quebec.

In 1867, modern Canada was created when the provinces of Quebec, Ontario, Nova Scotia, and New Brunswick confederated under the British North America Act. The new constitution guaranteed the rights of French Canadians. Section 133 of the Act permitted the use of French in …

♦ The Quebec legislature.

♦ Quebec courts.

♦ The Quebec Parliament.

In order to hold on to their French origins, the Québécois became, possibly, more French than the French. For the next century, Québécois nationalism grew, as did its Catholicism. Yet even so, their English-speaking countrymen quickly began to dominate commerce in major Quebec cities like Montréal.

The Québécois in the Twentieth Century

The era between 1950 and 1965 became known as the "Quiet Revolution" in Quebec. It was a time of social transformation as Quebec moved from a rural, religious society to a more modern, urban one. Things that had traditionally distinguished the Québécois—their religion and rural lifestyle—were vanishing. The French language became, seemingly, the only difference between Quebec and the rest of Canada.

But even so, Quebec refused to assimilate with the rest of Canada. Instead, it led to an increase in nationalism, as well as a newfound desire for separatism and independence. In 1968, the "Parti Québécois" emerged, advocating self-rule for Quebec. It was lead by Rene Lévesque.

Reliable Resources

We are Québécois. What that means first and foremost—and if it need be, all that it means—is that we are attached to this one corner of the earth where we can be completely ourselves; this Quebec, the only place where we have the unmistakable feeling that 'here we can really be at home.' Being ourselves is essentially a matter of keeping and developing a personality that has survived for three and a half centuries. At the core of this personality is the fact that we speak French.

—1968 speech by Rene Lévesque

Peacekeepers

One of the Parti Québécois's first moves was to pass a French-only law, even though French had already been made the sole official language of Quebec in 1974. Bill 101, the French Language Charter, reflected the Québécois's fear of becoming a minority in their own province.

At the same time, other, more radical groups began the requisite terror campaign. Bombing public places and kidnapping high profile Canadian and British officials, the radicals dramatized the emergence of French-Canadian nationalism. In 1970 alone for example, the Front de Libération du Québec kidnapped James Cross, the British High Commissioner in Montreal, and murdered Pierre Laporte, the Canadian Minister of Labour.

In 1976, the Parti Québécois came to power in Quebec on the promise of holding a referendum on sovereignty, and the issue of separation was finally put to Quebec voters in 1980: 59.5 percent voted against independence for Quebec.

Attempting to quell Quebec's dissatisfaction, Canada created a new constitution in 1982 that recognized the "distinctiveness" of Quebec. The Québécois weren't mollified though; Quebec was the only Canadian province not to approve the reformed constitution.

In 1995, the issue of Quebec's independence was put before the voters again, and this time lost by only one percent. As a result, it became quite clear that this conflict is not going away any time soon.

Lesson Learned

What is interesting is how differently the Canadians dealt with its separatist movement than other countries. In almost every other country discussed throughout this book, when the desire of one people to be free surfaces, some radical group emerges from its ranks, ready to kill and maim anyone in their way. The government then usually becomes correspondingly repressive by arresting, murdering, and torturing the rebels.

In Canada, however, the issue was dealt with in a civilized manner. Yes, there were some wanton acts of murder, but by and large, both the Québécois and the Canadians have handled the issue of Quebec separatism responsibly and civilly. There were no death squads. There were no paramilitary crackdowns. Rather, the issue was put to a vote, of all things.

In that, they are a model for the rest of us.

The Least You Need to Know

- Mexico is becoming increasingly militarized.
- The Zapatistas are demanding rights in Chiapas.
- The Québécois are demanding independence in Canada.

Chapter 24

Give Peace a Chance

In This Chapter

- ◆ Is change possible?
- ◆ The United Nations
- ◆ The Olympic Movement
- ◆ The Nobel Peace Prize
- ◆ Nongovernmental organizations
- ◆ Peace in our time

To read about so many conflicts and so much death, hatred, and animosity can be depressing. It is truly shocking what people do to one another in the name of some ideology, ethnicity, or for power.

But progress, too, is possible. Conflicts do get resolved and people can learn to live with one another. It should be comforting, then, to realize that although the bad guys get the most press, there are far more good guys than bad.

Change Is in the Air

No, it is not easy to make peace. You do not make peace with your friends; you make peace with your enemies. It is not an appetizing thought for most people. Yet evidence abounds that people do it all the time and that peace and progress are possible.

The Abolition of Slavery

Once, the African slave trade was one of the largest businesses in the world. Starting in about 1500, slaves were imported to the Western Hemisphere until the nineteenth century. In the United States, the importing of slaves was outlawed by Congress in 1808.

But the United States was actually only a small player in the overall slave trade that brought roughly 10 million Africans west. The numbers actually broke down this way:

♦ The United States imported about 650,000 slaves before 1808, or roughly 7 percent of the overall number of slaves.

♦ The Caribbean and Brazil imported the largest percentage of the 10 million African slaves—73 percent.

♦ The rest of South America accounted for 17 percent.

Slaves sold for about $1,500 in 1850, or in year 2000 dollars, about $18,000. They brought in an annual rate of return of about 10 percent. So the slave trade, in today's terms, would be a multibillion dollar enterprise.

And even though it was clearly abhorrent and repugnant, the slave trade lasted for more than 300 years. By the time the United States was ready to go to war over the issue, slavery had become an ingrained institution that kept the rural south economically viable in relation to the more industrial north.

What should encourage us all is that despite its vast economic underpinnings, despite racism and hatred, despite the fact that it was big business, more important was that slavery was disgusting and wrong. In a world in which money means so much, and morals often amount to so little, that is no small thing.

Landmine!

Carolina, which later separated into North and South Carolina, enacted one of the most stringent set of laws governing slaves in the United States. The hours of working slaves were set at no more than 15 hours per day between March 25 and September 25, and no more than 14 hours per day between September 25 and March 25.

By the end of the nineteenth century, slavery had been all but abolished in the Western Hemisphere (although it certainly thrived, and thrives, in other parts of the world). And it was not just the institution that was ended; it was the *idea* that people's lives could literally be bought and sold that was also eradicated.

If we can end that idea, is it not impossible to conclude that other ideas—things like hunger, war, or racism—could similarly be done away with? Sure, it sounds pie in the sky, but so did the abolition of slavery to that black field hand slaving in Mississippi in 1825.

Ding Dong, the Witch Is Dead!

The Soviet Union cast a giant, dark cloud over most of Europe for the last half of the twentieth century. It was, according to Ronald Reagan, "an Evil Empire," and certainly there was plenty of proof to back up that assertion:

- Soviet forced labor camps were first established in 1919. By 1934, the Gulag had several million inmates.

- Josef Stalin was one of the greatest tyrants of all time, killing 20 million of his own countrymen.

- On April 13, 1943, Germans discovered the mass graves of several thousand officers of the former Polish Army murdered on Stalin's orders.

- In 1968, Alexander Dubcek in Czechoslovakia set out to reform his Warsaw Pact country. For the first time since 1948, the Czech government proclaimed the legitimacy of basic human rights and liberties and objected to the persecution of people for their own political convictions. In response, the Soviets, on August 20, 1968, invaded Czechoslovakia, ending the so-called "Prague Spring."

By the 1980s, the Soviet Union had seemingly become a monolithic empire determined to keep its satellites of Albania, Bulgaria, Hungary, East Germany, Poland, Rumania, and Czechoslovakia in check at any cost.

What no one expected was that a visionary man of peace would come to lead the Soviet Union. Mikhail Gorbachev concluded that something had to change in the USSR, and he instituted a so-called "Sinatra Doctrine" that allowed the Warsaw Pact countries to do things their way.

That small opening was all that was needed. In the fall of 1989, Hungary decided to open its border with East Germany, heretofore a completely isolated country. That decision, that little crack in the iron curtain, was all the people of Eastern Europe needed to break free and eventually topple modern communism.

Hungary's decision to open its East German border allowed East Germans to enter Hungary, and then enter Austria, and finally land in West Germany, reuniting with long lost loved ones. What started out as a trickle of refugees quickly became an unstoppable flood of change that swept through Eastern Europe with surprising swiftness.

> ### Reliable Resources
>
> General Secretary Gorbachev, if you seek peace, if you seek prosperity for the Soviet Union and Eastern Europe, if you seek liberalization: Come here to this gate! Mr. Gorbachev, open this gate! Mr. Gorbachev, tear down this wall!
>
> —Ronald Reagan, remarks at the Brandenburg Gate, West Berlin, Germany, June 12, 1987

Here's how it played out in Germany. After weeks of discussion in East Germany about a new travel law, and after mass demonstrations against the government, a member of the East German government was asked—at 6:53 P.M. on November 9, 1989, at a press conference—when the new travel law would come into force. He stammered, "Well, as far as I can see … straightaway, immediately."

Thousands of East Berliners stormed to the border crossings. At the Berlin Wall, the people demanded that the border be opened, and at 10:30 P.M. it was opened. That was the end of the Berlin Wall. An onrush of East Berliner's streamed into West Berlin over, around, and through the Wall. Wild celebrations erupted in both countries throughout the night. The Berlin Wall had fallen, and Eastern Europe would finally be free of the yoke of communism and Soviet repression.

> ### Reliable Resources
>
> According to one participant, the night went like this: "Perhaps 7,000 people were pressed together, shouting, cheering, clapping. We pushed through the crowd. From the East German side we could hear the sound of heavy machines. With a giant drill, they were punching holes in the wall. Every time a drill poked through, everyone cheered. People shot off fireworks and emergency flares and rescue rockets. Many were using hammers to chip away at the wall. There were countless holes. At one place, a crowd of East German soldiers looked through a narrow hole. We reached through and shook hands. The Germans were drunk with joy."

Again we see that progress is possible, and peace is achievable. It seemed to many people that the mighty Soviet Union was insurmountable and would dominate Eastern Europe seemingly forever. What few expected was that it would fold like a house of cards.

If the Evil Empire could be defeated and freedom could be restored to its seven satellites, what else is possible? What other evils in this world can be eradicated?

Middle East Peace

If you want more proof that the impossible is possible, consider the Middle East. In the modern world, no two countries have gone to war against each other more often than Israel and Egypt. Yet these bitterest of enemies found a way to create peace for their people.

What it took is not all that different from what it took in the Soviet Union—brave, bold leaders who were willing to take a risk in hopes of a higher return. Menachem Begin and Anwar Sadat both risked ridicule at home, and in Sadat's case, his decision to make peace probably cost him his life.

By the same token, Sadat and Begin personify what is needed if the world is to ever be a more peaceful place: the power to make a change, the understanding that change is necessary, the realization that peace is not easy, and the willingness to lead people and change minds.

That last aspect, the ability to change minds, might be the most important ingredient of all. By and large, people are creatures of habit and indoctrination. Serbs are taught to hate Bosnians. Israelis are taught to hate Arabs. It takes a leader of extraordinary courage to lead his people down a new path and to teach them a new way of thinking.

The people of Israel and Egypt were fortunate to have once had men like that in charge. One can only wonder what, say, Yasser Arafat could have done had he taken a page out of the Sadat playbook.

Northern Ireland

Peace also requires a people who are willing to change. In Northern Ireland, the Catholics and Protestants got so tired of war that they concluded that peace had to be better. Doing so meant that they had to give up age-old animosities and beliefs about each other; not an easy thing to do either.

But it is to their everlasting credit that they are trying.

The United Nations

One of the very first efforts to create a world of greater tolerance and more understanding occurred in 1899 at the International Peace Conference. The Conference, held in The Hague, worked on methods for settling crises peacefully, preventing wars, and codifying rules of warfare. It adopted the Convention for the Pacific Settlement of International Disputes and established the Permanent Court of Arbitration.

The immediate forerunner of the United Nations was the League of Nations, the brainchild of President Woodrow Wilson. The League of Nations was established in 1919 under the Treaty of Versailles "to promote international cooperation and to achieve peace and security." But it was doomed to failure when an *isolationist* United States refused to join, and it ceased its activities after failing to prevent World War II.

Diplomatic Dialogue

When a person (or country) wants to stay out of foreign affairs and international relations, the person is said to be an **isolationist;** someone who wants their country to remain isolated. In this rapidly shrinking, interconnected world, isolationists are becoming dinosaurs.

In 1945, at the conclusion of World War II, representatives from 50 countries met in San Francisco to draw up the United Nations Charter. The Charter was signed on June 26, 1945, by the representatives from the 50 countries. Poland, which was not represented at the Conference, signed it later and became one of the original 51 Member States.

The United Nations officially came into existence on October 24, 1945, when the Charter had been ratified by China, France, the Soviet Union, the United Kingdom, the United States, and by a majority of other signatories.

The purpose behind the United Nations was to help stabilize international relations and give peace a more secure foundation. Indeed, peacekeeping has become one of its most vital functions. This function is critical in an oft dangerous world. As the organization puts it:

> United Nations peacekeepers—military personnel in their distinctive blue helmets or blue berets, civilian police, and a range of other civilians—help implement peace agreements, monitor ceasefires, create buffer zones, or support complex military and civilian functions essential to maintain peace and begin reconstruction and institution-building in societies devastated by war.

> Member states voluntarily provide troops and equipment—the United Nations has no army or civilian police—for which they are compensated from a special peace-keeping budget.

> The peacekeepers' strongest "weapon" is the impartiality with which they carry out their mandate. But peacekeeping is dangerous business; over 1,650 U.N. peacekeepers have died in the performance of their duties since 1948.

Maybe even more impressive is that since 1945, the United Nations has negotiated 172 peaceful settlements of various conflicts. Similarly, the United Nations has enabled people in many countries to participate in free and fair elections, including those held in Cambodia, Namibia, El Salvador, Eritrea, Mozambique, Nicaragua, South Africa, Kosovo, and East Timor. It also provides electoral advice, assistance, and monitoring of results.

The United Nations promotes peace in many other ways as well:

- The U.N. Development Programme (UNDP) designs and implements projects for agriculture, industry, education, and the environment. It supports more than 5,000 projects with a budget of $1.3 billion.
- The World Bank is at the forefront in supporting developing countries worldwide. It has loaned more than $300 billion for development projects since 1946.

- By investigating individual complaints of human rights abuses, the U.N. Human Rights Commission has focused world attention on cases of torture, disappearance, and arbitrary detention and has generated international pressure to be brought on governments to improve their human rights records.

- The United Nations, through the International Atomic Energy Agency, helps minimize the threat of nuclear war by inspecting nuclear reactors in 90 countries to ensure that nuclear materials are not diverted for military purposes.

- More than 30 million refugees fleeing war, famine, or persecution have received aid from the U.N. High Commissioner for Refugees since 1951.

- U.N. agencies have worked to make safe drinking water available to 1.3 billion people in rural areas since 1990.

- A 13-year effort by the World Health Organization resulted in the eradication of smallpox from the planet in 1980. In 1974, only 5 percent of children in developing countries were immunized against major diseases. Today, as a result of the efforts of UNICEF and WHO, there is an 80 per cent immunization rate, saving the lives of more than 3 million children each year.

(Source: UN: Major Achievements of the UN; www.un.org/aboutun/achieve.htm)

Reliable Resources

The United Nations and its related agencies have won the Nobel Peace Prize an amazing eight times:

1950—U.N. Middle East mediator

1954—U.N. refugee agency

1961—U.N. Secretary General

1965—UNICEF

1969—U.N. Labour Agency

1981—U.N. refugee agency

1988—U.N. peacekeepers

On December 10, 2001, the United Nations and its Secretary General, Kofi Annan, received the Nobel Peace Prize on the hundredth anniversary of the venerated award.

International Humanitarian Law

Another international movement that is a very encouraging sign for a more humane world is that of International Humanitarian Law (IHL). It may surprise you to learn that war is illegal. The Charter of the United Nations states that the threat or use of force against other States is unlawful and so, since 1945, war has no longer been an acceptable way to settle conflicts between states.

Yet even so, armed conflicts are permissible under international law under a few circumstances:

- In self defense
- During a civil war
- To maintain or restore international peace and security

And, as you have seen throughout this book far too much, war is still a fact of life. As such, there emerged a need for rules which limit the effects of war on civilians. That is the goal of IHL, with the Geneva Conventions as its primary expression, along with an important body of resulting law: Six major treaties with more than 600 articles place restrictions on the use of violence in wartime.

According to Hans-Peter Gasser, IHL can be summarized in a few principles:

- Persons who are not taking part in hostilities, or who no longer are, shall be protected and treated humanely. They shall be given appropriate care, without any discrimination.
- Captured combatants shall be treated humanely. They shall be protected against all acts of violence, especially torture. They have the right to a normal judicial procedure.
- No superfluous injury or unnecessary suffering shall be inflicted on the opponent.
- Neither civilian populations nor civilian objects shall be the target of military attacks.

According to Gasser, "these principles give expression to what the International Court of Justice has called 'elementary considerations of humanity,' and serve to remind us that even in war, there should be dignity."

Going for the Gold

International understanding can occur in other ways as well. The modern Olympic Games do much to promote world peace by bringing countries together in the spirit of friendly rivalry. By so doing, the Olympics prove time and again that there are many ways to interact internationally: war being just one of them.

The first Olympic Games were held in 776 B.C.E. At first, the sprint was the only event. Events like the discus and javelin throw were added later. These ancient Olympic Games were held for more than 1,000 years but were abolished in 394 C.E.

The Games were revived in 1896. As Baron Pierre de Coubertin, the father of the modern Olympic movement put it, "The idea of the revival of Olympic Games was the logical culmination of a great movement. The nineteenth century saw the taste for physical exercises revive everywhere. At the same time, the great inventions—the railways and the telegraph—abridged distances. People intermingled and have learned to know each other better."

In fact, the symbols that we associate with the Olympics were all chosen as symbols of peace and international understanding:

♦ The colored rings were conceived of by Baron Pierre de Coubertin. Each of the five rings symbolizes one of the five continents. The intertwining of the five rings symbolizes the conjunction of the continents during the Games and represents the ideal of international peace and brotherhood.

♦ The flame symbolizes purity. It lights the way for the athletes, showing them the importance of creating a lasting unity for all mankind.

♦ The festivities associated with the Games symbolize a united community of people who come together peacefully from different societies. Despite their various backgrounds, they all can contribute to a peaceful coexistence between nations.

A Noble Prize

The Nobel Peace Prize is one of the world's great honors. That the Nobel Committee honors peacemakers so is critical because it symbolizes just how important peacemaking is in this modern world.

The Nobel Peace Prize has been hailed as "the greatest honor a man can receive in this world." Since 1901, when the first Peace Prize was handed out, recipients have included Theodore Roosevelt, Albert Schweitzer, and Mother Teresa.

A popular misconception is that Alfred Nobel, as the inventor of dynamite, established the prize to assuage his guilt. But the truth is that the money Nobel made from dynamite came mostly from peacetime applications. In 2001, the prize was worth just about $1 million.

The Nobel Peace Prize honors people who are dedicated to peace and human rights in a world that at times seems to honor neither.

Landmine!

The Nobel Peace Prize has been controversial at times. In 1973, the prize was awarded to Henry Kissinger—who was then the U.S. Secretary of State—and Le Duc Tho of North Vietnam for their attempts to end the war in Vietnam. When a U.S. ambassador showed up to claim Kissinger's prize on his behalf, Norwegians, furious with the choice of Kissinger, pelted him with snowballs.

Nongovernmental Organizations

Nongovernmental Organizations (NGOs) are increasingly playing a vital role in peace-keeping and education throughout the world and should be a cause of optimism. NGOs are (usually) international nonprofit organizations working in conjunction with local peoples to create a better world. They perform a variety of critical peacemaking functions:

- **As an early warning system:** Because of their close work with local communities, NGOs are in a position to alert people of potential breakdowns in a country's government or among relations among domestic groups.

- **Human-rights monitoring:** NGOs play an important role by gathering information, sending out fact-finding missions, and so on.

- **Community-building:** NGOs play an important role in strengthening social systems by building needed infrastructure, working on public health, and training local leaders, for example.

- **Education:** This is a traditional role for NGOs and helps bring about conflict resolution.

Peace in Our Time

One reason why there is so much war and conflict in the world today is because people are identifying themselves ever more narrowly. Thus, for example, although they lived in relative peace and harmony when they identified themselves as one nation, when Yugoslavs splintered into five separate subnationalities, they were free to war upon each other precisely because there were now "others."

When a group identifies with some religion or country, it is far too easy to conclude that anyone not of that identity is the enemy:

- Arabs and Jews can hate each other.

- Islamic fundamentalists can hate Westerners.

- Hutus can murder the Tutsis who live next door.

> **Reliable Resources**
>
> Every kind of peaceful cooperation among men is primarily based on mutual trust and only secondarily on institutions such as courts of justice and police.
>
> —Albert Einstein

Interestingly, people in one's own group usually get a pass for actions that, if done by the others, would be cause for revenge. Thus, for example, it is considered to be valid self-defense to Palestinians when one of their own blows up a bunch of Israelis. However, that same action is thought to be murder when an Israeli kills Palestinians (and vice versa).

For all its faults, one reason why the United States is as stable as it is, is because constitutionally it is illegal to identify people because of their race or color. This doesn't mean that it doesn't happen, but it does mean that people in that heterogeneous society tend to think of themselves as Americans first and their subset nationality second. When you expand the scope of your identity, there are fewer people to blame and more people on your side.

Changing that narrow sort of thinking is exactly what creates peace. The United Nations, by fostering peaceful relations between countries, endeavors to change the way people think. The Olympics, by showing people competing peacefully, does the same thing.

When Israel and Egypt chose peace, it not only required their people to think differently, it also required brave leaders who were willing to take a risk on new and unpopular ideas. The leaders needed to, in fact, lead. When those living in Northern Ireland are willing to put aside their longstanding differences and animosities, they light the way for people in the rest of the world to change the way they think about their enemies as well. Enemies are not a requirement.

So one way to create a more peaceful world is for people to expand the scope of who they think they are, as well as to change the way they think about who they are. Noted futurist and inventor of the geodesic dome, Buckminster Fuller, did not consider himself a Californian (though he lived there), nor an American (though he lived there, too). He considered himself an "Earthian." It might seem idealistic, but killing others becomes far more difficult when they can be identified as part of your group.

Imagine how much less war there would be if more people expanded their identity similarly. If we can end slavery, if we can topple totalitarianism, if bitter enemies can learn to live in peace, if leaders can forge a new path, there is no telling what the planet Earth can do. The good guys can still win.

The Least You Need to Know

- The end of slavery and the fall of the Soviet Union prove that the impossible can be made possible.
- Difficult peace treaties also prove that progress is possible.
- The United Nations does much good, if often unheralded, work.
- The Olympics and the Nobel Peace Prize foster peace in their own way.
- Identity causes conflict.
- The good guys can still win.

Organizations

There are many concerned people who are trying to make the world a better place. Here is a list of the most prominent.

The United Nations
New York, NY 10017
212-963-7539
www.un.org

United Nations Children's Emergency
Fund (UNICEF)
333 East 38th Street—GC-6
New York, NY 10016
212-686-5522 (vox)
212-779-1679 (fax)
information@unicefusa.org

Human Rights Watch
350 Fifth Avenue, 34th floor
New York, NY 10118-3299
212-290-4700 (vox)
212-736-1300 (fax)
www.hrw.org

Amnesty International
322 8th Avenue
New York, NY 10001
212-807-8400
www.amnesty.org

Begin Sadat Center for Strategic
Studies (BESA)
Bar-Ilan University
Ramat Gan 52900
Israel
011-972-3-535-9198
besa@mail.biu.ac.il

The Carter Center
Office of Public Information
453 Freedom Parkway
Atlanta, GA 30307
404-331-3900
www.cartercenter.org

International Campaign to Ban
Landmines
110 Maryland Ave NE
Box 6, Suite 509
Washington, DC 20002
202-547-2667

Physicians for Social Responsibility
1875 Connecticut Avenue, NW
Suite 1012
Washington, DC 20009
202-667-4260 (vox)
202-667-4201 (fax)
www.psr.org.

International Olympic Committee
Château de Vidy
1007 Lausanne, VD
Switzerland
www.olympic.org

Appendix B

For More Information

This section provides a bibliography of the resources that have provided invaluable information and insights during my research for this book. If you are interested in learning more about any of the conflicts listed in this book (historical or otherwise), or about various peace efforts underway throughout the world, these resources should be useful.

Bibliographical Information

The World Wide Web is an invaluable resource for all kinds of information. The following links provide a good starting point for general information and facts about the countries discussed in this book.

Allafrica.com
www.allafrica.com
African news.

Center for Defence and International Security Studies
http://www.cdiss.org/hometemp.htm
Provides information about a wide range of defense and security issues relevant to both the UK and the international community.

Country Reports
www.emulateme.com/alphanationtext.htm
A site devoted to the history of every country on earth.

Crisis Web
www.crisisweb.org/
Anticipating and understanding conflicts.

Flashpoints
http://home.earthlink.net/~vehicool/countries-conflicts/countries-conflicts.html
Links to conflict briefings.

Global Issues that Affect Everyone
www.globalissues.org
This site provides a gateway to all kinds of global issues that ultimately affect us all.

Human Rights Watch
www.hrw.org
A good resource if you want to learn more about human rights violations and abuses worldwide, including the United States.

National Defense Council Foundation
www.ndcf.org/
Yearly updates of world conflicts.

Political Africa
www.africapolitical.com/
All Africa, all the time.

The BBC News Service
news.bbc.co.uk/
A great international news resource; the BBC search engine allows you to look up various countries—stories about them, background facts, and so on.

The Central Intelligence Agency's World Fact Book
www.cia.gov/cia/publications/factbook/index.html
An excellent overview of all countries.

The Federation of American Scientists
www.fas.org/man/dod-101/ops/war/
Great background information about world conflicts.

The History Guy
www.historyguy.com/new_and_recent_conflicts.html
A good source for more information about new and recent conflicts, listed country by country.

The United Nations
www.un.org/
Everything you need to know about the U.N.

Timetable of the History of Cuba
www.historyofcuba.com
Cuban history in a nutshell.

Unrepresented Nations and Peoples Organisation (UNPO)
www.unpo.org
Provides a forum for occupied nations, indigenous peoples, minorities, and even oppressed majorities who currently struggle to regain their lost countries and preserve their cultural identities.

Yahoo Regional Conflicts
dir.yahoo.com/Government/Politics/Regional_Conflicts
Yahoo's directory of conflict links.

Online Encyclopedias

Here is a list of search engines that are good for quick background checks and facts about countries and historical events or definitions of terms.

> ebooks.whsmithonline.co.uk/
> lexicorient.com/e.o/index.htm

www.bartleby.com/65/
www.encyclopedia.com/
www.humanitas-international.org/
www.lexisnexis.com
www.m-w.com/
www.onwar.com
www.pbs.org/wgbh/buildingbig/index.html
www.slider.com/index.htm
www.worldatlas.com

Web Bibliography

This section provides a chapter-by-chapter listing of the articles and links that provided invaluable insights and facts for my account of the state of world conflicts.

Chapter 1, "The World at War"

Council for a Livable World. "Foreign Aid and the Arms Trade: A Look at the Numbers."
www.clw.org/cat/foraid/faidexe.html

Crossett, Barbara. "Kofi Annan's Astonishing Facts!" *The New York Times*. September 27, 1998.
www.teachingforchange.org/News%20Items/un%20data.htm

Deen, Thalif. "Inequality Primary Cause of Wars, says Annan." InterPress Third World News Agency, 9 September 1999.
www.hartford-hwp.com/archives/27a/052.html

Fritz, Walter. "Peace Between Nations."
www.anice.net.ar/intsyst/peace.htm

Georgieff, Anthony. "Swedish Report Emphasizes Role of Poverty in War." Radio Free Europe/Radio Liberty.
www.rferl.org/nca/features/2000/06/F.RU.000620135251.html

Keegan, Sir John. "Eliminating the Causes of War."
www.pugwash.org/reports/pac/pac256/keegan.htm

Rummel, R.J. *Power Kills: Democracy as a Method of Nonviolence.* Transaction Publishers: 1997.
www.hawaii.edu/powerkills/

Chapter 2, "East Is East and West Is West"

Anon. "Attack on the USS Cole." Yemen Gateway.
www.al-bab.com/yemen/cole1.htm

Anon. "World Trade Center." PBS Online
www.pbs.org/wgbh/buildingbig/wonder/structure/world_trade.html

Armstrong, Karen. "The True, Peaceful Face of Islam." *Time*. October 1, 2001 Vol. 158 No. 15.
www.time.com/time/magazine/printout/0,8816,175987,00.html

Glossary of Islamic Terms and Concepts.
www.usc.edu/dept/MSA/reference/glossary.html

The International Policy Institute for Counter-Terrorism has put together the Osama bin Laden and al-Qaeda page, which provides an extensive listing of al-Qaeda-related reports and articles.
www.ict.org.il/articles/bombings.cfm

Islam: Empire of Faith. Companion website to the PBS film of the same name.
www.pbs.org/empires/islam/index.html

Symon, Fiona. "The Roots of Jihad." BBC News, Tuesday, 16 October, 2001.
news.bbc.co.uk/hi/english/world/middle_east/newsid_1603000/1603178.stm

Chapter 3, "The Middle East Mess"

Anon. "Camp David: Historic Moments." BBC News, Monday, 10 July, 2000.
news.bbc.co.uk/hi/english/world/middle_east/newsid_827000/827488.stm

Anon. "Failure of the Oslo Accords."
www.globalexchange.org/campaigns/palestine/oslo.html

Bard, Mitchell. "The Lebanon War." The Jewish Virtual Library.
www.us-israel.org/jsource/History/Lebanon_War.html

Beinin, Joel. "Camp David II." MERIP Press Information Notes, July 26, 2000.
www.merip.org/pins/pin26.html

Camp David Accords. September 17, 1978 192. The Camp David agreements, annexes, exchange of letters, 17 September 1978.
www.mfa.gov.il/mfa/go.asp?MFAH00ie0

Isseroff, Ami. "A Brief History of Israel and Palestine."
www.mideastweb.org/BriefHistory.htm

Lee, Roger. "The History Guy: Arab-Israeli Wars: Suez/Sinai War (1956)."
www.historyguy.com/suez_war_1956.html

Chapter 4, "A Wreck Called Iraq"

Butt, Gerald. "Saddam Hussein Profile." BBC News, Thursday, 4 January, 2001.
news.bbc.co.uk/hi/english/world/middle_east/newsid_1100000/1100529.stm

CNN Special Report. "The survival of Saddam Hussein."
www.cnn.com/SPECIALS/2001/gulf.war/unfinished/war/index4.html

Columbia Encyclopedia. "Iran-Iraq War."
www.bartleby.com/65/ir/IranIraq.html

Hooker, Richard. "Mesopotamia: The Sumerians."
www.wsu.edu:8080/~dee/MESO/SUMER.HTM

Jews For Justice In The Middle East. "The Origin of the Palestine-Israeli Conflict."
www.mediareviewnet.com/JewsForJustice.htm

Kuwait Information Office, "History of the Kuwait-Iraq Border Dispute."
www.kuwait-info.org/Gulf_War/history_kuwait_iraq_border_dispute.html

Malowany, Matthew. "Defiance in the Desert."
www.cbc.ca/news/indepth/iraq/index.html#backandhistory

VanDoodewaard, William. "Islam United? A Comparison of Shi'ite and Sunni Belief and Practice."
www.rim.org/muslim/shiite.htm

Chapter 5, "Never-Never Land: Kurdistan"

Allison, Graham T. "Bombing Afghanistan with Food." Boston Globe, October 14, 2001. www.ksg.harvard.edu/news/opeds/allison_afghanistan_war_bg_101401.htm

Anon. "Struggle in Turkey. The final goodbye from a Kurdish activist who was executed by the Islamic Republic of Iran on January 24, 2002." www.ukin.org/struggle/turkey.htm

Anon. "The Kurds in Iran: From the Mahabad Republic until Present." kurdweb.humanrights.de/keo/english/politics/analysis/analysis-04.html

Burkay, Kemal. "The Kurdish Question—Its History and Present Situation." members.aol.com/KHilfsvere/Kurds.html

CNN News. The Ocalan Trial: Triumph or Test of Turkish Policy on Kurds? www.cnn.com/SPECIALS/1999/ocalan/stories/overview/

Culturalorientation.net "The Kurds in History." www.culturalorientation.net/kurds/khist.html

Sancton, Thomas. "A Terrorist's Bitter End." *Time*, March 1, 1999. www.time.com/time/daily/special/ocalan/bitterend.html

Usher, Rod. "Nationalists Without a Nation." *Time*, March 01, 1999. www.time.com/time/magazine/intl/article/0,9171,1107990301-21232,00.html.,

Chapter 6, "Hotspots in Northern Africa"

Anon. "Sudan: A Historical Perspective." http://www.sudan.net/society/history.html

Astill, James. "Osama: The Sudan Years." The Guardian, October 17, 2001. www.guardian.co.uk/g2/story/0,3604,575396,00.html

Broder, Jonathan. "How *real* terrorists do it." www.salon.com/june97/news/news2970609.html

Davis, Karen. "Slave Trade Thrives in Sudan." www.s-t.com/daily/02-98/02-22-98/a02wn011.htm

Out There News. "Egypt: All under wraps until recently." www.megastories.com/islam/world/egypt.htm

Chapter 7, "Death Around the Horn"

FAS. "Ethiopia / Eritrea War." www.fas.org/man/dod-101/ops/war/eritrea.htm

Human Rights Watch. "Mengistu Haile Mariam." www.hrw.org/press/1999/nov/mengitsu.htm

Milner, Kate. "Flashback 1984: Portrait of a famine." BBC News Online, 6 April, 2000. news.bbc.co.uk/hi/english/world/africa/newsid_703000/703958.stm

Chapter 8, "Insanity in West Africa"

Anon. "Country profile: Liberia." BBC News, 20 May, 2002. news.bbc.co.uk/hi/english/world/africa/country_profiles/newsid_1043000/1043500.stm

Anon. "Q&A: Sierra Leone's hostages" BBC News, 10 August, 1999. news.bbc.co.uk/hi/english/special_report/1999/01/99/sierra_leone/newsid_252000/252822.stm

Anon. "Snapshot of issues surrounding Clinton's Nigeria visit." CNN, August 25, 2000. http://news.bbc.co.uk/hi/english/world/americas/newsid_756000/756309.stm

Blunt, Elizabeth. "The Guinea conflict explained." BBC News, February 13, 2001. news.bbc.co.uk/hi/english/world/africa/newsid_1167000/1167811.stm

FAS. "Movement of Democratic Forces in the Casamance (MFDC)." www.fas.org/irp/world/para/mfdc.htm

Human Rights Watch. "Sierra Leone Rebels Violating Peace Accord." www.hrw.org/press/1999/aug/sierra3008.htm

Rupert, James. "Nigerian Ruler Dies After Brutal Reign." Washington Post, June 9, 1998. www.washingtonpost.com/wp-srv/inatl/longterm/nigeria/stories/abacha060998.htm

Chapter 9, "Struggles in Central Africa"

Anon. "Angola." home.earthlink.net/~vehicool/countries-conflicts/Angola-web/angola_briefing_main.html

Anon. "Rwanda genocide inquiry to end in 2004." BBC News, 7 December, 2001. news.bbc.co.uk/hi/english/world/africa/newsid_1691000/1691954.stm

Chadwick, Alex. "Coltan Mining and Eastern Congo's Gorillas." www.npr.org/programs/re/archivesdate/2001/dec/20011220.coltan.html

Human Rights Watch. "Leave None to Tell the Story: Genocide in Rwanda." www.hrw.org/reports/1999/rwanda/index.htm#TopOfPage

Pearce, Justin. "Landmines: War's deadly legacy." BBC News, January 29, 1999. news.bbc.co.uk/hi/english/special_report/1999/01/99/angola/newsid_264000/264223.stm

Chapter 10, "All in the Family: North and South Korea"

Anon. "Profile: Kim Jong-il." BBC News, April 2, 2002. news.bbc.co.uk/hi/english/world/asia-pacific/newsid_1907000/1907197.stm

Anon. "Kim Dae-jung: Dedicated to reconciliation." CNN, June 14, 2001. www.cnn.com/2001/WORLD/asiapcf/east/06/12/bio.kim.daejung/

FAS. "Korean War." www.fas.org/man/dod-101/ops/korea.htm

Schnabel, James F. "United States Army in the Korean War: Policy and Direction: The First Year." www.army.mil/cmh-pg/books/p&d.htm

Chapter 11, "Enter the Dragon: China"

Anon. "China-Taiwan History." PBS Online News Hour, March 07, 2000. www.pbs.org/newshour/bb/asia/china/china-taiwan.html

Anon. "What You Need to Know About the Chinese Occupation of Tibet." www.freetibet.org/info/basics.htm

Holland Sentinel Archives. "Leaders who ordered Tiananmen crackdown feared arrest." www.thehollandsentinel.net/stories/010701/new_Leaders.html

Human Rights Watch. "China: Human Rights Concerns in Xinjiang." www.hrw.org/backgrounder/asia/china-bck1017.htm

Macan-Markar, Marwaan. "Asian governments seen exploiting September 11." www.thinkcentreasia.org/News/news012.html

O'Hanlon, Michael. "Can China Conquer Taiwan?"
www.brook.edu/dybdocroot/views/articles/ohanlon/2000fall_IS.htm

Smith, Charles R. "Rand Report Warns of Conflict with China." Newsmax.com, June 20, 2001.
www.newsmax.com/archives/articles/2001/6/19/205940.shtml

Chapter 12, "Cain and Abel: India and Pakistan"

Dhar, L. N. "An Outline of the History of Kashmir."
www.koausa.org/Crown/history.html

FAS. "Jammu and Kashmir."
www.fas.org/irp/world/india/threat/kashmir.htm

Kumar, Radha. "Sovereignty and Intervention: Opinions in South Asia."
www.pugwash.org/reports/rc/como_india.htm

Ramana, M. V. and A. H. Nayyar. "India, Pakistan and the Bomb."
www.sciam.com/2001/1201issue/1201ramana.html

Sahay, Tara Shankar. "India ready to take on Pakistan at two levels."
www.rediff.com/news/2001/dec/21parl.htm

Spaeth, Anthony. "India: Piercing the Armor." *Time*. September 11, 1995.
www.time.com/time/international/1995/950911/india.html

The Legacy Project. "India-Pakistan Partition."
www.legacy-project.org/events/display.html?ID=10

Chapter 13, "Religious and Ethnic Animosity in Indonesia"

Anon. "Dayaks broaden violent campaign in Borneo." CNN, February 26, 2001.
www.cnn.com/2001/WORLD/asiapcf/southeast/02/26/indonesia.killing02/

Arthurs, Clare. "Irian Jaya: A troubled history." BBC News, January 1, 2000.
news.bbc.co.uk/hi/english/world/asia-pacific/newsid_587000/587064.stm

FAS. "Timor."
www.fas.org/man/dod-101/ops/war/timor.htm

Karon, Tony. "Megawati: The Princess Who Settled for the Presidency." *Time*. July 27, 2001.
www.time.com/time/pow/article/0,8599,169130,00.html

Linder, Diane. "Ethnic Conflict in Kalimantan." ICE Case Studies.
www.american.edu/projects/mandala/TED/ice/kaliman.htm

McCarthy, Terry. "Chaos in the Islands." *Time*. January 17, 2000.
www.time.com/time/asia/magazine/2000/0117/indonesia.ambon.html

Nugent, Nicholas. "Roots of Sulawesi Conflict." BBC News, December 20, 2001.
news.bbc.co.uk/hi/english/world/asia-pacific/newsid_1719000/1719964.stm

U.S. Committee for Refugees. "Political History of Aceh."
www.refugees.org/news/crisis/indonesia/aceh.htm

Chapter 14, "More Asian Atrocities"

Anon. " Country Profile: Burma." February 25, 2002.
news.bbc.co.uk/hi/english/world/asia-pacific/country_profiles/newsid_1300000/1300003.stm

Anon. "Guide to Philippines conflict." BBC News, December 6, 2001.
news.bbc.co.uk/hi/english/world/asia-pacific/newsid_1695000/1695576.stm

Anon. "Row grows over disputed Spratly island." CNN, March 21, 2001.
www.cnn.com/2001/WORLD/asiapcf/east/03/21/China.Philippine.row/

Anon. "Sri Lanka: The ethnic divide." BBC News, May 16, 2000.
news.bbc.co.uk/hi/english/world/south_asia/newsid_514000/514577.stm

Anon. "Sri Lanka: An unwinnable war?" BBC News, April 27, 2000.
news.bbc.co.uk/hi/english/world/south_asia/newsid_620000/620631.stm

Gregorius, Arlene. "World: Asia-Pacific Profile: Aung San Suu Kyi." BBC News, July 29, 1998.
news.bbc.co.uk/hi/english/world/asia-pacific/newsid_140000/140955.stm

Havely, Joe. "Asia-Pacific Analysis: Flashpoint Spratly." BBC News, February 14, 1999.
news.bbc.co.uk/hi/english/world/asia-pacific/newsid_279000/279170.stm

Horn, Robert. "Burmese Democracy Leader Faces New Threat." *Time*, November 28, 2000.
www.time.com/time/asia/features/news/2000/11/27/burma.suu_kyi.html

Huang, Cheng-China. "Diaoyutai Islands Dispute."
www.american.edu/projects/mandala/TED/ice/DIAOYU.HTM

Iyer, Pico. "Woman of the Year: Corazon Aquino." *Time*, January 5, 1987.
www.time.com/time/special/moy/1986.html

Kelly, Todd C. "Vietnamese Claims to the Truong Sa Archipelago."
www.hawaii.edu/cseas/pubs/explore/v3/todd.html

Powell, Leigh. "Sprately Island Dispute."
http://www.american.edu/TED/SPRATLY.HTM

Chapter 15, "The Balkan Mess"

Simpson, Bob. "Milosevic's Yugoslavia." BBC News.
news.bbc.co.uk/hi/english/static/in_depth/europe/2000/milosevic_yugoslavia/croatia.stm

FAS. "Operation Deliberate Force."
www.fas.org/man/dod-101/ops/deliberate_force.htm

Judah, Tim. "Milosevic's legacy." BBC News June 30, 2001.
news.bbc.co.uk/hi/english/world/europe/newsid_1415000/1415683.stm

U.S. State Department Report. "Ethnic Cleansing in Kosovo: An Accounting."
www.state.gov/www/global/human_rights/kosovoii/document.html

Wood, Paul. "The downfall of Milosevic." BBC News April 1, 2001.
news.bbc.co.uk/hi/english/world/europe/newsid_1204000/1204857.stm

Chapter 16, "The Russian Bear"

Anon. " Destination Guantanamo Bay." BBC News, December 28, 2001.
news.bbc.co.uk/hi/english/world/americas/newsid_1731000/1731704.stm

Anon. "Arrests follow failed Paraguay coup." BBC News, May 20, 2001.
news.bbc.co.uk/hi/english/world/americas/newsid_756000/756309.stm

Anon. "The first bloody battle." BBC News, March 16, 2000.
news.bbc.co.uk/hi/english/world/europe/newsid_482000/482323.stm

Miller, Sarah K. "Crisis in the Caucasus; History of the conflict in Dagestan."
www.infoplease.com/spot/dagestan1.html

Valasek, Tomas. "Demystifying the Role of Islam in the Former Soviet South."
www.cdi.org/weekly/1999/issue33.html

Valasek, Tomas. "The Changing Face of the Chechnya War." Weekly Defense Monitor,
July 13, 2000.
www.cdi.org/weekly/2000/issue28.html

Chapter 17, "Northern Ireland Imbroglio"

Anon. "Ireland's Troubled History."
www.washingtonpost.com/wp-srv/inatl/longterm/nireland/overview.htm

Anon. "The Honorable George J. Mitchell."
www.us-irelandalliance.org/aboutmitchell.html

Chapter 18, "Smoldering European Conflicts"

Anon. "History of Basque Nationalism: Birth and Ideology of Euskadi Ta Askatasuna."
www.contrast.org/mirrors/ehj/html/birtheta.html

Anon. "Country profile: Armenia." BBC News, March 8, 2002.
news.bbc.co.uk/hi/english/world/europe/country_profiles/newsid_1108000/1108052.stm

Anon. "Terrorist handbook reveals 'secret of success.'" BBC News, May 21, 2001.
news.bbc.co.uk/hi/english/world/monitoring/media_reports/newsid_1343000/
1343250.stm

Anon. "Turkey foresees Cyprus settlement." BBC News, January 8, 2002.
news.bbc.co.uk/hi/english/world/europe/newsid_1749000/1749138.stm

FAS. "Nagorno-Karabakh."
www.fas.org/man/dod-101/ops/war/nagorno-karabakh.htm

Housden, Tom. "Cyprus: Years of division." BBC News, January 15, 2002.
http://news.bbc.co.uk/hi/english/world/europe/newsid_1760000/1760565.stm

"Q&A: Cyprus conflict explained." BBC News, January 15, 2002.
http://news.bbc.co.uk/hi/english/world/europe/newsid_1761000/1761585.stm

Schweimler, Daniel. "Proud Basques defend ancient culture." BBC News, December 6,
1999.
news.bbc.co.uk/hi/english/world/europe/newsid_548000/548545.stm

Chapter 19, "Columbia in Conflict"

Anon. "Country profile: Colombia." BBC News, May 1, 2002.
news.bbc.co.uk/hi/english/world/americas/country_profiles/newsid_1212000/1212798.stm

Anon. "The Colombian Drug Cartels."
gangstersinc.tripod.com/Car.html

Human Rights Watch. "Colombia."
www.hrw.org/wr2k1/americas/colombia.html

Meza, Ricardo Vargas. "The Revolutionary Armed Forces of Colombia (FARC) and the
Illicit Drug Trade."
www.tni.org/drugs/pubs/farc.htm

Chapter 20, "Hatred in Haiti"

Anon. "Country profile: Haiti." BBC News, March 19, 2002.
news.bbc.co.uk/hi/english/world/americas/country_profiles/newsid_1202000/1202772.stm

Anon. "Profile of H.E. Mr. Jean-Bertrand Aristide: President of the Republic of Haiti."
www.haiti.org/aristide-bio.htm

FAS. "Operation Uphold Democracy."
www.fas.org/man/dod-101/ops/uphold_democracy.htm

Sorre, Lucio. "Christopher Columbus."
http://www.castellobanfi.com/features/story_3.html

Chapter 21, "More Latin and South American Standoffs"

Anon. "Arrests follow failed Paraguay coup." BBC News, May 20, 2000.
news.bbc.co.uk/hi/english/world/americas/newsid_756000/756309.stm

Anon. "Country profile: Ecuador." BBC News, March 7, 2002.
news.bbc.co.uk/hi/english/world/americas/country_profiles/newsid_1212000/1212882.stm

Anon. "Peru's Fujimori resigns effective Tuesday, leaving Peru to debate a transition government." CNN, November 20, 2000.
www.cnn.com/2000/WORLD/americas/11/20/peru.fujimori.03/

Anon. "Timeline: Ecuador." BBC News, March 21, 2002.
news.bbc.co.uk/hi/english/world/americas/newsid_1212000/1212826.stm

Anon. "Timeline: Paraguay." BBC News, March 21, 2002.
news.bbc.co.uk/hi/english/world/americas/newsid_1224000/1224216.stm

Human Rights Watch. "Peru."
www.hrw.org/wr2k1/americas/peru.html

Izaguirre, Carlos Reyna. "Shining Path in the 21st Century: Actors in Search of a New Script."
http://www.hartford-hwp.com/archives/42a/016.html

Chapter 22, "Life in These United States"

Chomsky, Noam. "The Invasion of Panama."
http://www.zmag.org/chomsky/sam/sam-2-05.html

CNN. "Vietnam." (Episode script).
http://www.cnn.com/SPECIALS/cold.war/episodes/11/script.html

Kennedy, Bruce. "Dien Bien Phu 1954 battle changed Vietnam's history."
http://www.cnn.com/SPECIALS/cold.war/episodes/11/spotlight/

King, Martin Luther Jr. "The Casualties of the War in Vietnam."
www.stanford.edu/group/King/speeches/unpub/670225-001_The_Casualties_of_the_War_in_Vietnam.htm

Chapter 23, "Problems for America's Neighbors"

Anon. "The Beauty of Resistance."
www.globalexchange.org/campaigns/mexico/chiapas/communities/diary1.html

Anon. "Mexico; A chronology of key events." *Time*, March 21, 2002.
news.bbc.co.uk/hi/english/world/americas/newsid_1210000/1210779.stm

Anon. "So You Wanna Know about Quebec Separatism?"
http://www.soyouwanna.com/site/pros_cons/quebec/quebec.html

Cummings, Joe. "Drugs, Rebellion, and Mexico's Militarization."
www.mexconnect.com/mex_/travel/jcummings/jcdrugsmiltariz.html

Robberson, Tod. "Rebels Show Flair for Communicating." *Washington Post*, February 9, 1994.
www.washingtonpost.com/wp-srv/inatl/longterm/mexico/overview/keymarcos.htm

Whitbeck, Harris. "Mexico faces ironies of post-Cold War rebellion."
www.cnn.com/SPECIALS/cold.war/episodes/18/then.now/

Chapter 24, "Give Peace a Chance"

Gasser, Hans-Peter. "International humanitarian law and the protection of war victims."
www.ICRC.org

"History of the United Nations."
www.un.org/aboutun/history.htm

"Major Achievements of the United Nations."
www.un.org/aboutun/achieve.htm

"United Nations Peacekeeping: Some questions and answers."
www.un.org/Depts/dpko/dpko/ques.htm

Books

If you prefer a more traditional way of browsing for information and insights about the human path of war and conflict, check out these books.

Grenville, J.A.S. *A History of the World in the 20th Century*. Cambridge, Mass.: Harvard University Press, 2000.

Halberstam, David. *War in a Time of Peace*. New York: Scribner, 2001.

Kozodoy, Neal. *The Mideast Peace Process: An Autopsy*. San Francisco: Encounter Books, 2001.

Mandela, Nelson. *The Long Walk to Freedom: The Autobiography of Nelson Mandela*. New York: Little Brown & Co., 1995.

Mitchell, George J. *Making Peace*. Berkeley: University of California Press, 2001.

Shlaim, Avi. *The Iron Wall: Israel and the Arab World*. New York: W.W. Norton & Co., 2001.

Tolstoy, Leo. *War and Peace*. New York: Viking Press, 1982.

Tzu, Sun. *The Art of War*. Oxford, England: Oxford University Press, 1984.

Appendix C

Glossary

apartheid   Apartheid was the official state policy of South Africa that forcefully subjugated the African majority to the will of the European minority.

apparatchik   Under Communist rule, loyalty to the party was one of the most respected traits. An apparatchik was an unquestioningly loyal subordinate or bureaucrat.

archipelago   Any sea or broad sheet of water interspersed with many islands or with a group of islands.

Bolsheviks   The Bolsheviks (meaning "majority") split from the original Russian Socialist movement in 1903, and developed into a small, organized, revolutionary, Marxist group thereafter. In November 1917, they took over a country torn by civil war. Upon gaining power, the Bolsheviks renamed themselves the Communist Party of the Soviet Union (CPSU).

caliph   The person acting in Muhammad's place after his death; that is, the leader of Islam is called the caliph. Through history, there have been many caliphs. The last one however was removed by the Mongols when they conquered Baghdad in 1258. The term is rarely used for anyone else but the leader of the entire Muslim community.

communism   A system of social organization in which property (especially real property and the means of production) is held communally. Based on the works of Karl Marx, and interpreted by Vladimir Lenin, communism's aim is to overthrow capitalism by revolutionary means and establish a classless society. Communism must be distinguished from socialism, which seeks similar ends but by evolutionary rather than revolutionary means.

containment   In politics, containment refers to the foreign policy strategy pursued by the United States after World War II. The term suggested a policy of patient but firm and vigilant, long-term containment of communist expansion.

Convention on the Law of the Sea   A U.N.–sponsored agreement that establishes rules governing the uses of the world's oceans and their resources. The Convention resolves conflicting claims, interpretations, and measuring techniques by setting a 200-mile limit as the boundary of a country's continental shelf.

Crusades   A series of wars initiated by Christian warriors determined to win back their holy lands from the Muslims.

de facto   When a fact exists, whether it is legal or not, it is said to be de facto. For example, when two countries are in a de facto state of war, they are waging war, whether one country has actually declared war or not.

détente   From the French, détente is the relaxation of strained relations or tensions.

Drug Enforcement Agency (DEA)   A unit of the United States government charged with enforcing drug laws and eradicating illegal drugs. Since 1973, the DEA has grown significantly, especially during the last several years. The DEA has more than 4,000 agents, and its budget is roughly $1.5 billion.

domino theory   During the Cold War, it was the conventional wisdom that if one democratic state in a region fell to communism, all other democracies might, too, like so many dominos; hence the name domino theory.

Eastern Bloc countries   During the Cold War, much of the world was divided into two camps—the West (democratic countries) and the East (communist countries). Eastern Bloc countries were those that were part of the Soviet Union's Warsaw Pact and sphere of influence—countries like East Germany, Poland, Romania, and Czechoslovakia.

fascism   A system of government marked by centralization of authority under a dictator, stringent socioeconomic controls, and racism; suppression of the opposition through terror and censorship, and usually, a policy of belligerent nationalism are par for the course.

fatwa   A legal opinion or decree on a specific issue.

fiefdom   The estate or domain of a feudal lord. In modern times, the word has come to mean an area over which one dominant person exercises complete control.

gross domestic product   The value of all goods and services provided within the borders of a nation.

hegemony   In politics, hegemony is the overwhelming influence and authority of one country over another country or countries.

Imam   In Islam, an Imam is a recognized leader or a spiritual teacher.

in absentia   From the Latin, to be absent. When a person who is on trial is not present for the proceedings, that person is in absentia.

infidel   In the Islamic culture, an infidel is an unbeliever.

isolationist   A person (or country) who wants to stay out of foreign affairs and international relations. In this rapidly shrinking, interconnected world, isolationists are becoming dinosaurs.

Jim Crow laws   Laws that barred African Americans from access to voting and employment, as well as to public places such as restaurants, hotels, and other facilities.

mujahedeen   Someone who actively fights for Islam.

nation state   A political unit consisting of an autonomous state inhabited predominantly by a people sharing a common culture, history, or language.

Pan-Arabism   A modern Arab movement calling for political unification among Arab states. Since the Ottoman Turks rose to power and conquered the Middle East in the fourteenth century, there have been stirrings among Arabs for reunification as a means of reestablishing Arab political power.

paper tiger   A country that is comes off as dangerous and powerful, but is in fact timid and weak. The phrase was first used by Mao Tse Tung to describe the United States: "U.S. imperialism seems quite powerful, but in reality it isn't. It is very weak politically because it is divorced from the masses of the people and is disliked by everybody and by the American people too. In appearance it is very powerful, but in reality it is nothing to be afraid of: it is a paper tiger."

plebiscite   A direct vote in which a population exercises the right of self-determination.

protectorate   In international law, a relationship in which one state surrenders (or is forced to surrender) part of its sovereignty to another nation. In most cases, because a protected state usually has no access to diplomatic channels, it is in a poor position to resist attempts at increased control.

realpolitik   Politics based on practical and material factors rather than on theoretical or ethical objectives.

republic   The idea that a republic is a government of elected representatives is a modern interpretation. Historically, a republic referred to a government in which the leaders held authority granted by the people and ruled according to law.

Third World   In politics, the so-called First World refers to the highly developed industrialized nations often considered the westernized countries of the world. The Second World refers to the communist nations as a political and economic bloc. The Third World is the aggregate of the underdeveloped nations of the world. Some people even refer to a Forth World, meaning a group of nations, especially in Africa and Asia, characterized by extremely low per capita income and an absence of valuable natural resources.

trade embargo   A prohibition by a government on certain or all trade with a foreign nation. By preventing both imports and exports with that country, an embargo can sometimes be an effective way to punish one's enemies.

Warsaw Pact   To counter NATO, the Soviet Union, in 1955, created the Warsaw Pact. Participating countries included Albania, Bulgaria, Hungary, East Germany, Poland, Rumania, and the USSR. In July 1991, all members agreed to end the 36-year alliance.

Index